TRIATHLONING

FOR ORDINARY MORTALS™

TRIATHLONING

FOR ORDINARY MORTALS™

And Doing the Duathlon Too

UPDATED

Steven Jonas, MD, MPH, MS

Foreword by Donald B. Ardell, PhD

W. W. NORTON & COMPANY   NEW YORK LONDON

This book is not intended to be a substitute for medical advice. If there are
any doubts in your mind about the advisability of undertaking the exercise
programs described in this book, you should consult a physician.

For information about permission to reproduce selections from this book,
write to Permissions, W. W. Norton & Company, Inc.,
500 Fifth Avenue, New York, NY 10110

"The 8 Top Stretches," pages 116-17, courtesy of the
American Running Association.

Manufacturing by The Maple-Vail Book Manufacturing Group
Book design by Chris Welch
Production manager: Amanda Morrison

Library of Congress Cataloging-in-Publication Data

Jonas, Steven.
Triathloning for ordinary mortals : and doing the duathlon, too /
Steven Jonas; foreword by Donald B. Ardell. — Updated ed.
p. cm.
Includes bibliographical references and index.
ISBN-13: 978-0-393-32877-6 (pbk.)
ISBN-10: 0-393-32877-5 (pbk.)
1. Triathlon. 2. Aerobic exercises. I. Title.
GV1060.7.J66 2006
796.42'57—dc22
2006012380

W. W. Norton & Company, Inc.
500 Fifth Avenue, New York, N.Y. 10110
www.wwnorton.com

W. W. Norton & Company Ltd.
Castle House, 75/76 Wells Street, London W1T 3QT

1 2 3 4 5 6 7 8 9 0

For my darling Chezna, who has made the twilight
of my life into a new dawn.

Chezna and I after the finish of my 100th multi-sport race, the 1999 Mighty Montauk.

CONTENTS

FOREWORD

A competitor since 1983, I know triathloning. However, I'm not so sure about "ordinary mortals." What other kinds of mortals are there? Are there extraordinary mortals? If so, what distinguishes them from the ordinary types, and how many are doing triathlons? If there are mortals extraordinary as well as ordinary, are there not also sub-ordinary mortals? Who qualifies for each mortal type? Most important, which one am I? Other things being the same, I suppose I want to be an extraordinary mortal or, better yet, an extraordinary immortal! Maybe this book will answer these questions and point the way to glory in the sport and a life lived happily ever after, hopefully on the first page!

These were among my reactions when I first encountered Steve Jonas's book *Triathloning for Ordinary Mortals* almost twenty years ago.

"Why," you might ask, "would any sensible person harbor such jejune and ridiculous expectations of a book?" Well, for one of two reasons, I suppose. The first is that I am *not* a sensible person—I harbor unrealistic expectations all the time. The more likely explanation is that I know Dr. Steve Jonas! When he writes something, my expectations are sky-high—and justifiably so.

I soon realized that Steve wanted to make triathloning easier, safer, and more enjoyable for everyone. All the early stars of the sport, including Dave Scott, Scott Tinley, Scott Molina, Mike Pigg, and Mark Allen, among others, wrote articles and/or books for the highly competitive age-group types, like myself. But of the 62,000 individuals active enough in the sport (as of late 2005) to hold membership in USA Triathlon (USAT), the sport's governing body, a very small fraction expect podium finishes, save at small, local races, and most not even then, unless they are in advanced age-groups, like Steve and yours truly. The vast majority are, like Steve, enthusiasts of the sport who do triathlons for a special kind of pleasure, along with attractive side benefits, such as weight control, stress relief, excitement, camaraderie, and because it makes them so virtuous and good looking!

Thus, *Triathloning for Ordinary Mortals* is designed expressly with the triathlon Everyman and Everywoman in mind. Although I consider Dr. Steve Jonas an extraordinary man of remarkable talents and accomplishments in several fields (including medicine, political science, and wellness promotion), I also think he is the slowest triathlete I've ever known—and thus highly qualified to write about "ordinary mortalhood." I don't think there is more than a handful among this country's 62,000 triathletes who have finished a race that began at 7 A.M. at 3:20 A.M. You can read about this experience of Steve's on page 221. I did not have to—I was there, cheering him on. But, to be forthright about it, not at 3:20 A.M. I did my cheering earlier, when all the ordinary mortals were swimming, biking, and running about. But I've always been in awe of the good doctor for doing such a thing. If I had that kind of dedication, to quote the fighter Terry Malloy (Marlon Brando) in the 1954 classic movie *On the Waterfront*, "I coulda been a contender. I coulda been somebody, instead of a bum, which is what I am, let's face it." A 19-hour and 20-minute triathlon? As I told Steve that day, "Man, now *that* is an achievement."

There may be something you need to know about getting started in triathlons or a few ways to make triathloning easier, safer, and more enjoyable that Steve Jonas has not thought about and addressed in this book. Maybe, but I doubt it.

Be well.

—Donald B. Ardell
St. Petersburg, Florida

ACKNOWLEDGMENTS

First, many thanks to my editor at W. W. Norton, Nomi Victor (who, among other things, is a fellow graduate of Columbia College), for her combination of editorial excellence and consistent good cheer. She offered strong support for the creation of this twentieth-anniversary second edition, which I appreciated very much, and it has been a fun experience to work with her. I cannot let the opportunity pass to also remember my first editor at Norton, Eric Swenson, who gave me the chance to publish the original version of this book when the sport was young and I was thoroughly unknown in it. That taking of risk has produced good results over the years for both Norton and me. I also want to thank my copy editor for this book, Barbara Feller-Roth, who did such an outstanding job for me, and Adele McCarthy-Beauvais at Norton, who handled the publicity for the book with such expertise.

I thank Fred Feller, president of Carl Hart Bicycles of Middle Island, New York, for all the help, encouragement, material benefit, technical assistance on my various triathlon-related writing projects (including this one), and most importantly the friendship he has given me over the years. I also thank his son, Darren, who is following in his father's footsteps in all of the above.

I thank also my friend Dan Honig, president of the New York Triathlon Club, stalwart of multi-sport racing almost since its inception, for his friendship and support since my early days as a tri- and duathlete. And thanks to his loyal crew who have worked so many of the races that I have done over the years, especially Jim Borzell and Gary Bennett, who never fail to offer encouragement, especially as I take my time getting through the transitions.

I would like to thank the basketball coaching and broadcasting immortal Dr. Jack Ramsey, a triathlete himself, who wrote the forewords for the original edition and the updated and expanded version that appeared in 1999. This time around, it is my dear friend Dr. Don Ardell, the nationally recognized "Dean of Wellness" with whom I happen to share many professional interests, who graces these pages with his introductory prose. Most of the time, Don and I have competed in the same age-group. A big difference is that he is fast, a frequent All-American, national champion, and sometimes world champion in triathlon and duathlon, and I am slow. I refer to us as the "alpha and omega" of our age-group. But we both love multi-sport racing and have fun doing it, over and over again.

Special thanks to John Hanc, fitness writer nonpareil (primarily for *Newsday*, the Long Island, New York, daily), for his friendship, wise counsel, and many an excellent interview over the years.

I want to thank USA Triathlon for being there for our sport, and my old friends there, especially Mark Sisson and early executive director and my longtime friend Tim Yount, presently senior vice-president for marketing and communications, who both gave me so much support along the way, as well as my new friend there, Executive Director Skip Gilbert. Among my many friends who race, I want to mention especially the now-retired Frank Grasso, of my age-group in duathlon (whenever I saw him at a race, I knew that one possible trophy slot for me was gone), and Odd Sangeslund, as of this writing still racing at 78 (and still faster than I am), who provides such a great example for all of us of what you can do in sports if you keep your body and mind in shape. Thanks to all for their support and good cheer along the way.

Then there are my thanks to all of those triathletes and duathletes who over the years have approached me at and even during the races, and have written to me, to let me know personally that this book has helped them. It always gives me a thrill to have someone tell me directly that the book has affected their lives in a positive way. And thanks to the many others who have not communicated personally with me but who have obviously used the book and liked it so much that they have recommended it to their friends, colleagues, and family members.

My children, Jacob and Lillian, were there for my very first race back in 1983, and have continued to offer their good cheers and good wishes all along the way. Finally, there is my dear Chezna, who provides me with so much continued support and encouragement to keep on racing, and who, herself an exercise walker, joins me in the sport each spring, for the Spring Couples Relay in New York City's Central Park. The Dedication to this book says it all about what she has meant, means, and will always mean to me for as long as we continue to breathe.

ABOUT THE AUTHOR

Steven Jonas, MD, MPH, MS, is Professor of Preventive Medicine, School of Medicine at Stony Brook University (New York). He is a Fellow of the American College of Preventive Medicine, the New York Academy of Sciences (elected), the New York Academy of Medicine, and the American Public Health Association. He is editor in chief of the *American Medical Athletic Association Journal*, and a member of the editorial board of the American College of Sports Medicine (ACSM) *Health and Fitness Journal*. Over the course of an academic career that began in 1969, his research has focused on health care delivery systems analysis, the health of the public, and personal health, fitness, and wellness. He has authored, coauthored, edited, and coedited more than 25 books, published more than 135 papers in scientific journals, and written numerous articles in the popular literature. Since the late 1980s he has been a columnist for a number of triathlon publications. In 2005, he was appointed as a member of the Writers Bureau for *USA Triathlon Life*. Not athletic as a child, he took up skiing while in medical school and became a ski instructor certified at Level I by the Professional Ski Instructors of America in 1995. He became a runner at the age of 43. The rest of his athletic history is found throughout the pages of this book. He lives in Port Jefferson and New York, New York, has two children—Jacob, a basketball coach, and Lillian, a schoolteacher—and a stepson, Mark Newman, an architect.

PREFACE

I am delighted to have the opportunity to write the Preface to this book for the third time. The first edition came out in 1986, with an update in 1999. It began back then, and remains today, a book for the wide range of people who have heard about the triathlon—a distance race in which one swims, cycles, and runs in sequence—and are intrigued by the idea of participating in one. Many are also interested in the duathlon—a three-segment, two-sport race in which one does a run, then a bike, then another run. With the increasing popularity of duathlon (sometimes called "biathlon") a whole generation of non-swimmers has been able to get into the multi-sport racing act.

This book is not directed at the super-fit, low-body-fat, high-performance distance athlete. Rather it is for the person who is presently a recreational runner, cyclist, or swimmer (whether a racer or not), or even someone with no previous distance-sports racing experience, who is thinking about doing a triathlon or duathlon without turning the rest of his or her life upside down in the process, while at the same time having fun. It is also for the recreational triathlete/duathlete who is seeking guidance about how to train in a more organized way, perhaps how to choose races and equip him- or herself better, and how to have fun in the sport over the longer term without necessarily going fast. If you are a member of either of these groups, namely an "Ordinary Mortal" of the title, this book is for you.

For this edition, I significantly reorganized the content over the whole of the book and rearranged and rewrote major sections of the text. I updated the chapter on equipment to reflect the new technologies that benefit multi-sport racing on an ongoing basis. Chapter 9, "The Race," reflects my ever-increasing experience on the racecourses (160-plus multi-sport races, including 100-plus triathlons, at the time of this writing). In the new Chapter 11, I share with you many of the important lessons I learned beyond those of the races themselves as I now near twenty-five years in the sport. The occasional repetition is purposeful. Not everyone will read a book like this all the way through. I want to ensure that everyone is exposed to those important messages.

The first focus of the book remains on doing what in the first edition I called the "marathon-equivalent" race: a 1.5-kilometer swim, a 40-kilometer bike, and a 10-kilometer run. (In 2000, triathlon became an Olympic event for the first time. The race at these distances is now known as the Olympic- or international-distance triathlon.) In this edition, given the ever-increasing popularity of the shorter races—the Sprint-distance triathlon and the entry-level duathlon—I offer advice and specific training programs for doing them too. Following my training recommendations, many people will find races at the Olympic- and the Sprint/duathlon-distances very manageable, as long as they don't try to go too fast. At the same time, given that I have done a number of longer races since the time I wrote the original version of this book, I also show you, in Chapter 10, how to prepare to "go long" (again without—for the most part—turning your life upside down).

Chapter 1 introduces you to multi-sport racing and provides a set of criteria you can use to help you decide if it is for you. In Chapter 2 I describe my own journey from nonathleticism at age 43 to the starting line of my first triathlon at age 46. In Chapter 3 I offer criteria to use in choosing your own first race. In Chapter 4 I discuss some basic aspects of technique for the three triathlon sports. In Chapter 5, the longest one in the book, I set forth the basic principles of distance-sports training and racing as I see them. If you are just starting out in the distance sports, Chapter 6 shows you the requirements for establishing the "aerobic base" that you will need before you can safely undertake what I call the Triathloning for Ordinary Mortals Training Program (TFOMTP).

The original 5-hour-per-week, 13-week TFOMTP, the central feature of the book, designed to prepare you for the Olympic-distance triathlon, is presented in three different versions in Chapter 7. I also offer one each of a shorter variant, for doing a Sprint or a duathlon. I go over the equipment requirements in Chapter 8. In Chapter 9 I take you with me through the first triathlon I did back in 1983, offer some advice on racing itself (with more to come in Chapter 11), and take a look at what you will likely experience on the "morning after" your first race.

Chapter 10 examines "going long." It offers doable training programs for the half-ironman-distance (1.2-mile swim, 56-mile bike, 13.1-mile run) and the ironman-distance (2.4-mile swim, 112-mile bike, 26.2-mile run) races. In Chapter 11, you will find some more of the nuts and bolts of training and racing lore that I have accumulated over my close to quarter-century in the sport.

My central message back when I wrote the first edition of this book was a simple one. If you are a recreational distance-sports athlete, or would like to become one, and you set as your goal the completion of an Olympic-distance or a Sprint-distance triathlon, or an entry-level duathlon, happily and healthily, by investing a relatively modest amount of time, effort, and money, and following the TFOMTP, you can achieve that goal.

My own experience and that of the many people who have written to me and spoken with me at (and even during!) the races, and the much larger number who have used the book, confirms that conclusion. If the TFOMTP has worked for me and so many others, it can work for you too. I can assure you that when you cross the finish line of your first race, regardless of your time, you will experience feelings of accomplishment and self-satisfaction unlike any you have experienced before. In spirit, I will be there to greet you. Remember that day well, for never again will you do your very first multi-sport race. Good luck and have fun!

—Steven Jonas, MD, MPH, MS, FNYAS
Port Jefferson, New York, August 26, 2005

TRIATHLONING

FOR ORDINARY MORTALS™

I encourage all . . . triathletes to reach for your goals, whether they be to win or just to try. The trying is everything.
—*Dave Scott, six-time Hawaii Ironman champion*

AN INTRODUCTION TO TRIATHLON AND DUATHLON

"Life is what you do till the moment you die." It is this empowering, mind-expanding concept with which The Woman opens the musical-stage version of Nikos Kazant-zakis's classic inspirational story *Zorba the Greek*. What a challenge to us all. Life is in our hands. Life is what we do with our time, what we make of it, what we make of ourselves and others during our time on Earth. Living his own life along these lines, the late George Sheehan, MD, was a runner, cardiologist, philosopher, and inspirer of thousands of distance athletes from the 1970s into the 1990s. He talked about the triad of "energy, clarity, and self-esteem" as the principal personal outcomes of a program of regular running. They are characteristics of the mind that are produced by regular participation in any aerobic sport or combination of them. Aerobic exercise improves health and increases life expectancy—long-term physical results. But as George pointed out, perhaps more importantly it improves the *mental quality* of life, in the here and now. It makes life as we live it better from day to day, from month to month, and from year to year by adding, improving, building for us energy, clarity, and self-esteem.

The reason you are reading this book is your interest in the sport of triathlon and/or its offspring, duathlon. A triathlon is a race that has three segments, each one requiring competition in a different sport. Most commonly, the three sports are swimming, road cycling, and running, in that order. Occasionally triathlons include one or more other sports, such as canoeing, downhill or cross-country skiing, mountain biking, or kayaking. The duathlon (formerly, now much less frequently, called the "biathlon") has become increasingly popular. Like triathlons, duathlons have three segments. But they involve only two sports, usually cycling and running, rather than three. The common sequence is run-bike-run. Together triathloning and duathloning are known as "multi-sport racing."

Describing triathloning, Jim Curl, an early organizer of races around the country, put it well:

> It's a personal growth sport. Your body will change and you will feel great. It's about waking up in the morning and knowing that you've done something that you didn't know that you could do the day before. There aren't that many things around that will give you that sense of accomplishment that fast. In addition, nobody can take it away from you. It's just you.

I overheard it put even more succinctly at the rain-drenched starting line of the 1984 Brooklyn Biathlon, run for several years on the old Floyd Bennett Field by my good friend Dan Honig and his Big Apple Triathlon Club (now the New York Triathlon Club). Two women who appeared to be in their fifties were chatting. One said to the other: "Are you going to do the whole thing?" "Yes I am," came the reply, "God willing." God was willing. She did it.

Twenty years later, on the bike segment of the 2004 Pine Barrens Triathlon, held at Atsion State Park in central New Jersey, on the bike segment I passed a young lady who had obviously gotten out of the swim well ahead of me. She was riding the kind of bike that I had ridden as a child. It had a heavy steel frame with two tubes connecting the handlebar stem to the seat tube, and upright handlebars, balloon tires, and one speed. (Yes, it was a totally flat course.) "Are you having fun?" I called out as I was overtaking her. She nodded vigorously in the affirmative. "Are you going to finish?" I asked. "Yes, I am!" she replied. Indeed she did. And you can too.

Who This Book Is For

"Ruts long traveled"—it has been said—"grow comfortable." If you are reading this book, it is safe to assume that you want a new challenge and are at least thinking about trying this marvelous, zany, captivating, made-in-America phenomenon—the sport of triathloning. If you are an average recreational distance athlete of modest ability who would like to do a triathlon or a duathlon of relatively modest proportions, Chapter 7 shows you how to train up for the big event without turning the rest of your life upside down. Indeed, if you are already a regular exerciser at some level, you may not have to spend too much more time training than you already do, just organize it differently. If you are not yet an average recreational distance athlete of modest ability but would like to become one, with the goal in mind of doing a triathlon or a duathlon of modest proportions, Chapter 6 will show you how to get on the road to achieving that goal, from square one. If you are already a recreational triathlete, racing primarily to have fun, Chapter 7 will show you how to train better and more easily; Chapter 10 will show you how to train for longer races, if you would like to do that.

Whatever your present state of aerobic/athletic fitness and whatever race distance you are contemplating, this book is for you if your primary goals are to have fun, to meet a new challenge in your life, and to do it without upsetting the rest of your life. This book is about the nuts and bolts of the sport; about the knowledge, training, equipment, and mind-set you need to go the distance—whatever that distance may be—happily and healthily. Once you are into the sport, should you find that you have some speed potential and want to go faster, there are plenty of other books (see Appendix II for a few suggestions), and qualified coaches, too, that can help you realize that goal.

Believe me, there are many fast people in the sport, folks who can swim the mile in 18 to 20 minutes, then go 25 miles on the bike at 25 miles per hour, then do a 10-kilometer (10k) run in 35 minutes or so. You might have the ability to eventually become one of them. (I definitely do not—indeed, far from it.) If you are, I say go for it. Most of us do not come anywhere near those speeds, but we still have fun. And that, primarily, is what this book is about: having fun doing triathlons and duathlons.

Triathlon Categories

"Triathlon" is a late-twentieth-century word that sounds old due to its Greek root. It names a race that combines three distance sports done consecutively. Various combinations of sports are offered under the rubric "triathlon." The most common combination is the swim-bike-run event, in that order. These events are offered in a wide range of lengths. For example, the 2005 Pawling (New York) Triathlon consisted of a $^1/_3$-mile swim, a 13-mile bike, and a 3-mile run. Toward the other end of the spectrum is the Vineman, held in the wine country north of San Francisco, California; it's an "ironman"-distance event, comprising a 2.4-mile swim, a 112-mile bike, followed by a marathon (26.2 miles). For those who find the latter too tame, there is always the three-day Ultraman held on the Big Island of Hawaii. Competitors swim 6.2 miles on the first day, bike 171.4 miles on the second, and run 52.4 miles on the third.

The races of more modest proportions, which are the principal focus of this book, come in two classes. In the first are the "Sprint triathlon" and the "duathlon of customary length" (hereafter simply called "duathlon" even though, few and far between, there are also long duathlons). The Sprint triathlon distances are customarily a $^1/_4$- to $^1/_2$-mile swim, a 6- to 15-mile bike, and a 3- to 5-mile run. For the duathlon, the runs are generally 2 to 3 miles, the bike 8 to 15 miles. Because the latter races do not involve swimming, they are logistically simpler and require less equipment and equipment/clothing changes than triathlons, an advantage for the beginning multi-sport athlete.

The second class is the "Olympic"-distance triathlon, or the "marathon-equivalent" tri, a race that takes the average competitor 70 to 80 percent of the time it would take him or her to run a marathon. For the first twenty years or so of the sport, the distances of the marathon-equivalent triathlon varied somewhat. In the mid-1990s, the international governing body of the sport, the International Triathlon Union (ITU), began preparing for the sport's inclusion in the Olympic Games; this occurred for the first time at the Sydney, Australia, games of 2000. The standardized distances for this class of race were a 1.5-kilometer (0.93-mile) swim, followed by a 40-kilometer (24.8-mile) bike ride, concluding with a 10-kilometer (6.2-mile) run. Hence the name "Olympic-distance" for this variant.

As a beginner, you can realistically get started in multi-sport racing in either triathlon category or the customary duathlon distance. It all depends on how much time you want to put into your training and what kind of challenge you want to set for yourself for that first time out. You will find training programs of modest proportions for all three types of race in Chapter 7. More than twenty years ago, when I started to train for my first race—a race actually somewhat longer than the present-day Olympic-distance event—I developed for myself what became the basic Triathloning for Ordinary Mortals Training Program (TFOMTP). It worked for me then (see the next chapter) and still does.

At the time that I did my first race, there were no books designed specifically for beginners and the recreational triathlete. I decided to write this book as I was standing in the transition area (where one changes clothing and equipment between the three race segments) after finishing that first race and feeling very good about myself. With a few variations that I developed over time, I have been using essentially the same training program that I designed back in 1983 throughout my now nearly 25 years in the sport. The program and its variants have worked for me and for tens of thousands of other triathletes who have used the book since it first appeared in 1986. It never fails to be a most gratifying experience when someone comes up to me at a race and says some version of: "Are you the doc who wrote that book? You're the reason I'm here."

A Little History

The sport began on an informal basis in and around San Diego, California, under the leadership of David Pain and friends, as well as others, in the early 1970s. From then until the late 1980s, the races came in a bewildering variety of sizes and shapes. There was no standardization. Now, at least to a certain extent, there is. This has occurred in part because of the professionalization of the sport at the upper end, by its acceptance as an Olympic sport, and by the adoption of standard distances for the amateur "age-group" championships, both national and world. Nevertheless, there are races, particularly those designed to attract a local or regional group of competitors, that are set up to fit a certain available course and/or group of central facilities that form the physical focus of this logistically complicated enterprise. Thus, in certain instances, the available course distances themselves dictate the length of the race legs.

A special category is the "ironman"-distance. The original was the product of an historical accident. In 1978, a United States Navy commander, John Collins, thought that it might be fun to take three of the Hawaiian Islands' premier distance-race distances, string the distances together, and ask competitors to do them consecutively. The Waikiki Rough Water Swim happened to be for 2.4 miles; the Oahu Bike Race happened to be for 115 miles (but for that first Ironman, the bike course was shortened by 3 miles to fit the starting point for the marathon leg that had been decided upon); and the Honolulu Marathon was, well, a marathon. Fifteen men entered the new, combination event. Twelve finished. The prize for the winner was a six-pack of beer. The race was repeated the next year with 50 entrants, although only 15 competed due to bad weather. The race grew in popularity, and by the early 1980s it was being held twice a year.

A special event signaled the development of the next stage of the sport: it was the women's finish of the February 1982 Ironman Triathlon, starting on Kona Pier in Hawaii. That finish, which was very dramatic, happened to be televised on ABC's *Wide World of Sports*. With about ¼ mile to go in the last leg of the marathon, Julie Moss, who had been leading the female group by a wide margin, collapsed. Completely out of glycogen (the body's stored form of carbohydrates), her leg muscles felt as if they had turned to rubber. She rested briefly, got up, ran for a bit, and collapsed again. She repeated the cycle several times until she was within about 10 yards of the finish. She could not rise again. This gallant woman then proceeded to crawl toward the line. Before she got there, however, Kathleen McCartney, who had been second and far behind, passed her and won the race. (She then disappeared into the mists of triathlon history. There! You now have the answer to a classic triathlon trivia question: Who won the famous "Julie Moss" race?) Julie continued to crawl and took second place. She also etched herself indelibly into the memories of millions of Americans who watched that telecast and subsequent repeats of it. For some reason that I cannot recall, I happened to be among them. I was not contemplating doing even a 5-kilometer road race at that time. But I did see gallant Julie, and the memory stayed with me (and has to this day). Many times in talking to nonathletes about triathloning, they tell me about that particular episode. They may know little else about the sport, but they do remember Julie.

Whether coincidentally or not, triathloning then took off. By the 1983 season, an estimated 1,000 triathlons were being held all over the country, involving an estimated 250,000 entrants (many individuals doing more than one race). On the day I did my first race—September 10, 1983—at least thirteen other races were being run at the same time. Thus about 5,000 people, most of them amateurs, were triathloning that day. In 2005 it is likely that at least 250,000 individuals did at least one multi-sport race.

Although races of many lengths were held in the early "proliferative period," USA Triathlon (USAT), the sport's governing body in the United States, now defines four event categories. The Sprint- and the Olympic-distances were described above. The races in the ironman range—a 2.4-mile swim, a 112-mile bike ride, and a 26.2-mile run—comprise the "Ultra Course" category (not to be confused with the "Ultraman"). The "Long Course" category consists of races in the range from the half-ironman-distances of a 1.2-mile swim, a 56-mile bike, and a 13.1-mile run up to about two-thirds of the ironman-distances.

Is Triathloning for You?

Your Enjoyment Quotient

If you have bought this book, you have probably already come to the conclusion that, yes, multi-sport racing may well be for you. Nevertheless, let's go over the basic criteria. If you are contemplating becoming or are just beginning as a distance athlete, you must believe that you will enjoy one or more triathloning sport. The "from scratch" training program sequence set out in Chapter 6 is designed to give you the best chance of making that belief a reality. By the way, age should not be considered a barrier. At the yearly U.S. National Age-Group Championships, male and female competitors are routinely older than 70 and a number of them are faster than racers in several five-year age-groups (65 to 69, 60 to 64, et cetera) below them. At the 2002 ITU Age-Group World Championship in Cancún, Mexico, an Olympic-distance event, one finisher, Roman Jezek of Canada, was in the 85-plus age-group.

The word "enjoy" in the context of distance sports has different meanings for different people. Some distance athletes enjoy their sports while they are doing them, most of the time. They feel good while they are running, for example. They get into a private mind-world. They say they do not have or they do not feel or they just ignore any aches or pains that may crop up. The cyclist enjoys the speed, the breeze in the face, the rhythmic turning of the pedals. The swimmer enjoys the buoyancy, the quiet noise of the breathing and stroking, the private mind-world like that of the runner. Others actually enjoy doing the sport itself only occasionally. They do feel the pain, they do get bored, and they do have trouble getting under way in the morning. However, they do it regularly, on an ongoing basis, because they know what other physical and mental benefits they derive from the activity. There is the enjoyment that doing distance sports brings to the larger context of life, the enjoyment drawn from what performing a distance sport on a regular basis does for you as a whole person. I have never met a distance athlete who does not enjoy what he or she is doing at least in this sense.

In an article written a long time ago in the *New York Running News*, Sofia Shafquat reported on a series of interviews with runners on the question "Is running fun?" The answers were quite varied, and are, I think, still valid. A 24-year-old male summed it up well: "Running is what you make it. It could be fun or it could be torturous." To me, this is an important concept that applies to multi-sport racing and training as well. To make it a positive, enjoyable experience, you must remain in control of your training and your racing. *You* must run your training program and your racing schedule and experiences, not the other way round. If you let them run you, you will have a hard time finding enjoyment. An important corollary is that if the experience is to be enjoyable, you must set reasonable, realistic, attainable goals for yourself. If the experience is not going to be enjoyable in one sense or another, why do it?

Technical Ability

The second criterion for being able to respond to the question "Is triathloning for you?" with a "yes" is that you must be physically able to do each of the three sports, even if you are not yet trained in any of them. This does not mean that you need to be an expert in any of the sports. Running, except as done by top competitors, is not a technically complicated sport. Harold Schwab, owner of the 2nd Wind running-shoe store in Setauket, New York, was a world-class hurdler and a recreational marathoner. He was asked about technique by a beginning runner who had just bought his first pair of running shoes. Harold put it simply: "Stand up straight, hold your arms comfortably, then go right, left, right, left." There is a bit more to it than that (see Chapter 4), but unless you try something like the "Pose Method" (which I do not do), for the recreational triathlete there is not too much more. By the way, if you do not like, or cannot for one reason or another, run, you may walk the run legs of the triathlon and duathlon. It is specifically provided for in the USAT rules (Article VI, 6.1; see the USAT Web site—www.usatriathlon.org).

Cycling, when done well, is a highly technical sport that requires a great deal of mental concentration. However, for the beginner triathlete, the most important aspects of cycling are safety and comfort. You must be comfortable on your machine and you must ride safely. Once you get to know your bike—a process that takes some time—you can then start to learn about technique, build up your miles, and gradually increase your speed, if that is of interest to you.

The beginner triathlete must also know how to swim—safely. Obviously, the beginner duathlete does not have to know how to swim, which is one reason why duathlons have become so popular. Like cycling, swimming when done well is a highly technical sport requiring a great deal of mental concentration. However, previous experience in distance swimming is not a prerequisite for triathloning. Nor, necessarily, is mastery of the stroke used by the top triathletes—the freestyle (Australian crawl). Any stroke is permitted in the swim leg, and you may use any combination of strokes that works for you. I learned how to swim as a child. I was thought to have good swimming form (by my parents at least), but I never raced and never swam for distance. After my twelfth year, I did little swimming of any kind. For my first triathlon, the 1983 Mighty Hamptons at Sag Harbor, New York, I went in the water for training exactly nine times, as I recount in more detail in Chapter 2. Swimming slowly, I had no trouble with the swim leg because I was in good shape aerobically. I still swim slowly, all freestyle, doing the mile in about 43 minutes. However, I am comfortable in the water, never get out of breath, and get out of the water ready to get on the bike and have a good ride.

Available Time

The third criterion for deciding if triathloning is for you is whether you have or can make available the time to train. I talk more about training time in Chapter 5, but the basic requirements are as follows. Before you start specific triathlon or duathlon training, it is best that you have done or plan to do your principal sport or sports at the aerobic level for $2^1/_2$ to 3 hours per week (that is, total workout time for all the sports you are doing, together) for 2 to 6 months. This weekly total of $2^1/_2$ to 3 hours of aerobic work will establish your aerobic base (see Chapter 5). Once you've done that, for the Sprint/duathlon race distances you need to spend an average of $3^1/_2$ hours per week training for 13 weeks leading up to that first race. For an Olympic-distance triathlon, the requirement is an average of 5 hours per week for 13 weeks. The workout schedules are spelled out in the Triathloning for Ordinary Mortals Training Program (see Chapter 7). The TFOMTP has several variants, depending upon what distance you have chosen for your first race, and—once you are into the sport(s)—how you like to apportion your training time among them during each week.

The programs are described in detail, with day-by-day training tables. Depending upon the variant you choose, they require five or six workouts per week over 5 to 6 days, with 1 or 2 days of rest each week. It will be best for your lifestyle and your body if you can schedule your workouts pretty much at the same time each day. Unless you happen to own your own pool or live by open water that is safe to swim in, that rule does not apply to the swim. If, like most of us, you will be doing your swim training in a pool, its hours of operation will determine when you swim.

Although to become a triathlete, and remain one, you need to commit time on a regular basis, the time commitment necessary is not one that most people interested in distance sports will find inordinate.

Regularity and Consistency

In your training, regularity and consistency are central to success. You need to be able to commit to achieving both. Regularity is training on a schedule that is spaced out over a majority of the days of the week. You cannot be a successful regular exerciser, much less a multi-sport racer, if you train only on the weekends. Such an approach almost invariably leads to pain, eventual injury, a lack of cardiorespiratory conditioning, frustration—even anger—and quitting. Consistency is following a schedule in which the individual workout times do not vary widely within any one week (except for a few specific race-preparation longer ones). In other words, even if you work out five or six times a week but do most of the required minutes in one or two weekend workouts, you are inviting the same problems that lack of regularity brings. I come back to these two important elements of productive training in more detail in Chapter 5.

If you are already a distance athlete, you know that the exercise itself is usually not a problem. It is *not* getting out there to exercise that most often creates problems. As I am fond of saying to professionals and the general public, "The hard part of regular exercise is the 'regular,' not the 'exercise.'" You must be prepared to push yourself when necessary to achieve regularity. Consistency is also essential. It is better to spend less time per workout more often than to spend more time per workout less often. Rod Dixon, winner of the 1983 New York Marathon, once offered his "Ten Rules of Running" (see page 124). Rod's first rule is: "Emphasize consistency in your training program." This is a theme to which I return—consistently.

Finishing Happily and Healthily

If you are to be comfortable with what I recommend in this book, your goal should be simply to finish your first triathlon or duathlon happily and healthily. You should want to do the race just for the sake of doing it. You should be able to *realistically* define success for yourself in this venture in terms of your abilities and available time. You will do best if you are truly happy doing what you can do, not trying to do what you realistically cannot do or what someone else can do or thinks you can or ought to be able to do. In this book, I stress the goal of *finishing* a triathlon or duathlon—of whatever length—happily and healthily, without worrying about your time and where you place. If winning is important to you (and you have some reasonable potential for doing so), that can come later, with the help of other books and programs. This book and my program introduce you to the sport with the goal of enjoyment for its own sake. Once you have done that first race or first three races, there will be plenty of opportunity to see if you want to, and might be able to, accomplish other possible goals, such as going faster or going longer.

A Quick Word on Equipment Requirements

Many people come to triathlon from running, and some come from pool swimming. Triathlon is a "stuff" (read, equipment) sport, unlike running or pool swimming. Readers who are coming to triathlon from another distance sport (other than cycling) should be aware of some basic equipment demands for triathlon/duathlon racing, although they can be quite modest at the beginning, especially if you already own a serviceable bike or can borrow one (that fits) from a friend or family member. Chapter 8 provides some ideas about equipment. You should read it before acquiring a $3,000 bicycle, or building your own lap swimming pool in the backyard.

What Is a "Real" Triathlon?

Some people regard doing a triathlon of less magnitude than the ironman-distance as an achievement not worth mentioning. The ironman focus is currently a central feature of one of the two leading triathlon magazines. By implication, at least, the constant focus seemed to make races at the shorter distances somehow less worthy—a prime example of setting goals for others rather than yourself. It happens that I have started five races at the ironman-distance and finished three. The experience was a life-changing one for me, as you will see later in the book. However, I had the time—each time—to train, and I really wanted to have the experience for me, not for anyone else. Doing an ironman is not good for everyone, nor is everyone physically and/or mentally capable of it. And not everyone *wants* to do it. For one thing, the training alone puts a great deal more wear and tear on the body than does training for the shorter events.

The central point of the Triathloning for Ordinary Mortals approach to the sport is that any multi-sport race you do, of whatever length, is for *you* a great achievement. It is *your real* triathlon or duathlon. Ironman is not the gold standard of the sport. The race that *you* do is. In terms of the overall population, few people do or have done what you are setting out to do, at whatever distance. If the race you are doing is your first, that's a challenge regardless of distance. If it's your 100th, that's a challenge too, if only in the sense that you kept on training and kept on racing to get to 100, regardless of distance or how fast you went. Dave Horning, a professional triathlete and longtime race director, presently with Enviro-Sports Productions, won his share of big races and trained hard for them. In describing the 1984 Liberty to Liberty Triathlon (a 2-mile swim, 90-mile bike, 6-mile run from New Jersey's Liberty State Park to Philadelphia's Liberty Bell) before a meeting of the Big Apple Triathlon Club, Dave said, "If it's not fun, there is no point in doing it." I could not agree more.

The Advantages of Triathlon as a Distance Sport

Some people may look at triathloning as the refuge for the road-race runner, especially the marathoner, who is tired of running and wants to do something else. I am certainly not knocking marathoning. In fact, I think it is a great experience (which I have had ten times, including three that I ran at the end of ironman-distance triathlons), one not to be missed. It is just that exercising aerobically in three different sports for a given period of time is easier than exercising aerobically for the same amount of time in one sport. This is especially true if that one sport is running.

This is true for several reasons. First of all, swimming and cycling, neither of which involves pounding, are easier on the body than running. Second, in a triathlon you are spending about 20 percent of your time with the bulk of your body weight supported by water, and another 50 percent or so of the time sitting down. Third, triathloning is a colorful and busy event. In marathoning, it's "right, left, right, left" for 26 miles. In triathloning, you have to be concerned with logistics and equipment, two clothing changes, lots of hustle and bustle, and usually some complications to the course. Fourth, a triathlon offers variety in about as much time as it would take you to run a marathon, which is an Olympic-distance event. The boredom that can accompany the later stages of a marathon has little chance to set in while triathloning. Finally, if you are concerned about where you will place at the finish, strength in one triathlon sport can make up for weakness in another.

The Pros and Cons of the Three Sports

When I started out, I believed that running was the basic sport of triathloning. Running, because it involves constant pounding of the body, is the most demanding physically. To do triathlons and duathlons, you must run. You cannot consider triathloning or duathloning as a refuge from running.

Although physically demanding, running does have its advantages as a training sport, and the triathlete would do well to look at it in this light. Running does not require a special place. Running shoes do not get flat tires. Running is cheap, and its equipment demands are simple. It requires the least total time to get a good workout. It is relatively safe. Its equipment is highly portable. (When traveling, nothing is more fun than going for an easy morning run in a new city.) If you like socializing while exercising, running offers you the best opportunity to do so. Swimming is by nature a solo sport, and you need a special place to do it. As for safe side-by-side bicycle riding, most highways do not lend themselves to it.

The late Jim Fixx, one of the great popularizers of distance running, put it succinctly in the first paragraph of his magnum opus, *The Complete Book of Running:* "One gray November morning I [met] . . . an old man shuffling along slowly, using a cane. As I ran by him, I called out, 'Good morning!' [He responded:] 'Say, what do you gain by running?' I hollered back: 'It makes you feel good!'"

Even one of the best-known political figures of the twentieth century, a man not ordinarily thought of in the context of distance sports, considered them important. He gave them a political as well as a physical and psychological meaning. In 1918, Mao Tse-tung wrote: "In general, any form of exercise, if pursued continuously, will help to train us in perseverance. Long-distance running is particularly good." That was written long before distance-running shoes were developed. Although Mao became rather obese in his later years, I suppose that that experience with running in his younger days helped him to prepare for the Long March.

Running has many health benefits, as is well known. It is good for the cardiovascular system in a variety of ways. As for the gastrointestinal system, I have yet to meet a constipated runner, although some would certainly like to be just before and/or *during* a race. All that bouncing does loosen things up. Running is a major factor in successful weight control. Running seems to improve a person's ability to handle stress. That has certainly been my own experience and has been reported by many runners.

There is a biochemical basis to that finding: running teaches the body how to handle—in a positive, productive way—substances that are produced by both running and stressful situations. Running may ameliorate depression. It has an important social aspect, especially for members of running clubs and/or people who race frequently. All of these pluses, with the possible exception of the GI tract benefits, result from any distance sport done regularly.

Running has the disadvantage of inflicting a regular pounding on your legs. Overuse or overtraining injuries constitute the major physical risks of running. There are many such injuries, ranging from minor aches and pains to chondromalacia patellae ("runner's knee," which is softening of the kneecap cartilage), plantar fasciitis (inflammation of the bottom covering of the foot muscles), Achilles tendonitis, pulled muscles, shin splints, blisters, stress fractures, and numerous others. Virtually all of these problems result from doing too much running. They can be healed by rest combined with other interventions as appropriate, such as physical therapy, ultrasound, ice application, special stretching exercises, weight lifting, massage, and medications.

You can get overuse and wear-and-tear injuries in any of the three triathlon sports. However, with the exception of risking "swimmer's shoulder," swimming is generally good for the body. Much of your weight is supported by the water, there is no pounding, and there are no hard surfaces against which you could twist a body part. In cycling, although a knee injury can come from riding in too high a gear at too low a pedaling rate and traumatic injuries can result from falling off your machine, there is no pounding or twisting.

As for answering the question "What is the basic sport of triathlon?" although I used to believe that it is running, I now realize that it is any of the three—or none. Runners can learn to ride and swim; cyclists and swimmers can learn the other two sports as well. If right now you do none of them, you can fairly quickly learn enough about the two or three necessary to do your first duathlon or triathlon.

Cross-Training and Balance

Finally we come to the subject of "cross-training" and its product: balance. Cross-training is the combination of two or more aerobic distance sports in one training program. Many single-sport athletes already occasionally train in another sport simply to reduce musculoskeletal stress, strengthen additional muscle groups, diminish boredom, and add some balance to their training. I started on the road to triathloning in the fall of 1981 when I bought my first 10-speed bike after I had been running for about a year. I had never even heard of triathloning at the time. I doubt that I was familiar with the term "cross-training" either. However, even at only 15 to 20 miles of running per week, I wanted to get some relief from the constant pounding of the sport while maintaining my aerobic base. Although I was absolutely fascinated by Julie Moss's feat in February 1982, it wasn't until the following September—when I heard about the Mighty Hamptons, a triathlon of reasonable length—that the first faint flicker of "maybe I could try that someday" crossed my mind. I found that cross-training is a benefit in itself and an entrée into triathloning.

The goal of the distance athlete should obviously be to achieve as many of the positives and incur as few of the negatives from doing the sports as possible. Balancing the disciplines and limiting your running seem to be the keys to doing this. For most of us, running 15 to 25 miles per week is reasonable. More than that rapidly increases the risk of injury. Cross-training introduces balance into your training regimen. A major Navajo precept is an excellent one to strive for: "[When there is] balance between the individual and his total physical and social environment . . . good health is the result; an upset in this equilibrium causes disease."

In preparing for a triathlon, cross-training in effect becomes formalized; thus, balance in your athletics, in your workouts, becomes institutionalized. Virtually all of the benefits of running relate to extended aerobic exercise. Virtually all of its cons relate to extended running itself. Thus triathloning gives you the benefits and diminishes your risk of incurring the negatives. What could be better? Cross-training leads to total-body fitness—not merely running or swimming or biking fitness—and it reduces the risk of overuse injury in each of the three sports.

Conclusion

Are you looking for a new athletic experience or even your first serious athletic experience? If you are already a regular exerciser and perhaps a single-sport racer, are you tired or bored with doing nothing but running or biking or swimming? Are you thinking about trying a triathlon or a duathlon? Obviously your answer to the last question is yes, or you would not be reading this book. The pathway is open for you to get into it. Welcome, welcome, and enjoy the journey.

THE ROAD TO
SAG HARBOR

The difference between a jogger and a runner
is a race entry blank. —*George Sheehan, MD*

I did my first triathlon on September 10, 1983, at the age of 46. It was the Mighty Hamptons, held at Sag Harbor, New York. A little less than four years earlier, in December 1979, I had started down the road that would eventually lead to the starting line of that event. It was hardly a straight road, and it did not begin with exercise. Nevertheless, it lead me to that line. I had received a letter from a Texas physician named Charles "Charlie" Ogilvie, DO. I did not know it at the time, but that letter would change my life in more ways than one. Charlie was then chairman of the Department of Medical Humanities at the Texas College of Osteopathic Medicine (TCOM) in Fort Worth. With the late I. M. "Kim" Korr, PhD, a neurophysiologist and medical educator, Charlie was leading a movement to make major changes in the medical education program at TCOM.

Kim and Charlie believed in the health-oriented precepts of the original osteopathic tradition as created by Dr. Andrew Taylor Still in the latter third of the nineteenth century. They were in the process of designing a program to convert the curriculum at TCOM from the disease-oriented mode—common to modern osteopathic and allopathic (MD) medical education—to a health-oriented one. About a year before, without knowing anything about osteopathic medicine, much less what was happening at TCOM, I had published a book recommending that all medical education in the United States be changed from the traditional disease-focused mode to what I called "Health-Oriented Physician Education." Charlie had read the book, and had discovered that we were thinking along precisely the same lines. His letter inquired if I might be interested in discussing developments at TCOM with an eye toward assisting them in their endeavors. I leaped at the chance. In March 1980, I made a visit to the college and gave a talk. Shortly thereafter, I was asked to become a consultant to the college. I began work there in June 1980.

Charlie was then 62 years old. Although he had run track in college, he had gotten increasingly out of shape and rather heavy during his medical career. Taking a serious look at his own body and what had become of it, he began running again at age 59, this time for distance. By the time I met him, he was lean and hard, a marathoner training 70 to 80 miles a week. He almost always won his age-group in the races he entered, and often finished ahead of the winners of several of the next-younger age-groups. In 1983, at age 65, he did ten marathons, about a month apart. His marathon personal record is 3:03,* a pace of less than 7 minutes per mile for the distance. Truly remarkable.

At TCOM, I began working with Charlie on the professional level as a consultant. Soon I felt that I was learning more from him than he was learning from me. Soon, too, I was also being influenced by Charlie on the level of my personal health, though always by example, never by direction. At that time, I was 43 years old. My risk factors[†] for cardiovascular disease, cancer, and the other major killers were low. My blood pressure was also low. I had never smoked cigarettes. I rarely drank alcoholic beverages. I was overweight but not significantly so. My ability to handle stress was improving, and I always wore my automobile seat belt.

---

* A personal record, or personal best, is an athlete's own best time for a race at a particular distance or on a particular course.

[†] A risk factor is an element in one's environment, personal behavior, or genetic makeup that increases one's chance of contracting a particular disease.

However, my diet was fairly high in fat and cholesterol, and I did not exercise.

In the TCOM context, the latter was the biggest issue for me. Exercising regularly is the most visible health-promoting activity one can engage in. Many TCOM faculty members were regular exercisers. Here I was, a consultant on health and prevention in medical education, and I was not a regular exerciser. I started thinking about becoming one. I was sure that I would hate doing it, but it would be important politically at TCOM to be able to say that I was exercising regularly. After all, I said to myself, I had heard that 20 minutes three times a week were the magic numbers, the minimum exercise then recommended by the American College of Sports Medicine (ACSM). That did not seem too bad— or hard for that matter. Over the summer and into the fall of 1980, no one, especially not Charlie, put any pressure on me. It was never mentioned. Although many on the faculty were in good shape, several members of the college's top leadership were not, so it was unlikely that I would be pressured into exercising. However, I was thinking about it. Then I had my moment of personal awakening—not, as it happened, at TCOM.

In October 1980, I was in Detroit for the annual meetings of the American Public Health Association, the Association of Teachers of Preventive Medicine, and the American College of Preventive Medicine. Many of the sessions took place in Cobo Hall, a large arena with floors connected by ramps. On a Tuesday morning at about half past eight, on my way to a seminar at which I was going to make a presentation on how to lobby government officials and legislators on behalf of public health and preventive medicine, I walked up one flight on one of those ramps. When I got to the top, I was huffing and puffing.

For years after such (minimal) exertion, I had found myself huffing and puffing and done nothing about it. But this time I said to myself: "This is it. I've had enough of this. I've never been in shape in my life, but that's going to change. When I get home, I'm going to begin running. I know that I'm going to hate it, but I'm going to do that ACSM minimum."

I had had my moment of self-discovery. It is an experience that many folks, including many of you who are reading this book, have had at one time or another, when the time was right. Why it happens at all, and why it happens at one particular time and not another, no one knows. But it does happen. On that day, at that time, in that circumstance, I was ready for that experience, for that big step ahead that took place first in my mind—the place that all positive personal behavior change begins.

I Become a Runner

The high school outdoor track in my community, Port Jefferson, New York, was about three blocks from where I lived at the time. The Saturday morning after I returned from those professional meetings, I laced on a pair of old low-top basketball shoes. I did not buy running shoes. I knew that it was not good to run in sneakers, but I was not at all convinced that I would continue this running business. I had several pieces of almost-new sports equipment around the house, including a pair of soccer cleats. All had been bought in bursts of enthusiasm for various new sports, my participation in which had proven to be short lived. Therefore, I was not buying any more equipment until I had convinced myself that this time I would stick with it. I put on the sneakers and walked over to the track. Being a sailor, and occasionally racing my boat, I had a digital stopwatch that I used for timing the race starts. So I began to run, slowly, just about three weeks before my forty-fourth birthday.

I followed Bob Glover's "Run Easy" walk-run-walk program designed for beginners. I think I lasted about 12 minutes on that first day. It was very difficult. Nevertheless, I did manage to stick with it. Following my moment of self-discovery, I discovered something inside me that I did not know was there: I could stick with exercising if I really wanted to. By the end of the first month, even as the weather got colder, I was hooked. I had gotten over the hurdle that was supposed to be the most difficult one, the 1-month mark, and I was actually enjoying myself. I went out and bought my first pair of running shoes. I started lengthening my workout sessions: 25 minutes, 30 minutes, 35 minutes. I went from three workouts per week to four.

Snow fell. The track, with which I was starting to become bored anyway, became difficult to run on. I left it and started running around a "superblock"—about 0.6 mile long—near my home. It took 5 to 6 minutes for me to cover one lap. The weather got colder. I put on more clothing—so much that I sweated profusely. I must have looked like the Michelin Man, but I was actually having fun. I was learning to run—and, even more importantly, learning to exercise regularly—in the winter. If this is fun, I thought, wait until I get to run in short pants. I took my first run out on the road. I ran about 2 miles after a 2-mile warm-up. Was this really me?

At the end of March 1981, my family and I went to Los Angeles for my brother-in-law's wedding. I took my running stuff with me. The temperature was hovering around 70°F. I went running in shorts for the first time. I was like a kid with a new toy. This was really it! I was now doing 35 to 45 minutes per workout, four or five workouts per week.

Springtime arrived at home. One beautiful Sunday morning I went out and ran a total of 8 miles on the track and road. I did not do them consecutively, and there was a lot of chitchatting as I hooked up with various other runners jogging around the track. However, I had done 8 miles, and had a really hard time tearing myself away from the physical activity. I was actually getting in shape.

I passed the 6-month mark, considered the second major time hurdle in exercising regularly. I did notice a further change in my body around that time. The frequency of shin splints and minor muscle pulls in my legs that I had been experiencing dropped off sharply. My aerobic capacity was improving markedly. Although my enjoyment of the running itself was highly variable, I was enjoying the mental and physical good feelings of the "afterward" more and more. I was really into it. Considering my previous sports background, this was rather amazing to me.

As a child, I had been a virtual nonathlete. I was small and slow. I had no aptitude for the hand-eye coordination sports (and still do not). Although my father had been a fine athlete in the 1920s—a high school 60-minute two-way (offense and defense) football player and, in fact, county quarter-mile sprint champion—the genes for that quality did not seem to have been passed to me. One exception was downhill skiing. I took it up while in medical school in 1959. It was the first sport I had tried that I could actually do. I fell in love with it. By the mid-1990s I had become proficient enough to qualify as a ski instructor and be certified at Level I by the Professional Ski Instructors of America. A skier now for 45-plus years, I teach regularly on a part-time basis at a ski area in Colorado. In the mid-1970s, I took up sailing and enjoyed that sport greatly too. Skiing and sailing have a lot in common—they both involve a sense of balance and require no hand-eye coordination—although sailing involves intense physical activity only on rare occasions (usually associated with pure panic), and skiing is aerobic only in short spurts. So running, the quintessential aerobic/physical-conditioning sport, was an entirely new experience for me.

By the summer of 1981, I had become a regular runner, working out four or five times a week for 30 to 60 minutes at a time. People would occasionally ask me about racing. "No, not for me," I would respond. "I'm doing this for my health and because it makes me feel good." To put some variety into my workouts, that fall I bought the first 10-speed bike I had ever owned. Before the activity had even been formally named, I was engaging in a bit of the cross-training that I spoke about in Chapter 1.

That year I watched the New York City Marathon on television for the first time. I saw the exciting record-setting finishes of Allison Roe and Alberto Salazar. I watched the shots of the "back-of-the-packers" too. I had a slight flicker of personal interest. However, that little restraining voice that we all have inside our heads said "impossible," and that was the end of that.

As winter rolled around, I decided to try something new. I joined a local "body shop" and took up lifting free weights (barbells and dumbbells). I was really getting into my body.

Starting to Race

For reasons that are still unclear to me, that next spring I decided to enter my first running race. It was a 5-miler held in a neighboring community on Memorial Day 1982. My objective was to break 50 minutes. I did 42:21. I had a glorious time. I experienced the runner's high at the end. The particular feeling of satisfaction you get when you finish a distance race was of course something I had never experienced before. Throughout that summer, I continued running and cycling, doing a total time equivalent to 20 to 25 miles of running per week.

In October 1982 I ran my first 10k (6.2 mile) road race. I set a goal of 56 minutes. It was a great day weatherwise, and the course was almost flat. By the halfway mark, I was really getting pumped up. I flew (for me, everything is relative) through the last 2 miles and finished in 50:10. I broke down and wept. I could not believe that I had finished that distance at a minute per mile less than the pace I thought I would run.

The Sunday before Thanksgiving, I did a local "Turkey Trot." I managed 7:40s for 5 miles. After two years of running and three whole races, I was a racer. I could barely wait for the next racing season to begin. (As I have gotten older, even though I am much better conditioned by training and racing regularly, I have not seen running times anything close to those for many years. Did I mention that I was getting older?)

At the end of the 1982 racing season, I joined the Port Jefferson Road Runners Club. It was to become a major influence in my life. The club held group runs on Sunday mornings. Among other things, several members were already training for the 1983 *Newsday* Long Island Marathon, held in May. One of my new buddies asked me about marathoning. "No way," I said. "Too far, too much training, too much pain. You have to be nuts to do a marathon. I'll be happy to do some 10ks next season, but that's it." Little did I know how quickly I would change my mind on the subject of marathoning (either becoming crazy myself or realizing that, no, it was not nuts to do one). As far as triathloning was concerned, the word was not yet even in my vocabulary.

As one is wont to do when running with a club, I fell in with someone who trained at about the same pace I did (9:30- to 10-minute miles) for a distance that I was comfortable with for my then-long run, 6 to 8 miles. Ed Miller was an architect who lived in Port Jefferson. He had started running only the previous September. He was already planning to run the *Newsday* Long Island Marathon in May.

He was planning to run the *Newsday* Long Island Marathon in *May*? How the devil was he going to do that, given that he had just started running the previous September? He told me about a very interesting book by Ardy Friedberg called *How to Run Your First Marathon*. It provided a 22-week program that could be started by someone running no more than 20 minutes three times a week. Completion of the program would, according to Ardy, enable almost any user to finish a marathon, provided that he or she did not attempt to run it at too fast a pace.

I did not know it at the time, but Ed Miller was telling me not only about a marathon-training program that was feasible and doable for me, he was telling me about what would become the basis for my own first triathlon training program. The latter would enable me to complete the 1983 Mighty Hamptons Triathlon and would then evolve into the Triathloning for Ordinary Mortals Training Programs, one of which you will be using for your own race preparation (see Chapter 7). At any rate, Ed was talking about marathons and I was listening. "Why don't I try it?" I thought. But the little restraining voice inside of me said, "No. Too much time, too much training, too much pain." The idea of trying it remained there, nevertheless. A week or two later my curiosity got the better of me, and I asked Ed if he could bring the book along one Sunday.

A week or two after that, I was pursuing what looked like a reasonable, doable program, as designed by Friedberg. It was based on minutes, not miles, which makes training much easier. When you feel good, you run fast. When you feel not so good, you run more slowly. You do not have to measure courses. You just go out for half the required time, turn around, and come back. Overall, the program required an average of just over 4 hours per week for 15 weeks, with a graded pattern of gradually increasing and decreasing weekly times leading to a peak two weeks before the race. The major concepts underlying Ardy's program were "hard/easy,"* scheduled rest, and build up/cut back/build up further. They're discussed in more depth in Chapters 5 and 7.

* Hard/easy refers to a regular alternation of workouts that are difficult and challenging in length and/or intensity with ones that are less so.

Between my winter weight-lifting program and running, I was already working out 3 to 4 hours per week. If I wanted to try a marathon, I could hop in at Week 8 of Ardy's program, which required 220 minutes per week over 5 days, then go on to finish a schedule that did not take that much total time and had only one run of more than 2 hours in it. The little restraining voice again said "no." "But," said competitive me, "if *he* [that is, Ed Miller] could do it, I can do it. I *can* do it." After all, *he* had been running only since the previous September. I had been at it for $2^1/_2$ years. Just like that I crossed the line from "I will never do a marathon" to "Yes, I'm training for my first marathon." I thought, "There, little voice. That wasn't so hard, was it?"

Triathlon Thoughts

By the time I started following Ardy's program, it was already too late to prepare for the 1983 *Newsday* Long Island Marathon in early May. So I set my sights on doing one that fall. As a first test of my long-distance racing ability, I would do a 20-mile race, from the north shore of Long Island to the south shore—Port Jefferson to Patchogue—in mid-June.

As my running time increased during my training, I tapered off the weight training. Overall, my program was going well. I had gotten on Ardy's program and was sticking with it consistently. Then in mid-May I had a really wild idea. I saw an announcement for the 1983 Mighty Hamptons Triathlon, to be held the Saturday after Labor Day. I remembered Julie Moss in Hawaii. I remembered hearing about the 1982 Mighty Hamptons, and that New York City Marathon champion Allison Roe had won it. "I can bicycle," I thought. "My running is getting better, I can handle the increased training time, and I can swim." Looking at the distances involved for that particular race (1.5-mile swim, 25-mile bike, 10-mile run) and projecting completion times for each segment, I figured that it should take me just about as long to finish the Mighty Hamptons as it would to do a marathon in 4:20 or so. (In the end I was just about right—for the actual racing time. I did a 4:46, which happened to include 23 minutes [!] for changing my clothes between the swim and the bike, and the bike and the run.

More on that in Chapter 9.) And here I was already doing marathon-distance training for the run.

The little restraining voice spoke up again. "You can swim? What do you mean you can swim? You mean you know *how* to swim. What makes you think you can go a mile and a half in the water, *then* cycle 25 miles, *then* run 10? You haven't swum in years, and you have *never* swum for distance!" "I know, I know," I said to the little voice, "but this triathlon thing sounds like fun. I'll make a deal with you. I'll send in my entry to Mighty Hamptons. If I get in and if I finish the 20-mile road race, *then* I'll try the swimming. Maybe, just maybe, my aerobic conditioning will carry me through. I promise that if I can't do the swimming, I'll pull out of the race. I don't want to drown me *or* you." "All right, all right," the little voice said, and retreated once again. After all, it knew that it had lost every debate about distance racing since the subject had first come up.

Training for My First

On June 18, 1983, I did that 20-miler in 3:13, slightly under a 10-minute-per-mile pace. Shortly thereafter, I received my acceptance to the Mighty Hamptons Triathlon. Now I *had* to see if I could still swim.

My first swim workout was on July 7 in a pool. I did half a mile in half an hour. I alternated strokes by lap, doing crawl, sidestroke, and elementary backstroke. I discovered that because I was in aerobic shape, I could do the distance without getting worn out if I did not try to go too fast. Paradoxical as it may seem, I progressed rapidly by going slowly. I got up to a mile by the third workout. I dropped the sidestroke by the sixth, splitting time evenly between the crawl and the elementary backstroke. I was taking more than 50 minutes to cover a mile, but I was doing it, and I was comfortable at the end of the workout. I felt that I could do the race. I then designed for myself a balanced swim-bike-run training program based on the concepts in Ardy Friedberg's marathon training program.

In addition to the six pool swims, I did a total of three open-water swims in preparation for that first triathlon. In the first of them, I swam comfortably for an hour in fresh water, turning over on my back when I needed to take it easy for a bit, and resting at the halfway mark. In the second, I swam in tidal salt water for about 70 minutes without stopping, returning to my starting point against an outgoing tide. I went slowly, alternating strokes. I felt good and didn't wear myself out. I followed my running/cycling program closely. I had a good August. About two and a half weeks before the race, I went out to the racecourse and did my third open-water swim: 1.2 miles of its 1.5-mile length. I knew then that I could do the swim in the race. I also knew then that if I finished the swim without becoming a physical wreck, I could complete the bike and the run. Things were looking very good.

Two weeks before the race, I biked 25 miles, then ran 10 miles on a very hot Sunday morning. I was ready. I tapered my training over the next two weeks. I had my bike, all 30-odd pounds of it, "race prepared" at my bike shop. I pulled together all the necessary bits and pieces of equipment and clothing. I packed very carefully, trying hard not to fall into my usual pattern (even back then) of forgetfulness. On the morning before the race, I loaded my bike into my car and took off for Sag Harbor. Upon arrival, I checked into a guesthouse, then checked myself and my bike into the race. I sorted out all of the paraphernalia. I took my bike over to the transition area, the place where you set up your bike and change from the swim to the bike, and the bike to the run. I put my bike into its assigned space on the bike rack. I was really going to do this thing.

Doing It

The next morning I was up bright and early. I felt good and only slightly nervous as I made my way to the race site. I laid out my equipment carefully at my assigned transition-area spot. The swim was on a point-to-point course, not an out-and-back or loop course, which is much more common now. Along with most of the other competitors, I decided to walk the mile or so to the start of the swim rather than using one of the buses provided for transport. The walk gave us a chance to stretch out, to chitchat, to relax. I got to the starting line and prepared for the swim. Almost four years before, Charlie Ogilvie's letter had set me off down the road to that starting line. Until six months before the race date, neither I nor anyone I knew could have imagined that I would be at that place. But there I was. I entered the water, and I finished the race. I describe the experience in detail in Chapter 9. It was a great one.

Next Steps

Following the Mighty Hamptons, I was on an emotional high for about two weeks. I cast around for another event that I could do before the season ended. Three weeks later, I was at Barnegat Light, New Jersey, to do the Ricoh East Coast Championship Triathlon, an event similar in length to the Mighty Hamptons. Between the two I did a metric century (100k) on my bike at near race pace* in an American Heart Association cyclethon. I was flying.

As part of my preparation for the Mighty Hamptons, I had read the three books then in print about the sport. Each was helpful in its own way. But they were all peak-performance oriented, for the athlete who was fast or wanted to be. None was specifically addressed to beginners and/or recreational triathletes who were out there to have fun, to finish happily and healthily, at whatever speeds were comfortable for themselves that day. Being a writer, I started thinking about writing such a book, designed for people like me and you—Ordinary Mortals who just happen to want to be triathletes.

Immediately after the Barnegat Light race, I began training for my first marathon—the White Rock in Dallas, Texas, held on December 4, 1983—using Ardy Friedberg's original program. I completed the race in a slow, comfortable 4:31, running most of the way. For the first time in my life, I thought of myself as an athlete. Although I was slow, I was steady. Unlike Charlie, a man blessed with speed and the perseverance and will to take advantage of it, I was not driven to try to win my age-group, and I thought it unlikely that I ever would be, or indeed could be. (That

* Race pace is the speed at which one does an event.

thought, I have found out as my age-group cohort has become ever smaller, was wrong; see Chapter 11.) Simply doing it was my thing, just as it is for the overwhelming majority of competitors in these open distance events. That has rewards all its own.

For me, the single most important message of this book is this. I formerly was a complete nonathlete. Over the years in multi-sport racing I have had much fun, I have conditioned my body, I have developed my mind, I have improved my health, I have changed my self-concept, I have made many friends, I have had many unique experiences. I have become an athlete. And I have had so much fun along the way. If I could do this, you can too. Now, on to the how-to.

CHOOSING YOUR FIRST
TRIATHLON OR DUATHLON

The world is moving so fast now-a-days that a
man who says it can't be done is generally
interrupted by someone doing it.
—*Elbert Hubbard,* The Complete Triathlon

Triathlons come in a variety of lengths and combinations of
events. The standard combination is swim-bike-run, in that
order. Duathlons are generally run-bike-run. There is a
logic to the order of the segments in both types of race. In
triathlons, the potential for serious mishap is greatest in the swim
leg. This is why triathlons invariably begin with it. The athletes
are physically fresh and hopefully more mentally alert than at any
other time during the race. Further, because the skill/speed range
among triathlete swimmers varies widely, the swim leg spreads
the athletes over the distance. This is important for traffic control
on the bike leg. Once the athletes get on their bikes—racing on
often-narrow roads with usually regular traffic as well—there is
much less likelihood of developing bike packs and traffic jams.
Even when the bike course is closed to automotive traffic, spreading out the competitors for the bike leg reduces the occurrence of
drafting* on the bike.

---

* "Drafting" is riding closely enough behind a cyclist in front of you to take
advantage of his or her blocking of the wind. It is a central element of pure bike
racing, such as that found in events ranging from the local criterium (multi-lap

This spreading out is accentuated when there is a wave start for the swim. In a wave start, entrants are divided into groups, sometimes randomly by race number, sometimes by age and sex. (The rules of USA Triathlon require that the age-groups be set up at five-year intervals, to include the age of the oldest entrant. These rules apply only to USAT-sanctioned races,* however. Non-sanctioned races can set the age-groupings at whatever intervals they desire, and often have a single 60- or 65-plus age-group for all of the older folks.) The waves are then started into the swim at (usually) 3- to 5-minute intervals. Wave starts are becoming more common, even in smaller races.

The bike leg is placed second, because during it racers will occupy the most road length for the longest period of time. Because the bike courses are usually on open, public roads, the authorities always like to have them clear of racers as early in the day after the start as feasible. Occasionally there are cutoff times, after which slow cyclists are instructed by the police to return to the transition area. The bike leg is usually the longest in time duration for all racers, regardless of speed, and is physically the easiest, except on very hilly courses. In biking, as opposed to swimming and running, when you get tired you can always rest while continuing to move forward, by coasting while going downhill or even on the flat. The run, then, is last, because it provides a clean, safe race finish.

The Consistency of Triathlon

The sports of triathlon and duathlon are remarkable in that their structural essence has changed little since they first came on the scene. There are still three segments in all but a few specialized

---

circuit race) to the Tour de France. Although drafting does occur from time to time in crowded races, it is officially prohibited in duathlon and in all but a few professional and Olympic-level triathlons.

* "USAT sanctioned" means that the race will be run using USAT rules, that USAT is providing the liability insurance for the race organizer, and that USAT membership (see page 73), on an annual basis or with a one-day ticket, is required for entry.

races. Each competitor's finishing time is still his or her overall time, including the time spent "in transition"—changing clothing and equipment between each segment. There are a few "stage" races—such as the Liberty to Liberty Long Course triathlon between New York City and Philadelphia, held on Memorial Day weekend, in which the swim, bike, and run legs are stand-alones—but they are few and far between. As noted above, with the exception of a limited number of races done by professionals only, no drafting is allowed during the bike segment, as has been the case since the sport was first developed.

There are many more duathlons and Sprint triathlons than there were when I started out, and there are many more "iron-man" and "half-iron" races too. But they all still have the same format that they have always had. Thus, in contrast to football and basketball, in which important rules are changed all the time, for amateurs ("age-groupers," as we are commonly called) triathlon and duathlon are developing a timeless essence. In this sense, multi-sport racing has much in common with the true game of major league baseball as it is played in the National League (as contrasted with the diluted variety that is played in the American League). True, baseball players are getting bigger, faster, and better conditioned. The ball may have been "juiced" over the years. But home to first is still 90 feet, as it was when the game was created in the nineteenth century. It is still $60\frac{1}{2}$ feet from the pitcher's mound to home. The bats are still made of wood. You are still out after three strikes, and still get to walk to first after four balls. Going over the plate, the ball is still neither a ball nor a strike until the umpire says it is one or the other. And although strategies and tactics have changed some over the years, the incredibly intricate rules of the game have changed little.

Although the essence of triathlon has changed little, if at all, there have been some important developments over the past twenty-five years. The number of races, at a wide range of dis-tances, has increased markedly. The proliferation of Sprints and duathlons has made it much easier for first-timers to get into the sport and for recreational, relatively light-training triathletes like me to stay in it. There have been major advances in equipment technology and design—for the wet suits now used by a majority of racers in the swim, for the bicycles, for the running shoes, and for the clothing you will likely be wearing in the races once you get into the sport. (See Chapter 8 on equipment.) There have been significant changes in the training regimens of the top triathletes, so at the high end faster and faster finishing times are being achieved.

Another change that has occurred is in the names given to the three general groupings of race distances for triathlons. "Tiny tri's" have thankfully come to be called "Sprints." The "Short Course," what I called the "marathon-equivalent event" in the first edition of this book, has become the "Olympic"-distance. In USAT terminology, "Long Course" now refers to the "half-ironman" events (1.2-mile swim, 56-mile bike, 13.1-mile run) and those of similar distances. "Ultra Course" races are now those at the "ironman-distance"—the 2.4-mile swim, 112-mile bike, 26.2-mile run event, or close to it. Not all Ultra Course events at the standard distances are referred to as "Ironman" (capitalized), however. The trademark for "Ironman" is held by the World Triathlon Corporation (WTC), sponsors of the Ironman World Championship held in Hawaii every year, and a series of ironman-distance races held in different countries around the world every year. Non-WTC ironman-distance races, such as the Great Floridian held outside of Orlando every year, go by a variety of names. "Tinman," a term I always regarded as pejorative, implying that any triathlon not composed of the ironman-distances was not a "real" triathlon, has thankfully just about disappeared.

The 2006 season marks my twenty-fourth in triathlon/ duathlon competition. I have participated in more than 165 multi-sport races, including more than a hundred triathlons. Since my first race in 1983, with occasional slight variations, I have continued to use the Triathloning for Ordinary Mortals Training Program (TFOMTP) that I developed in my first full season. I have had continuing success with it. I have finished almost every race I entered, happily and healthily. Many multi-sport racers and thousands of others have had apparent success with the program too. These outcomes confirm the conclusion that I came to during my early training and racing experiences and drew upon while writing the first edition of this book. For finishing Olympic-distance triathlons happily and healthily, if not necessarily quickly, the TFOMTP average of 5 hours per week for 13 weeks works very well.

Doin' the Du'

If you are thinking about getting started in multi-sport racing but don't look forward to training in three sports, or you are looking for a shorter event that is not as demanding as a Sprint triathlon but is still a challenge, or you are weak in or not thrilled with swimming, or you want to do a multi-sport event that is logistically simpler than a triathlon, or are most comfortable on the bike and perfectly happy to do the bulk of your training on it, or any combination of the above, think about "doin' the du'." Duathlons are two-sport races usually having three segments—commonly the run-bike-run sequence. The usual distances are 2 to 3 miles for each of the run segments and 12 to 18 miles on the bike. The duathlon is easier than the triathlon for most people. The format also appeals to race directors: duathlons are obviously significantly easier and cheaper to set up and manage than are triathlons. Thus, duathlon is now well established in most parts of the country. I have done more than sixty duathlons, including several long ones.

Duathlons are sometimes called "biathlons," although the latter name has gradually disappeared from the multi-sport race vocabulary in many parts of the country. There was some controversy over the name. When the event first appeared in very limited numbers in the early 1980s, it was called the "biathlon," because "tri" and "bi" both come from the Greek language. But as the international campaign to gain inclusion for triathlon in the Olympics got under way in the late 1980s, the need to come up with a new name for its two-sport offspring became apparent. In the Winter Olympics there is a well-established Nordic event that combines cross-country skiing and target shooting known as the "biathlon." Understandably, the International Biathlon Union did not want another event in the Olympics— either summer or winter—connected with an event that has the same name as theirs. USA Triathlon (at that time called the Triathlon Federation USA), as well as the triathlon governing bodies of a number of other countries around the world, worked hard to gain acceptance for triathlon to the Olympics. As part of their application, they officially adopted the name "duathlon" for the two-sport races (inserting a Latin prefix into an otherwise Greek word). Not everyone has accepted the change. Many non-USA-Triathlon-sanctioned two-sport races, run by race directors who have no direct connection with the USAT/ Olympic movement, are still called "biathlons." My good friend Dan Honig, founder and owner of the New York Triathlon Club (formerly the Big Apple Triathlon Club), if not the sole inventor of duathlon, was a major force in its early development. He still calls the half dozen or so of these events he runs every year "biathlons."

Regardless of what it is called, it's a fun race. It is quite manageable for many people. The logistics are much simpler than they are for triathlon. Along with no swim, there is no swim stuff to be concerned with. Almost all duathlons have just one transition/ finish area (some triathlons have two, although that number is decreasing), and making the first-to-second-leg transition is obviously easier and faster in duathlon than in triathlon. Because there is no worry about water temperature, in many parts of the country the duathlon season is considerably longer than the triathlon season. Duathlon can be your gateway to triathlon. Or if swimming is just not your thing, duathlon can be your multisport race format of choice.

Because the runs are short, many competitors (including me) wear their bike clothing for the whole race. On the cold, windy days of early spring or late fall, sometimes I add a wind shell and tights to make things more comfortable, especially on the bike segment. On a hot summer day, you may want to doff the bike shirt and wear a singlet on the run, especially the second one. (For more details on clothing, see Chapter 8.) Because I'm not concerned with saving a couple of minutes in transition, and I like to be thoroughly comfortable on the bike, I usually change from my running shoes to my bike cleats and back again. However, in duathlon many people ride wearing their running shoes. They use the flat strapless pedals found on entry-level road and mountain bikes, or the pedals with straps that can be tightened over their running shoes, or one of the platform devices that can be attached to "clipless" pedals (for more information, see Chapter 8).

Choosing Your First Race

Tri or Du?

There are several criteria to use for choosing your first race. First, will it be a triathlon or a duathlon? Ability and interest in swimming are obviously the central considerations here, as is available time to train. (Note that the training programs for the Sprint triathlon and the standard-distance duathlon are of the same length; see Chapter 7.) Second, if you choose triathlon, of what length? Important factors are how much time you have available for training; your previous distance-sports experience, if any; the availability of races that are convenient for you in terms of the calendar and distance from where you live; and how much you are ready to challenge yourself.

Race Length

A calculation that could help you make the decision about length is to figure out approximately how long it will take you to do a race with given distances. You obviously need to know the rate of speed at which you do each event. If your experience is like mine and that of many of my friends, in the race you will probably do the swim at a rate 2 to 4 minutes per mile faster than your training pace, the bike at or slightly above your training pace, and the run at 1 to 2 minutes per mile more slowly than your training pace. The Olympic-distance Triathloning for Ordinary Mortals Training Program (TFOMTP) will prepare most people who use one of its three options to engage in up to $4\frac{1}{2}$ hours of consecutive aerobic exercise. In addition, you will spend a total of 5 to 10 minutes in transition between events. Thus, unless you are very slow (that is, even slower than I am!), the standard TFOMTP will prepare you to do an Olympic-distance event in not much more than four hours, maximum. The Sprint/duathlon TFOMTP will prepare you to do one of these races in plus/minus two hours, maximum. If you are naturally faster than I am, you will naturally go faster, even in your first race.

Racecourse

In addition to length, you will want to consider the many other characteristics of the course itself. For the swim, will it be in salt or fresh water? Most triathlon swims are held in natural bodies of water, although occasionally they are done in pools. Salt water means ocean, bay, or tidal river. It also means extra buoyancy, which I find helpful. If the race is in open ocean, you must be prepared to deal with the possibility of breakers, tides, and an undertow. If the swim is in a bay, it is unlikely that you will have to worry about breakers, but there are still tides, currents, and waves to deal with. For example, in many of the twelve times that I have

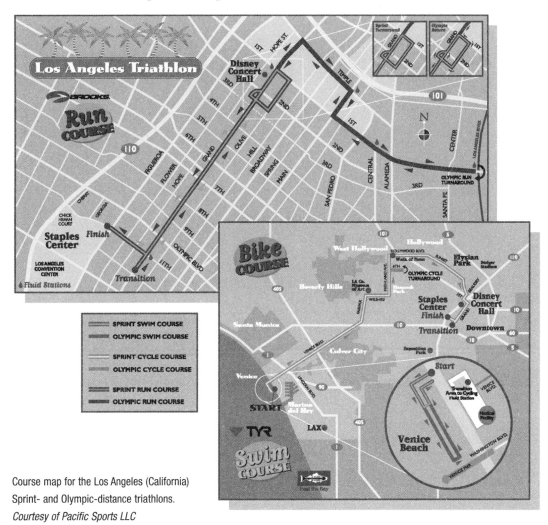

Course map for the Los Angeles (California) Sprint- and Olympic-distance triathlons.
Courtesy of Pacific Sports LLC

done the Mighty Hamptons Triathlon at Sag Harbor, New York, we had to swim into a tide and windblown waves coming from the same direction. Luckily I happen to breathe to that side. I was able to time my swim stroke so that I was breathing at the top of each wave. But it took concentration.

Then there are currents. In the 2001 New York City Triathlon, the downstream Hudson River current for the point-to-point swim course was running at a brisk pace that day. A couple of hundred yards before the finish, I actually made a 90-degree left turn toward the shoreline in order to be carried on a diagonal line towards the exit ramp. Otherwise I would have had to go straight downstream into a safety barrier, then scramble along it to exit the water. However, everybody had a good swim time that day.

I have also experienced "uphill" ocean swims going in one direction when there was a current running lateral to the beach. You do get a nice ride going "downhill" the other way, however. The Town of Hempstead (Sprint) Triathlon at Lido Beach, New York, in 1989 was a good example of this. Fresh water is in and of itself more pleasant than salt water, especially if you happen to take in a mouthful every now and then. But fresh water doesn't have the buoyancy of salt water. And the unpleasantness of some lake bottoms and what grows out of them can negate the pleasantness of the water. A couple of practice sessions on my lawn would have helped me deal with the eelgrass and floating weeds in certain races in shallow lakes.

Water temperature is also an important consideration. Below 70°F, water starts to feel distinctly cold even after you have been swimming for a while. Because you will likely not be using a wet suit for your first race, if possible choose a race in which the water temperature will be at 70°F or above. For temperatures more than one or two degrees below that, you may want to consider using a wet suit. Some of the better bike shops and some dive shops rent them. For some races, your registration materials will have information about available wet suit rentals in the area. At the occasional very large race with an expo set up for a day or two before the race, such as St. Anthony's in Saint Petersburg, Florida, you will find wet suits available for rent from one or more of the merchants displaying there. Of course, different people react to the

That's me coming out of the water during my 100th triathlon, at Kingston, New York, July 14, 2005. *Photo by Chezna Newman*

same water temperature in different ways. My layer of subskin body fat, which I cannot get rid of even after all my years of training, does help insulate me in cool-water swimming.

For the bike and the run, the course criteria to take into account are similar. Is the course a single loop or laps? The former is more interesting, but the latter may make the race more comfortable and seem to go faster as you begin to deal with familiar terrain. If the course is hilly, just how hilly is it? My personal preference is for mildly to moderately hilly courses. I train for the bike and run on hills, and I'm used to them. After you have worked your way up a hill on your bike, you can always get an exhilarating ride down the other side. On the other hand, on flat terrain, as at the 2004 New Jersey Pine Barrens (Sprint) Triathlon at Atsion State Park and the 2005 Belle Plain (Sprint) Triathlon and

Duathlon at Belle Plain State Forest, New Jersey, you have to keep going at a constant pace. This can be a real bother, especially on the bike.

What is the road surface like? Do you have to be extra-prepared for flat tires on the bike leg? Will any running be done on uneven surfaces? What about shade? When the sun is shining brightly, the temperature is 85°F, and the humidity is 90 percent, running on a tree-lined road will be a lot more comfortable than running through a wide-open stretch of farmland. The time of day of the start is an important consideration too. Generally in my experience, the earlier the start the better, even if it means arising on race day in the dark.

Racing Ability

Another criterion to use in deciding when you are ready and what length to try is to take the race-pace test developed some years ago by Dr. E. C. Frederick and Stephen Kiesling. To happily and healthily finish an Olympic-distance triathlon you should be able to do the following over a maximum 5-day span: swim 1k (0.6 mile) in no more than 31 minutes (a 52-minute-per-mile pace), cycle 12k (7.5 miles) in no more than 34 minutes (a 13-minute-per-mile pace), and run 5k (3 miles) in no more than 35 minutes (an 11.7-minute-per-mile pace).

You might want to take this test before you start the TFOMTP if you have already established your aerobic base, or after you have established it through the Basic Aerobic Fitness Program (BAFP; see Chapters 5 and 6). If you pass the test and then do the TFOMTP, you should be able to finish an Olympic-distance triathlon very comfortably. If you fail by a good deal, set your sights on a Sprint or a duathlon for your first race. If you fail by only a little, say in one event, try the test again during the sixth week of the TFOMTP. If you pass on the second try, you will probably do just fine in an Olympic-distance triathlon. If not, and you do want to do longer races eventually, in your subsequent training, work on improving your speed as well as your endurance. Of course if you have previous racing or time-trial experience in one or more of the sports, you do not have to formally take the full test, but rather can just plug in previous performances. Obviously, you must weigh all the variables for yourself and make the choice that suits you best, the one with which you are most mentally and physically comfortable.

Date

This is obviously a major consideration. You must have enough time to train properly. The TFOMTP requires 13 weeks. It assumes that, before you start it, you have been doing aerobic exercise consistently and regularly for $2\frac{1}{2}$ to 3 hours per week for 2 to 6 months. It also assumes that before you start the TFOMTP, you know how to safely ride a bicycle. The date that you choose for your first race, should it be a triathlon, will also be determined by how well you swim using one or more of the strokes that can be employed effectively over long distances (crawl/freestyle, side-stroke, breast stroke, elementary backstroke, or back crawl). Obviously, if you need time to learn how to swim or to bring your skill level up to one that you are comfortable with, that will be a factor in determining the date of your first planned race.

Depending upon how much you have to learn as well as how much time you spend getting into aerobic shape, your date will be anywhere from 3 months to 1 year from the time that you decide to become a triathlete or duathlete. If you think that you are going to need 9 to 12 months to prepare, choose an established race or two in the current season, and write to them, enclosing a stamped, self-addressed envelope, asking for the current year's race information and to be placed on the mailing list for the following year; or look them up on the Web (see page 71 for the URLs of several major triathlon calendar Web sites). Then you can attend this year's triathlon or duathlon as a spectator, or better yet as a volunteer; extra hands, even just showing up on race day, are almost always much appreciated.

You will also have to consider the length of the training season in your part of the country in making your choice of event. Some people run, ride, and swim year-round. I am not one of them. Partly because winter in the northeastern United States means consistently cool to cold weather for three to five months, and partly because I believe in cyclical training, I generally go indoors for the winter. (For more detail on my winter training program, see Chapter 5). Further, although I did it some when I was younger, presently I do not like bike riding in cold weather even when the roads are dry. I find cold headwinds frustrating and hurtful. Even with booties on, my feet feel like blocks of ice. Thus, if you are like me and you pay attention to the temperature in deciding upon your training regimen, you will want to allow at least 13 weeks of predictably decent weather before doing your first triathlon. As noted above, water temperature for the swim is also a factor here. To avoid really cold water, I never do my first triathlon of the season before early to mid-June. I usually do a couple of duathlons in the spring as tune-ups—spring training, as it were.

Distance from Home

Travel time is also a major consideration. You obviously must transport your bicycle to the race. Once you are into the sport, traveling over a distance to a race is great fun, but I suggest not doing that for your first race. For this one, advisable to pick a race nearby, one that you can drive to if not ride your bike to. With the proliferation of races, you will often find something reasonably close to home. Some race directors send out a list of available accommodations with your notice of acceptance, or post the list on their Web site. Some are able to negotiate special rates with local hostelries for triathletes. If a list is not provided, find the town nearest the race site on the map and go to your personal favorite hotel-booking service (or Web site). In any case, if you need to stay overnight, be sure to make your reservations some time in advance. Accommodations convenient to the race tend to fill early, and many races are held in locations that do not have many such facilities.

The Bike

The bike you use can be of the road or mountain bike variety. In either case, preferably it will be equipped with multiple gears and derailleur gear-shifters (see Chapter 8), although people have started out with old-fashioned 3-speeds and even—on a flat bike course—1-speeds. If you start out with a mountain bike or a 3-speed, after your first few races you may well want to get yourself a road bike. However, there are folks who have a mountain bike, enjoy riding it (mountain bikes tend to be more comfortable than road bikes and do better going up hills), and cannot afford or simply don't want to buy a road bike, who happily race on a regular basis on it. You will find much more information on bikes in Chapter 8.

Finding Your First Multi-Sport Race

There are many places to look for your first race. Two national triathlon publications, *Inside Triathlon* and *Triathlete* (see Appendix II), have race calendars, usually in every issue, and a Web site (www.insidetri.com and www.triathletemag.com, respectively) with readily accessible calendars. USAT-sanctioned races are listed in the organization's magazine for members, *USA Triathlon Life*.

The largest calendars in the magazines themselves appear in late winter/early spring, in plenty of time for you to plan your racing season. (Some parts of the country have regional multi-sport racing publications.) You can also find race notices at pro bike shops and running-shoe stores. A number of local/regional triathlon clubs or organizations around the country put on races. Mine, the New York Triathlon Club, has a busy race calendar (www.nytc.org). Local triathlon

---

Race Calendars Online

www.insidetri.com

www.triathletemag.com

www.nytc.org

www.usatriathlon.org, then click on "clubs"

www.trifind.com

www.lin-mark.com

www.active.com

www.danskin.com/triathlon.html

---

clubs are listed by state and city at the USA Triathlon Web site, www.usatriathlon.org. The Danskin company runs a nationwide series of women-only triathlons (Sally Edwards, pro) that has become increasingly popular (www.danskin.com/triathlon.html). Also on the Web are a number of organizations with race calendars that provide online registration services for race organizers who have signed up with them. A comprehensive list can be found at The American Triathlon Calendar (www.trifind.com), which has links to many of the listed races' own Web sites. Among the organizations that provide online registration are, in the Northeast, Lin-Mark Computer Sports (www.lin-mark.com); nationally, there is Active.com (www.active.com/triathlon).

Registration/Entry

By 2005 more and more races were providing for Web-based registration or, as Lin-Mark does, offering the option of printing out the registration form from their Web site, then mailing it in. Confirmation is sent to your e-mail address. Some races, such as those of the New York Triathlon Club, provide morning-of-the-race registration. But you do want to check the Web site of such races to make sure that entry is still open before getting up early on that Saturday or Sunday morning.

Until the Web explosion around the turn of the century, the way to enter a triathlon in advance was through the mail. It is still possible to do this, but for a decreasing number of triathlons and duathlons. Nevertheless, here's the drill. Once you have made your choice of race, send for the application (be sure to enclose a stamped, self-addressed envelope), then return it—with a check for the required amount—as soon as you can. Some of the better known races, such as St. Anthony's in Saint Petersburg, Florida, and the Central Park Triathlon in New York City, fill some months before they are held. Do not wait to receive a written acceptance to start your training. Sometimes acceptances are not mailed out until a week or two before the race. Appearance of your canceled check for the registration fee is an excellent indication of acceptance. However, if you have heard nothing, after a decent interval you can telephone the race director for confirmation. If you are worried about getting in, it may well pay to apply to two events being held at around the same time to be sure of doing at least one. Who knows, if your training goes well and the events are at least two weeks apart, you might end up doing both.

As you know from the previous chapter, in my first triathlon season, I did my second race three weeks after my first, and between the two I did a metric century (100k) at just below race pace on my bike. In my second season, I did three marathon-equivalent races in a four-week period; feeling fine at the end, I ran a marathon six weeks later. I was no Superman. I just followed the TFOMTP and did the races at a comfortable pace. (In 2005 I was still able to "double"—that is, do two Sprint triathlons, about 2 hours each, on consecutive days one weekend, at age 68.) At any rate, when you do get that first race acceptance, you are well on your way to having one of the great experiences of your life—completing your first triathlon or duathlon.

Check-in Requirements

You have to check in for each race to pick up your race numbers and, usually, a goodie bag including at least a race T-shirt. (Race numbers include at least one for you and one for your bike. Sometimes you also have to put a number on the front of your helmet. All triathlons require "body-marking"—using a felt-tipped pen to write your number on at least one limb. At most races you need to show a photo ID. For USAT-sanctioned races, you have to show your USAT membership card or buy a one-day entry (in 2005, it cost $9). Some triathlons and duathlons provide for morning-of-the-race check-in, a great convenience. However, many races, especially those that are USAT-sanctioned, require you to check in prior to the race. The race directions tell you when and where to do this, often providing more than one place and/or more than one time. Some races provide a secure, guarded area where you can safely leave your bike overnight.

USA Triathlon Membership

I strongly recommend joining USA Triathlon, the sport's national organization. First and most important, you will be supporting the body that has played a major role in the growth and development of triathlon and duathlon across the nation. USAT constantly promotes the sport and works to increase its visibility in the media; establishes, maintains, and enforces the rules that make the sports uniform and enhance race safety across the country; has a national training and certification program for coaches; sponsors and provides training for the U.S. Olympic triathlon team; offers a comprehensive insurance program for race directors (a central element of the "race-sanctioning" function); and represents the United States in the International Triathlon Union. You benefit by joining an enthusiastic fellowship, and saving money if you do four or more sanctioned races during a season. For members, registration for a sanctioned race is free; nonmembers must obtain a one-day license (which cost $9 in 2005). Furthermore, regardless of the number of sanctioned races you do, you will save the time and inconvenience of getting that one-day pass for even just one race.

At the basic membership level (there are two higher ones; see the Web site, www.usatriathlon.org), for the $30 fee (as of 2005) members receive, among other benefits, excess accident insurance while participating in USAT-sanctioned events, a subscription to *USA Triathlon Life*, a Choice Hotels discount card, a free trial issue of the *USA Triathlon Performance Coaching Newsletter*, a copy of the official USA Triathlon Rulebook, and inclusion in the USA Triathlon national ranking system after competing in at least three USAT-sanctioned events in one of the two disciplines: triathlon or duathlon.

Conclusion

Making the choice of which duathlon or triathlon to do for your first race becomes easier each year as more multi-sport races are developed in all parts of the country. You should have an ample number from which to choose, regardless of where you live. The major factors to consider are length, combination of events, distance from home/convenience, cost (of the event itself and of travel/accommodations), time of year/time for training, course characteristics, fresh water/salt water and water temperature, and of course your own ability. The choice you make will obviously be the result of the balancing and weighing of these factors and some others not on my list that may well occur to you. Whichever race you choose, if you train for it properly, the odds are that you will finish happily and healthily. The experience of that first race will be unforgettable, as mine still is for me, no matter how many more you do. And you may well become a regular at some level, as do so many folks who try it once.

RUN, PACEWALK, BIKE, AND SWIM: TECHNIQUE

I have two good doctors—my right leg and my left.
—*Anonymous*

When I wrote the first edition of this book in 1985, I did not consider myself an expert on technique in any of the three principal sports of triathloning: running, cycling, and swimming. I still don't. However, I do each sport reasonably well, and well enough to have finished happily and healthily for all of these years. Good technique is an important contributor to good race performance, whether that term is defined by speed, comfort, mechanical efficiency, injury prevention and control, longevity in the sport (as in my case in particular), or some combination of the above. Certainly, if you want to go faster in your races, and have the time and bodily equipment to do so, by all means go for it. Good technique is an important element of going faster. But if you simply want to stay in the sport to have fun without going fast, as I do, good technique—at a modest pace to be sure—is equally as important.

In this chapter, I offer you my thoughts on good technique in each of the three sports, drawn from my reading, conversations with experts, and experience—considerations that have stood me in good stead for my 24-plus years of racing. However, please understand that I am not setting myself up as a technical expert in any of the three sports. For higher-level technical expertise than I offer here, you will have to seek additional guidance. At the end of this chapter, I review some of the other principal sources of advice on technique.

Some General Thoughts on Technique

On Good Technique

In distance sports, as in medicine and sailing, there is often more than one way to do it right, although frequently someone who offers guidance will insist that his or hers is the only way to do it. There are also many different ways to do it wrong. Regardless of the correct way (or ways), you should make sure that what you are doing does not fall into the "bad" category. How then do you judge?

Good technique in the distance sports produces efficiency. You cover maximum distance at good speed for any given expenditure of energy. Good technique also enables you to do this with the most comfort. For long races, this translates as experiencing the least pain. Doing distance sports can hurt. At the paces I talk about, the pain level is not that high, and far from unendurable or incapacitating. However, there may be *some* pain. Good technique keeps the hurting down to the lowest possible level. If speed is of concern to you, good technique will enable you to go as fast as your cardiovascular and musculoskeletal conditioning and your genetic makeup have equipped you to go. Good technique is also one of the keys to injury prevention. For example, running with your feet splayed can lead to knee injury; cycling in too high a gear and too low a cadence (your pedal-turning rate) can lead to the same thing.

On Bad Technique

Bad technique has effects generally opposite to those of good technique. One of the problems is, however, that the athlete is not necessarily aware that he or she is doing anything that is counterproductive. If bad technique leads to immediate discomfort—as it does, for example, when you cycle with the seat so low that your quads (front thigh muscles) never get stretched out—you of course recognize it right away: it hurts. Even if you do not know the source of the discomfort, you know that you are uncomfortable and hopefully will seek advice from a book, a magazine, a Web site article (such as those offered by active.com and *Inside Triathlon* at www.insidetri.com), a friend, or a coach. However, unless you have an experienced person watch you, you may make a technical error that decreases your efficiency but does not cause pain, and you may never know that you are doing anything wrong. Technical errors in swimming are often of this variety.

Recreational triathletes are not likely to swim fast enough to get into the pain or out-of-breath zone, because of the well-placed fear of getting into trouble and not having the option of stopping for a rest while on the water. Unlike in swimming, on the bike and the run you can stop at any point if you have to. Thus, many of us (I certainly) tend to take it relatively easy while swimming. If you are swimming with poor technique, the usual outcome is not pain but loss of efficiency, wasting of energy, decline in speed, and possibly some feelings of anxiety. Other than in the latter case, this state of affairs could continue over a long period of time without you knowing it. "I'm a slow swimmer and I will just have to live with that fact," you might say. Alternatively, in an effort to speed up, you might put in a lot of extra training time that could have been saved if only you were using correct technique, which would make speeding up easier.

Bad technique in the other two sports—cycling and running—can slow you down for simple mechanical reasons. Cycling in too upright a position increases wind resistance. If you run with too short a stride you will obviously cover less distance with each step. Because there is a limit to how fast we can make our legs go, a shorter stride can mean a slower rate of speed. Finally, if good technique protects against injury, it follows that bad technique increases your risk of being injured.

Overtraining

Overtraining also increases the risk of injury. The three most important telltale signs of overtraining are feeling fatigued frequently throughout the day; having the "I really don't want to" response too often just before a scheduled workout; feeling stressed out by "having to" train; and perhaps by feeling compelled to try to go faster. Injury and overtraining are the most frequent causes of quitting for the regular distance athlete. Thus, you should correct bad technique and make sure that you do not overtrain.

On Breathing

While exercising you should breathe through your mouth, primarily using your diaphragm (the horizontal tissue at the bottom of your rib cage that separates it from your abdomen). You will occasionally want to fill your lungs fully with air by consciously expanding your upper rib cage and raising your shoulders. However, diaphragmatic breathing is the key to good, beneficial sports breathing. If you are running fast enough to raise your respiratory rate significantly, you will want to fall into a rhythmic pattern. When I am moving right along, I will breathe in for two steps, out for two steps. Breathing in for one step, out for one step means that I am working too hard and will not be able to hold that pace for long. Breathing in for three steps and out for three steps is a leisurely pace for me. If I am breathing less hard than that on a training run (and on the easy days, I am breathing less hard than that), I do not bother with maintaining a rhythm.

When I am pushing hard and getting tired in running, biking, and swimming, I find that a pattern of quick, full inspirations followed by long, slow, complete expirations—essentially blowing as much air out of my lungs as I can for a few breaths—is helpful for recovery. This cleans out carbon dioxide (CO_2) from the lower reaches of the lungs, where it can accumulate with less than full expiration. The less CO_2 there is clogging up all of those little breathing sacs (alveoli) in your lungs, the more surface area there is available for oxygen (O_2) to cross into the bloodstream. Ergo, I feel better shortly, even while continuing to move forward. Develop your own variation of the pattern and try it. It should work for you too.

On Running Technique

In Chapter 1, I said that one running-shoe storeowner, a runner himself, told me that running is mainly a matter of right, left, right, left. However, if you sit down to talk with other experts (and him too), you will find that there is a bit more to it. Foot strike is the single most important component of running technique. Although there are several different good approaches, for most recreational distance athletes the best one seems to be "heel-ball." You land on the outside edge of your heel first, then quickly roll along the outside edge of your foot, rotating inward as the ball of your foot comes in contact with the ground, then driving off the ball and big toe into the next stride. Keep your toes pointed straight ahead. You do not want to run solely on the balls of your feet, nor do you want to land hard on your heels, then slap the rest of your foot down on the ground. There is enough pounding and jarring in running when it is done well; you do not want to do anything to accentuate it. Run lightly and in balance.

Your arms should be bent at the elbows. Arm swing should be straight ahead, not across your chest. As in walking, the arm going forward is the one opposite the leg going forward at the same time. The bulk of the arm swing should be at the elbow, not the shoulder. If you are at all like me, you will find it unnatural to run with *no* shoulder swing at all, but the shoulders should come into play in a significant way only when you are driving up a hill. Keep your hands partially open and cupped. Neither clench your fists nor let your hands and fingers flop around aimlessly; both waste energy. A quiet upper body is one of the keys to effective running.

Stand up straight, but do not lock yourself into an erect posture. Bending at the waist inhibits movement of the diaphragm, the major muscle that you want to use for breathing. Making yourself rigidly upright, especially at the shoulders, produces only spasm and pain. From time to time, I have had a problem with shoulder cramping. When I get into the right gait and do not develop shoulder pain, the run is much more fun. As in everything else, the keys are balance, balance, and balance. Hold your head erect. All the books tell you to keep your gaze level, off in the distance. That is good for posture. However, if you are at all like me, you will also be concerned about road conditions immediately in front of you: cracks, bumps, broken glass, holes, discarded mattresses, dead animals, animal droppings, and the like. Compromise. Keep your head up, but cast your eyes down from time to time, and try not to bend your neck.

Going up *and* coming down hills can present some problems. Because I live in a hilly area and train on hills, I actually like them. In a race, often when others are slowing down on a hill, I am trying to speed up or at least maintain my rate of speed. I shorten my stride, bend slightly forward at the waist, pick up my pace, maintain heel-ball foot strike, and drive forward with my arms at the shoulders. My breathing rate increases, my quads begin to burn, but boy does it feel great at the top, especially if I have managed to pass a few people on the way up. Visualization is a technique that I have used successfully in hill climbing, especially in races.

Visualization

On the way up, try to see yourself at the top of the hill, and try to feel yourself there too. Try to imagine what it will be like to be at the top and then to be relaxing with the pain easing in your muscles as you glide down the other side.

I used this technique with some success in my first marathon— the White Rock, in Dallas, Texas, in December 1983. The course was generally flat except for some hills at miles 8 to 12 on the way out. Those same hills turned up at miles 18 to 22 on the way back. If you were going to "hit the wall" (literally run out of energy and feel just terrible), I guess the race organizers wanted you to do so with a vengeance. At any rate, I was going through this first marathon on my planned 9:30- to 10:00-minute pace and was having a good time. At about mile 17, I fell in with a pleasant young woman from Tulsa, Oklahoma. She was struggling a bit as we got into the hilly section. Using visualization, I talked both her and myself right through the hills. "Power up with your arms, see yourself at the top; feel yourself gliding down the other side." I did not even think about the wall, nor apparently did she. We both finished the race happily and healthily.

I have also used the technique many times in long triathlons. In those circumstances, I focused not so much on the specifics of terrain but on, for example, getting to a turnaround and saying to myself, "OK, that's halfway home. Downhill from here." Even on the outbound leg, I start talking myself through it by saying, "OK, that's halfway to halfway." Or, feeling hot, a bit tired, a bit achy, saying to myself, "Just see yourself crossing the finish line, think about how good you are going to feel having made it, and walking around with a nice cold drink in your hand."

For going downhill, gliding—not pounding—is the key, unless you really want to make up time. If you do want to go really fast, you have to lengthen your stride. But even as you try to maintain heel-ball, you will find yourself coming down pretty hard. In any case, lean forward slightly from the hips, but do not bend forward at the waist. Leaning backward, as I did as a beginner, is also a no-no. It acts as a brake, robbing you of the benefits of gravity's pull, and increases the pressure on your heels. Do not flail your arms. Keep them going as you do when running on the flat. Increase your stride length by raising your knees—pushing off well and getting more bounce up—not by reaching out farther in front. However, when coming down really steep hills, you actually have to shorten your stride to stay in control. The most important thing about running downhill is, in fact, to stay in control. Your prime objectives should be to stay on your feet, stay in balance, and avoid injury, even if it means losing a few seconds here and there.

On Walking

Suppose you don't like to run, or simply cannot for one reason or another. Can you still do triathlons or duathlons? You sure can. Try walking. It is specifically permitted by the USA Triathlon rules (Article VI, 6.1). You can just do regular walking. At a brisk pace you can do about 15 minutes for the mile. If you use one of the athletic walking gaits, you can increase your speed considerably while still incurring much less wear and tear on your body than you do when running. There is no secret here. In running, with each step there is always an instant when you are airborne. In any walking gait, by definition your rear foot is still on the ground when your front foot comes down. Thus, in walking the weight bearing is split with each step, sharply diminishing the jarring and pounding that for many people accompanies running.

You can try race walking. It can be a fast gait (how do 7-minute miles sound?), although the technique takes some time to learn, and it is rule centered. Why not consider what I call PaceWalking* (also known as striding, health walking, power walking, exercise walking, aerobic walking, and fitness walking)? I have done it in a number of triathlons and duathlons and in the 1989 New York City Marathon; I managed sub-11-minute miles for the distance, not too far off my personal best running.

There are two PaceWalking gaits: Exercise PaceWalking and the PaceWalking Race Gait. They are both simple. In Exercise Pace-Walking, you walk fast with a purposeful stride of medium length. With each step, you land on your heel, feet pointing straight ahead, then roll forward along the outside of your foot and push off with your toes. You can rotate your hip forward with the forward motion of the leg on the same side, something akin to what race walkers do. But that is not essential. Your back should be comfortably straight, shoulders dropped and relaxed, head up. Keeping your elbows comfortably bent, you swing your arms forward and back, strongly, with purpose. For balance your arm swing should emphasize the back-, not the fore swing. With some practice, you may be able to Exercise PaceWalk at about a 12-minute-per-mile clip.

The PaceWalking Race Gait is jogging while keeping one foot on the ground at all times. Your body is relaxed, bent forward slightly at the waist. Your arm swing is not accentuated. You just do whatever you need to do for balance and rhythm. As long as your rear foot is still on the ground when you come down on your front foot, you are by definition walking. There are no rules for the PaceWalking Race Gait. Just maintain a gentle rock and roll, and have fun. Try both PaceWalking gaits. You may really enjoy the sport, as are an increasing number of people. In addition, as you catch some worn-out formerly running shufflers toward the end of a triathlon run leg, you will feel pretty good about racing with it too.

---

* In 1988 I published a book, with coauthor Peter Radetsky, entitled *PaceWalking: The Balanced Way to Aerobic Health* (New York: Crown). Long out of print, it is still available used from the popular Web bookstores.

On Cycling

For the beginning triathlete, the most important consideration in cycling technique is not found in the mechanics of the body but in the fit and comfort of your bike (see also Chapter 8). If a bike is too big or too small, if the seat is incorrectly adjusted, if the handlebars are too high or too low, if the handlebar stem is too long or too short, your technique really does not matter; you cannot ride the bike properly. There are many lengthy treatises on bike fit published in cycling books and magazines. If you are handy and have a great deal of patience, you can fit your own bike to yourself—assuming that you have the correct frame size and component lengths to begin with. To my mind, the easiest and best way to ensure that your bike fits right is to have it taken care of in a good pro bike shop. How do you know whether the bike shop you are standing in is a pro shop? See Chapter 8 for their characteristics.

Once you have a bike that fits, you have to turn your attention to the three points of attachment between you and it: seat, handlebars, and pedals. The fore-and-aft adjustment of the seat is critical. Once the seat is placed correctly, two important techniques are moving back on it to increase thrust in hill climbing, and moving back on it when braking in order to increase the weight over the rear wheel, which you want to brake first. Your seat must be placed far enough back on the seat post so that these maneuvers can be carried out without discomfort.

The position of your hands on the handlebars is very important. There are three places you can put them: on the drops (the downward-curving sections of the handlebars), on the brake hoods (the mounts found on the front of each handlebar to which the brake handles are attached, and through which they are connected to the brake cables), or on the tops (the flat, upper section of the handlebars that connects the drops to the stem, or turning post). On virtually all contemporary bicycles, the levers that control the gear-shifting mechanisms—the front and rear derailleurs (see illustration, page 84)—are integrated with the brake hoods and handles. (For an understanding of the bike and the incredible number of working parts that are put into a limited amount of

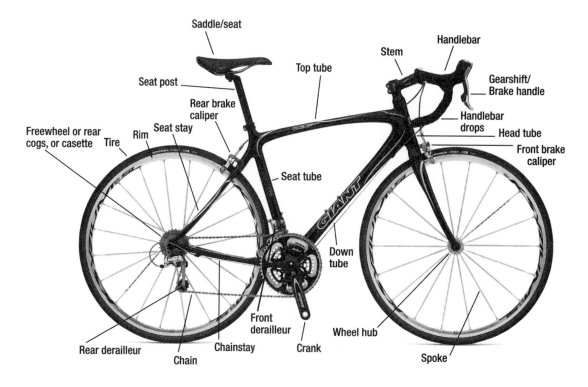

The standard road bike, a Giant 2006 OCR Composite. *Photo courtesy of Giant Bicycle*

space, see also Chapter 8.) The usual riding position is with your hands on the brake hoods or just back toward your body from them. This position gives you the maximum turning control and allows you to reach the brakes quickly if necessary. You let your hand rest on the hood, thumb to the inside, fingers to the outside. For more security, you can grasp the underside of the hood with your index and middle fingers. Your back is moderately bent, reducing wind resistance, but not so bent over as to be uncomfortable over the long haul.

With your hands on the drops, you have maximum braking control and power. You also have good turning control. It is the most aerodynamic position, and thus is the position of choice for going into a headwind and for picking up speed when you need to. With experience, I became used to the drops; even as I have gotten older and less flexible, I spend more time on the drops than I used to. The most aerodynamic position is achieved using aero

Here I am in the 2002 New York City Triathlon, "hands on the hoods." *Photo by official photographer, 2002 NYC Triathlon*

bars—forward extensions from the midpoint of the handlebars. I have used aero bars infrequently, because I am more comfortable using the classic road bars for more balance and control, but I do discuss them briefly in Chapter 8.

For a change of position to get comfortable during a long bike segment, you can ride with your hands on the tops from time to time. It is comfortable because your back is straight, you are relatively upright, and, believe it or not, the pressure on your bottom is the least. These are the reasons why leisurely bike riding in the 7 to 10 mph range is usually done in this position. However, as speed goes up, so does wind resistance. Upright is a no-no at 15 to 20 mph. Furthermore, with your hands close together on the tops, you have the least turning control and your hands are the farthest away from the brakes. Back in June 1984, I learned this lesson the hard way.

Out on a training ride, I was going through a busy intersection very slowly, making a left-hand turn. I had my hands on the tops instead of on the hoods or the drops. As I made my way through traffic at slow speed, the front wheel began to wobble. With my hands on the tops, I could neither stop the bike with the brakes nor effectively control the wobble because my hands were too close together. I tipped over to the right, instinctively stuck out my right arm in an attempt to break the fall, and sustained a shoulder dislocation and a fracture of one of the protrusions at the upper end of my upper arm bone. The injury was the result of a low-speed accident that was entirely my own fault. It would not have happened if my hands had been on the hoods or the drops.

The third point of attachment between you and the bike is at the pedals. Pedal considerations are mainly in the equipment realm rather than the technique realm. Thus, I deal with them primarily in Chapter 8. I will say one thing here about a pedaling technique called "ankling," which calls for active ankle flexion through the downstroke. Although used by many top bike racers, many expert cyclist triathletes advise against it for triathloning. For one thing, it stresses the Achilles tendon, something that you do not want to do if you are a runner. Generally, it is recommended that the sole of your foot be kept more or less parallel with the ground throughout the whole pedaling cycle except on the upstroke, in which the heel is elevated slightly as you pull up.

The most important element in the mechanics of cycling is the rate at which you turn the pedals. This rate is directly related to the gear that you select. The key to successful cycling is being in a relatively low gear, pedaling at a relatively high cadence. This is the road version of the exercise called "spinning," which has become popular in many a gym bike workstation. For the triathlete, the cadence range to aim for is 80 to 100 rpm. It takes some practice to learn this technique for the road. Leisure-time cyclists are not used to pedaling that fast. (Gym-trained spinners have a definite advantage here.) But believe it or not, pedaling that fast does mean less leg-muscle work (in the long run, or ride), less fatigue, and more cardiovascular efficiency. The stroke should be smooth, not jerky, and with each leg, you should be pulling on the upstroke as well as pushing on the downstroke. Pedaling at 70 rpm or less means more fatigue, more pain, and more risk of knee injury. But getting comfortable at a high cadence takes some time.

Do not rush it. You will eventually find a target cadence between 80 and 100 that you are comfortable with. You can count your cadence using a stopwatch, or you can get a tiny handlebar-mounted bike computer that, along with providing a good deal of other data, does the cadence counting for you (see Chapter 8). To help you get comfortable with maintaining a cadence over 80, you need to learn to shift gears constantly as the terrain changes, so that you can stay at or near your target spinning rate regardless of the incline or decline pitch of any particular hill. As you get even better and more conditioned, you will be able to reduce your gear shifting and stay in your target rpm range by adding muscle power as needed.

Shifting gears takes a bit of practice. You must be pedaling to shift gears on any bike equipped with derailleur shifting. Derailleur shifting is the system that moves the bike chain that connects the pedals with the rear wheels over two sets of metal-toothed rings of different sizes and numbers of teeth. One set, the chain rings—either two or three of them—are attached at their center to the cranks, the arms that are in turn attached to the pedals. The other, called the "rear cogs" or the "freewheel cogs," or the "cassette," is mounted on the rear-wheel axle. When the chain is on the larger front ring, the gear is higher—that is, the pressure needed to turn the pedals is greater. The same holds when the chain is on a smaller cog on the rear wheel. And vice versa: the smaller the front chain ring and the larger the rear cog in use, the lower the gear and the less pressure needed to turn the pedals.

The key to shifting success is doing it when there is as little pressure on the pedals as possible, while at the same time turning the cranks. It sounds contradictory, but practice will demonstrate how it works. The key to successful gear shifting on the hills is advance planning. Downshift early so that you don't get caught cranking at 20 rpm with searing quads (the muscles on the front of your thighs) and knees feeling as though they are about to pop (they aren't, but they can feel that way). Think ahead. If you get into a reasonable gear and are spinning at a reasonable cadence *before* you start up a hill, should you have to downshift again the bike will have enough forward momentum to enable you to release the pressure on the pedals for an instant while continuing to crank. Then you can downshift. Above all, remember that good bike pedaling is not a macho thing. Suffering up a hill in too high a gear impresses no one except your knees and quads, and they are likely to hate you for it. Likewise, on the flat if you are spinning at 90 rpm in a middle gear, you will pass many a cyclist grinding away at 60 rpm in top gear. In addition, you will be expending significantly less energy than he or she is.

Gear selection can be a complicated, sometimes arcane matter. Bike gears are quantified in "gear inches." The number of gear inches for any combination of front chain ring and rear freewheel cog connected by the chain is determined as follows. Divide the number of teeth on the chain ring by the number of teeth on the freewheel cog. Then multiply the result by the diameter of the bicycle's wheels in inches, usually 27. This figure is the number of gear inches you will be pedaling in for that combination of sprockets. Once you know the number of teeth on the respective sprockets, however, you do not have to go through the arithmetic yourself. Gear-inch tables covering any conceivable combination are available in cycling books and bike shop catalogs, and at your friendly dealer. Once you know the gear inches for your 10 or 18 or 27 chain-ring/rear-cog combinations, you know which ones are duplicative and you know in which order to go as you shift up and down through the range. Obviously, the larger the gear-inch number, the higher the gear, and vice versa. If you use a modern bike computer, such as the Shimano Flight Deck, it will tell you what your various gear inches are as you shift through the gears.

Now, all that being said, I feel that the best guide to proper gear selection when riding is feel and being in the right cadence range for any given pitch of hill, up or down. I have not looked at gear-inch tables for a long time. I am very familiar with my bike and have developed a shifting pattern that feels right and helps to keep me within my desired cadence range.

Braking is fairly simple: rear-wheel brake (controlled by the right brake handle) first, then the front-wheel brake (controlled by the left brake handle). Front wheel first can lead to painful outcomes if you happen to somersault over the handlebars. Try to anticipate situations. Bikes are inherently unstable. Slow down going into turns, especially sharp ones. Lose a few seconds rather than risk injury. You get the most leverage on the brake handles with your hands on the drops, but you can reach the brake handles with your hands on the hoods. By the way, long treatises have been written on turning and cornering. Suffice it to say here that the key to success is not to have the inside pedal in the 6 o'clock position.

On Hill Climbing

I have already mentioned the importance of thinking ahead, shifting early, and maintaining your cadence. Equip your bike with a large enough rear-wheel cog so that, in combination with your small chain ring up front, you will have a gear low enough to get you up any hill that you are likely to encounter, without grinding away at a low rpm. Keep your hands on the brake hoods. This practice will give you maximum steering control and maximum diaphragmatic expansion capability. Also, you will add power if you grip the hoods, looping your index and third fingers under them, pulling up with the arm on the same side as that of the leg going through the downstroke.

Standing up in the saddle can add tremendously to the power of any downstroke. Done correctly, your hands will be gripping the brake hoods and your torso will be over the handlebars. You can get more power without standing by shifting back on the saddle and moving your hands to the tops for the greatest leverage. Obviously, if you take my advice, you will do the latter only if you are sure that you will not have to brake or turn while your hands are up there. As for going downhill, be careful. In training rides on busy public roads with sometimes bumpy, obstacle-strewn shoulders, I rarely let 'er rip. Even in a race, I do so only on smooth-surface roads closed to vehicular traffic. I would rather lose a bit of time than significantly increase my risk of injury.

Whether racing or training, I have learned that for safety on the bike it is a good idea to come into all intersections with your hands on the brake hoods and handles, so you have virtually instant access to the brakes. In a race, when you are entering an intersection that is controlled by law enforcement officials or volunteers or both, slow down at least a bit to make absolutely sure that a motor vehicle is not barreling into the intersection. It is an extremely rare event, but there have been a few instances in which motor vehicles have gone through even police controls at intersections on a racecourse, causing severe injury, even death, to a cyclist.

The development of indexed shifting (which creates the "click" that you hear when shifting any modern bike) and the integration of shift levers with the brake handles on many modern bikes has made gear shifting much easier to do than it was back in the days of down-tube-mounted shift levers. I suggest taking advantage of that facility. Shifting frequently on a hilly course can make it easier to maintain the steady pedaling pace at a reasonably high cadence that reduces the effort needed on the ride. The integration of shift levers and brake handles has also made it easier to shift hand positions on the ride, adding to your comfort level.

On Swimming

Swimming is the technically most complex of the three triathlon sports. It is the one in which I am technically the weakest. Strangely enough, it is the one in which my relative performance is the best. This is not because I am a fast swimmer, but only because so many recreational triathletes swim even more slowly than I do.

Why is swimming the most complex triathlon sport? First of all, swimming well is a skill that takes time to learn. Much practice of form is needed, aside from conditioning. Second, the immediate benefit to overall race performance from swimming faster is not great. In the Olympic-distance triathlon, the swim distance is slightly under a mile, taking the average recreational triathlete 25 to 40 minutes. Presently it takes me 42 to 45 minutes. (Suppose you improve by 15 percent, a large amount. You may gain up to 6 minutes. With much less practice and a little planning, you can save the same amount of time in the transition from one event to another. A similar percentage improvement in the bike portion of the race could net you 12 minutes or more). A third factor in relatively poor swim performance by recreational triathletes is that boredom is a major problem in swim training. However, swimming with good, or at least decent, technique regardless of speed will help your performance in the other two legs of the race by conserving muscular and cardiovascular energy. Thus, it is worthwhile to learn how to swim with at least decent, comfortable technique, although achieving that objective may not be at the top of your priority list.

When you start out in swim training as a beginner triathlete, I strongly recommend using different strokes during each workout. Do not try to do the whole workout crawl (freestyle) right off the bat. That will come. When I started swim training for triathlons in the pool, I was doing one lap crawl, and one lap sidestroke, and one lap elementary backstroke. After a few workouts, I dropped the sidestroke and went to crawl for half the time, then elementary backstroke for the balance. For many years now, I have done my workouts exclusively in the crawl. However, if you are more comfortable doing the breaststroke or the sidestroke or even the back crawl (although, in the races, staying on course may present a bit of a problem here), then by all means do it. I now race exclusively using the crawl with one exception. After passing the age of 60, I found that I could actually get seasick in a rough-water swim. My solution to this problem has been to turn to the sidestroke, in which I can keep my head out of the water, which seems to ward off seasickness. (Taking an anti-nausea medication before the race helps, too, as long as it does not have drowsiness as a side effect.) In addition, I sometimes use sidestroke for a breather now and then in the longer races. However, this stroke is significantly slower than the crawl. For navigational purposes in open-water swims, you should learn one stroke, breast or lifesaving crawl, that you can use for brief intervals to enable you to hold your head out of the water and look straight ahead.

Whatever stroke you are doing, concentrate on using the upper body. Doing that will help your performance in the other two segments of the race, dependent as they are on leg power. Swimming the crawl places you in a private world that you must get used to if you are going to be a successful swimmer. It is quiet and noisy at the same time. It is quiet in the sense that the outside world is almost totally excluded. The noises that you do hear are those of your own breathing and your passage through the water. Your vision is limited, too, even if you are wearing goggles (and you certainly should be). When swimming you see only a small segment of the world above water level, on the side on which you breathe, for the brief intervals that your head is out of the water. Compounding the problem is the fact that when swimming you must breathe in a rhythmic fashion, only when your head is out of the water. Unlike the experience in biking and running, your breathing is confined, and feelings of claustrophobia can develop. (If they do, just turn over on your back and take a blow.) Of course, millions of people swim correctly, happily, and successfully. You can too. If you are not already a swimmer, it will just take time and practice.

Most triathletes do most of their swim training in a pool. This is fine for endurance and speed. It can be done in consecutive laps, and it can be done in "sets." A set is a specified distance or number of lengths/laps. Interval training is doing sets repetitively with short rest periods in between. They can help relieve boredom. Sets done as interval training, with increased speed, will also help you to lower your time if that is an objective. I seldom do any of these multi-sets anymore, preferring to go at a comfortable pace for whatever time I have on the schedule for that particular workout. If I am using a format, the "countdown 10" (number 4 at left) is my favorite. It is always nice to know that, with one exception, the next set will have fewer lengths than the one I am presently doing.

If the swim portion of your first triathlon is in open water, it is a good idea to do some open-water swimming in addition to pool swimming. The type of open water that you choose to swim

---

Some Set Patterns for a 25-Yard Pool

1. "Dome 4," for 800 yards, a bit under half a mile. *1-2-3-4-4-4-4-4-3-2-1*. That is, you do one length, then two lengths, then three lengths, and so on. These are not "laps," by the way. A lap is defined as an out-and-back round-trip. A length is just that: one length of the pool. Rest 10–15 seconds between segments.

2. "Dome 6," for 1,500 yards, slightly under the Olympic triathlon swim distance of 1,500 meters. *1-2-3-4-5-6-6-6-6-6-5-4-3-2-1*. Rest 10–15 seconds between segments.

3. "Ladder 16," for 1,600 yards, slightly under a mile. *4-8-10-14-12-8-4*. That is, you do four lengths, then eight lengths, and so on. Rest 20–30 seconds between sets.

4. "Countdown 10," for 1,500 yards: *10-9-8-7-6-5-5-4-3-2-1*. Rest 5–10 seconds between sets.

in should be the same as you will be swimming in for your race: freshwater lake, river, saltwater bay, or ocean. There are several reasons for doing some open-water training. First, you will need practice in swimming continuously, uninterrupted by making turns and doing push-offs. Second, if you will be racing in salt water, you need to get used to it. I like it because of the buoyancy. Some people do not like salt water because of the unpleasant sensation you get when you swallow some. There is also the matter of tides, currents, and waves (referred to in the previous chapter). Third, you need to get used to the racing-water temperature, usually colder than that encountered in a pool. Lastly, you will benefit from having some practice in open-water navigating. Thus, open-water swimming in triathlon training is not just for conditioning but for technical reasons. However, make sure that you do any open-water swimming safely, in sight of a lifeguard whenever possible.

Other Sources of Advice and Counsel

Magazines

Triathlete and *Inside Triathlon,* the two national monthly magazines on the market in 2006, are both strong on technique. I have frequently found their technical articles to be very helpful. There are also several single-sport magazines that publish useful technical articles on a regular basis. *Runner's World* is the main running magazine; *Bicycling* magazine is still the leader in that sport. Both also provide useful technical information on their Web sites, as does Active.com.

Books

The publishing world is replete with books on running. My own favorites are listed in Appendix II, along with some of the leading books on cycling and swimming. You can go to a bookstore with a good sports-book section. Browse. Take your time. These days, of course, you can also browse on the Web, with your favorite Web bookstore, although you cannot go through a book there as you can in a bookstore. In either case you can pick an author or two with whom you are comfortable. You can easily build up a nice little reference library for yourself.

I used *The Runner's Handbook* by Bob Glover and Jack Shepherd to introduce me to running. The edition available in 2005 was written in 1996, with Shelly-lynn Florence Glover. I found the section on technique in Bob Glover's *The Competitive Runner's Handbook* (the 1999 revised edition) particularly useful. I think that the late Jimmy Fixx's classic *The Complete Book of Running* will always be a fine guide to the sport, and who can be a runner and not read George Sheehan? Of the running books of the 1990s, I highly recommend *The Essential Runner* by my good friend John Hanc.

Two helpful introductory cycling books by Dr. Arnold Baker are *The Essential Cyclist* and *Smart Cycling: Successful Training and Racing for Riders of All Levels*. Another helpful book on bike racing is Davis Phinney and Connie Carpenter's *Training for Cycling*. The standard text for the beginning and intermediate swimmer is Jane Katz's most excellent *Swimming for Total Fitness*. It is well written and well thought out, and it covers technique and exercise programming well. A top-notch, comprehensive guidebook for the triathlete who is serious about speed is Joe Friel's *The Triathlete's Training Bible*. My other triathlon book, *The Essential Triathlete*, offers a slightly different perspective than this one does, although the guiding philosophy is the same. As you may have surmised by now, the Globe Pequot Press (www.globepequot.com) has an "Essential" series, under their imprint The Lyons Press. Well worth reading are John Hanc's *The Essential Marathoner* and Steve Tarpinian's *The Essential Swimmer*. Steve's book *The Triathlete's Guide to Swim Training* is also recommended.

Verbal Sources

The best way to learn about technique in detail is with private, hands-on coaching. It can be expensive, but if you have particular needs or desires, it can be worth the investment. (I have never used a coach, but that is simply because, in terms of my goals in the sport, I am happy with what I have been able to do on my own for 24 years.) Places to look for a coach include the Web (type in "Triathlon coaches" on your favorite search engine), ads in triathlon magazines, and bulletin boards at your pro bike or running-shoe shop. Classes in one or more of the sports may be offered in the adult education program of a local high school, college, or university, a Y, a sports club, or a running-shoe, bicycle, or sporting-goods store. Adult summer camps for triathloning are offered in various parts of the country, and can be located in the same ways.

USA Triathlon runs an extensive triathlon coach certification program. It was established in 1996 by my friend and colleague George Dallam, PhD, coach of the top U.S. male finisher at the 2004 Olympics, Hunter Kemper. Coaches are certified at three levels. There is a comprehensive training program, with increasingly demanding requirements for training, examination, and continuing education. As of 2006, there were more than 650 USAT-certified coaches in the United States. As a former member of the USAT Coaching Commission myself (primarily for my editorial—not my coaching or triathloning—skills, I should tell you), I recommend that if you decide to engage a personal coach, you seek one who is certified and comes with good references.

Conclusion

For efficiency and saving of energy, speed, and injury prevention, good technique is important in all three triathlon sports. Good technique should be learned and practiced. However, it should not be forgotten that the most important aspect of training, for the beginning triathlete, is aerobic conditioning. Following one of the Triathloning for Ordinary Mortals Training Programs will get you into shape so you can finish your first triathlon, or duathlon, happily and healthily. Be concerned with technique, but at the same time do not get hung up on it. Be concerned first and foremost with consistency and regularity in your training, and their product—a significant improvement in your overall aerobic fitness, the subject of the next three chapters.

TRAINING BASICS FOR TRIATHLON AND DUATHLON

Consistency is the hobgoblin of small minds—
except in training.
—*Ralph Waldo Emerson, modified by Steven Jonas*

Y ou have decided to do a triathlon or a duathlon. If you are starting from scratch, you will find a helpful guide to doing that in the next chapter, which presents my Basic Aerobic Fitness Program (BAFP). If you are ready to get right into race training, that means that you can already do each of the sports required for your chosen race or you have allowed enough time in your preparation to learn what you will need to learn about technique. If you are already in reasonably good aerobic shape, or already plan to get there by following the BAFP, you will likely have decided what type of race you will do for your first, picked out the actual race, and will be ready to start one of the variants of the Triathloning for Ordinary Mortals Training Program (TFOMTP), found in Chapter 7.

Thus, depending upon your present state of personal fitness, the big day is anywhere from a matter of months to a year or more off. At any rate, at this point you are ready to begin working out. This chapter presents a set of basic training principles that provide the foundation for each of the training programs described in the following two chapters. They apply regardless of your present level of physical and mental fitness, and regardless of whether you will be starting with the BAFP or are in pretty decent shape and will be going right into one of the TFOMTPs.

Assuming that for 2 to 6 months you have been doing 15 to 20 miles per week of running or its equivalent, the 13-week TFOMTP that is appropriate for the type of race and the distance you have chosen will enable you to comfortably complete that first Sprint or Olympic-distance triathlon, or a duathlon. The variables in deciding whether 2 months of preparation before starting the TFOMTP is enough for you or if you will need more include age, health status, fitness level now, previous racing and race-training experience, and eagerness to get going. You can certainly be the judge of where you stand on this scale. How you feel after a few weeks on the BAFP will also be helpful in determining how much time on it is right for you before you start the TFOMTP.

The Basic Principles of Training for the TFOM Approach to the Sports

First and Foremost: Consistency and Regularity

"Consistency" refers to the length of your training sessions. It should not vary widely from one session to the next. One of the prime goals of training is to improve musculoskeletal and cardiovascular fitness. (Musculoskeletal fitness is the ability to do increased physical work over time using one or more major muscle groups. Cardiovascular fitness is the increased ability of the heart to beat faster and pump more blood with each beat, within the limits of healthy functioning, over time.) You cannot improve fitness in these areas with training sessions of widely varying length. Exercise physiology research has shown that your body will not respond well to such an approach, which significantly increases the risk of injury and illness.

You should increase the length of your training sessions gradually, not in great leaps. You will see that I have designed the BAFP and the TFOMTP with this principle in mind. As you move through any of the training programs, it is a good idea to follow the recommended distribution of time among each session pretty closely. I have worked out those times with the aim of helping you establish consistency. Do not try to do a 10-minute session, then a 40, then a 70. You will only increase the chance of hurting yourself. If at some point you need to make up time, do it in sessions that are consistent in length with what you are otherwise doing at the time.

"Regularity" refers to the distribution of training sessions during the week and the distribution of workout weeks over the course of the year. Both should be fairly even. It is a good idea to follow the suggested training session plans pretty closely. Why? Well, in many of the lighter weeks you *could* pack the bulk of the minutes into the weekends. However, this approach will benefit neither your muscles nor your heart nearly as much as a more regular distribution will. It could actually be harmful to exercise heavily on the weekends only, getting your heart rate up to a really high level only then (say 80 to 85 percent of your theoretical maximum; see "Aerobic Exercise," page 107). Such intermittent episodes of a noticeably increased heart rate could significantly increase your risk of sudden death from a heart attack. An uneven distribution of training sessions over the course of a week may also wreak havoc on your musculoskeletal system. Muscles worked out on a regular basis, on alternate days at least, go through a cycle of buildup, breakdown, and further buildup— the process that leads to increased endurance and strength. Muscles worked out only intermittently will hurt after those intermittent training sessions, but will not develop increased strength and endurance. It is regularity of training that does that for you.

Regularity also refers to exercising on a year-round basis (with a couple of scheduled total pauses as well; see pages 120–22). If you are like most regular exercisers, you will not regard this as a chore. You will become positively hooked. You will want to do it. It is likely that if you have carefully and gradually become a regular exerciser, you will begin to feel not so good if you stop exercising for any considerable time. I know. That is what happens to me every fall after the season here in the Northeast when I try to take two weeks completely off (see "Winter Training," page 114).

Regularity in training is necessary for success, whether in simply working out or in racing on a regular basis. For most people, the toughest thing to handle in becoming and being a regular exerciser is the regular, not the exercise. However, it is only regular—not irregular—exercise that is beneficial, for health in general and racing in particular. Why? First of all, none of the exercise-related mental or physical health benefits can be derived from exercising if it is not done regularly. Second, as noted, irregular exercise often leads to excess exercise-related pain and increases the risk of exercise-related injury, and pain and injury lead to a failure to feel good and feel good about yourself—two of the most important benefits of regular exercise. They also interfere with the achievement of other exercise-related goals, such as becoming a multi-sport racer. If you exercise irregularly, the chances of quitting altogether increase significantly. Thus, it is obvious that consistency and regularity are central elements to achieving success using the BAFP and the TFOMTP.

Training for Time, Not Speed or Distance

Cardiorespiratory (heart and lungs) and muscular fitness and endurance are essential for success at any level in the distance sports. The key elements in developing both are aerobic work and the time spent doing it. The technical skills and athletic proficiency discussed in the last chapter are important, too, of course, especially if and when you decide to try to go faster. But for most readers of this book, the goal is to complete your chosen race happily and healthily, to simply cross the finish line and have fun getting there. So it was for me at the start of my triathlon days and has remained so ever since in triathlon and duathlon. You will need to achieve a level of aerobic fitness that will enable you to exercise for the amount of time necessary to complete the race, at the speeds you can handle for that amount of time. Because winning is not a concern, speed per se is not a factor. Endurance is. The central focus of your training then becomes being able to go the distances that you need to go in each of the sports, for the amount of time you require to get there, at speeds you are comfortable with.

The key variable in this approach to triathlon training is the amount of time you can devote, consistently and regularly, to aerobic training. Thus, the training programs that I recommend are always set out in minutes of aerobic exercise to be done, not distance to be covered. This feature is central to my approach to training, because it does for you what is needed to get you where you want to go, at least at the beginning of your multi-sport racing career. Minutes—at whatever speeds work for you—not miles define the workout sessions.

As noted previously, I first discovered this approach back in the 1980s in Ardy Friedberg's book *How to Run Your First Marathon*. In all of the years that I have been doing triathlons and duathlons since then, I have used the same approach. As I have said before, the training program that I use now is just about the same as the one I designed for myself as I entered my first full season of triathlon racing in 1984. It still works for me, has worked for the many thousands of others who have used it over the years, and has been adapted for use in many other triathlon/duathlon training programs that have been published over the years. I have found it to be psychologically comfortable and logistically simple. It has gotten me just where I want to go in almost all of my races: across that finish line with a smile on my face. (The northeastern race director and swimming and triathlon coach Steve Tarpinian once said that I was the only triathlete he had ever seen who crossed the finish line with a smile on his face every time—well, Steve, *almost* every time.)

In your cycling and run training, you will generally do out-

and-back courses, at least until you find loops that take about the amount of time required for a particular day's workout. With the minutes approach, you do not have to measure a variety of routes with your (often inaccurate) automobile odometer. In swimming, you do not have to count laps in the pool or worry about what hard-to-measure open-water distances actually are. Most important, on each day of training, you go at the pace that is comfortable for you for that day.

I have fast days and I have slow days. Many variables of weather, temperature, mood, and physical body state produce these differences. On the fast days, I go farther than I do on the slow days. However, in my approach to racing, as long as I put in my minutes, the particular distance that I cover in a particular workout does not matter. Without having mileage to worry about, as long as I have raised my heart rate into the aerobic range for a significant portion of the workout, I feel that I have had a good one.

Obviously, the time spent working out should be distributed among the three (or two) sports, so that the sport-specific muscle groups each get a significant amount of exercise work and strengthening. However, the specific balance among the sports is not critical. For example, suppose on the program you have a bike ride scheduled for a particular day and it happens to be raining. You do not like riding in the rain because of the safety factor. You certainly can go for a swim or a run (assuming that you do not mind running in the rain), just as long as you do the number of minutes scheduled.

I train at a rather slow pace in each sport: 10.5 to 11.5 minutes per mile running (5.0 to 5.5 mph), 13 to 14 minutes per mile PaceWalking (4.2 to 4.5 mph), 3.5 to 4 minutes per mile cycling (15 to 17 mph), and about 40 to 45 minutes per mile (1.3 to 1.5 mph) swimming. Thus, for me the rates are (approximately) 2.5 miles cycling = 1 mile running = 0.25 mile swimming. So if someone asks me, "Well, how many miles did you run today?" and it happens that I went cycling for an hour, I can comfortably say, "Oh, the equivalent of about five to five and a half miles of running." Another common medium of conversational exchange among distance athletes is miles per week. When I am in training for a triathlon, I average 300 minutes of aerobic exercise per week in all three sports for 13 weeks. Thus, at my usual pace, I am doing the equivalent of 26 to 30 miles of running per week. When someone asks you how much you do, it is much easier to say "Thirty miles per week" than to go into a long, involved explanation of minutes, aerobic work, and equivalencies, such as the one that you have just finished reading.

Tailor Your Training Program to Fit Your Lifestyle

From my own experience and from that of many recreational distance athletes with whom I have spoken, I have learned that central to achieving consistency in your training over time is adopting a training program that fits *your* lifestyle and *your* pattern of daily living. For me, for all of these years that I have used the TFOMTP, this is one of its major attractions. The time commitment for the TFOMTP is not overwhelming. Most of the long workouts are scheduled for weekends. For the most part, the during-the-week sessions are short enough that you should be able to work them in around family, school, and/or work obligations. The fact that, as you will see, there are only five or six workouts per week means that flexibility is built into the program.

After you have used the TFOMTP to help you cross that finish line happily and healthily, should you want to go for speed and should you have the capability of doing so, you can always get into a program designed to achieve that goal. As previously noted, there is a great deal of information on going fast and faster in triathlon magazines and books on the sport, on the Web, and from an increasing number of triathlon coaches. In my view, if you want to go fast, if you are physically and technically capable of doing that, and if you can find the time in your daily schedule without turning everything else in your life upside down, I say, go for it. I still suggest that the goals you set for yourself, success as you define it for yourself, should be realistically achievable for you, and include finishing happily and healthily—just more quickly.

As you already know if you have done or are presently doing any regular exercise, the total time required for it is certainly more than what you spend doing the actual exercise itself. You have to dress and perhaps stretch beforehand, cool down and shower afterward. Unless you have a pool in your backyard, you will have to travel to get to one. Unless you have a mini-gym in your basement, as I do, you will have to travel to get to a gym. Thus, although the time requirement is not overwhelming, it is significant. You must be prepared to make that commitment.

Carefully choosing your workout times will help. I like to get up early and exercise before going to work. Among other things, morning exercise usually sets me up for the day (although I swim in the pool at my health club after work). Some folks are able to fit in their workouts during the middle of the day. Others like to fit them in after they get home from work. However, if you have a family, that will usually mean delaying dinner for everyone or eating on your own. Either of these practices could create family-life problems. Thus, you have to give some careful thought to the best time of day to work out. For swimming in particular, the TFOM approach to training does not call for a great deal of it, just enough to get you through that segment of the race. Overall, with travel time, for most people the swim workout is the most time consuming of the three. Thus I try to minimize daily-living-pattern disruption by not scheduling too many of them.

I find that planning out my workout schedule several months in advance is useful. Within the general guidelines of time of day and place to work out, you can then plan around known events in your work and family life that might otherwise interfere with your training. Planning my training schedule well in advance also permits me to juggle workouts around other commitments and still get in the required number of minutes per week. I might not be able to do so if I waited until the last minute each week to set up my schedule.

Where to Train

Beginning runners usually start out on a track at a local high school or college. The surface is comfortable, the distance is measured, and there is no traffic. However, once you get up to 3 miles or so per workout, about 30 to 35 minutes, if you are like most of the rest of us, you will find that the track experience becomes increasingly boring, then BORING, then virtually impossible to do

Here are my rearview mirrors, even at the ITU Age-Group Worlds in 2004. *Photo by Brightroom Event Photography*

Madeira ITU Triathlon Age Group World Championships
Madeira, Portugal - 8 May 2004

(unless you decide to do speed/interval training; see the training books listed in Appendix II). You must then consider the alternatives. I live in a semirural area and find running on public roads very comfortable. I try to stay off the main ones and almost always run against traffic. I hardly ever run at night, so the safety level is good. Broad boulevards in older cities can have safe sidewalks bothered by cross streets only at infrequent intervals. City running can be done in the street, but against traffic and with great care and attention.

Cycling is a bit more of a problem in terms of safety. Smooth road surface is desirable in cycling—for comfort and flat-tire avoidance. The smoother surfaces are usually found on busier roads. To enhance safety, I generally stay on the shoulders, use a rearview mirror, and concentrate on the traffic at all times. I would not recommend trying to do bike workouts on city streets, but then again I have never tried it. If you have no other choice, you will have to. In that case, a rearview mirror of the helmet or handlebar-mounted type is a must for safety.

Most people do most of their swim training in a pool. Effective swim training in the pool requires fixed swim lanes with tight lines attached to floats. You cannot go into a community pool at general swim time and expect to do laps for 45 minutes while dealing with the interference presented by bathers, splashers, divers, handstanders, small children, two-lap speeders, and assorted show-offs and admirers. Pools that provide lane swimming can be found in schools, colleges, Y's, community recreation facilities, and health and fitness clubs. Costs vary widely. Lane swimming takes a bit of getting used to. Most pools have some kind of speed-rate pattern, ranging from slow in the lanes on one side of the pool to swim-team fast in the lanes on the other. After you have been swum over by speed demons or kicked in the face a few times by slow swimmers who won't let you pass, you will find the right lane for you. Once you do locate your niche, you will find lane swimming comfortable.

As part of race preparation, I highly recommend a few open-water swims. This will acclimate you to such factors as water temperature, salt water, tides, currents, and waves. Most importantly, in all types of open water—even including flat calm, warm lakes—you will need to be able to swim in a long, straight line. You do this by periodically raising your head and looking ahead to sight on landmarks (during the race, you sight on the colored buoys put out to mark the course).

Training and Travel

As I have grown older, I have greatly reduced my professional travel. However, when I did travel for professional reasons, I tried to stay on whichever training schedule I was using at the time. I found it most enjoyable to get out for an early morning or late afternoon run in a different city now and then, even if I had been there before. Many hotels have gyms in which you can get some sort of a workout, should the timing for going outside not work for you or if there is simply no place to run or walk safely in the neighborhood. This does necessitate taking the necessary workout shoes and clothing with you, of course. As far as training while on vacation is concerned, I generally take workout clothing with me, but I do not worry too much about staying on schedule. Doing so can be disruptive for traveling companions; and the vacations that my wife and I go on, it happens, always involve a great deal of walking, which does help to maintain my conditioning.

As far as particular places to work out are concerned, in many cities in the United States and abroad, there are parks that have special running/cycling paths and/or vehicular roads that are closed to automobile traffic at specified times. Waterfront, river-side, and park paths can be ideal for workouts, as in New York, Chicago, Washington, D.C., Philadelphia, Fort Worth, London, and Paris, for example. In the United States, in Fort Worth I just loved to run along the Trinity Trail on the banks of the Trinity River. This path is (or at least was in the early 1980s when I used it on a regular basis) for runners and bikers only; it is quiet and smoothly paved for the most part, has no traffic, and has measured miles. Even though I am an advocate of training by time, not distance, and seldom run measured courses at home, it was fun and useful to check my training pace on the Trinity Trail once in a while.

In Philadelphia, I loved to run over to the Fine Arts Museum and bound up its steps with the *Rocky* theme playing in my head. I then headed out along the Schuylkill River on a beautiful path, usually in the company of a flock of local runners. Speaking of flocks of runners, Central Park—in my birthplace, New York City—must be mecca for the recreational distance athlete. Running is delightful and picturesque on the park drives, which have dedicated running lanes open at all times, as well as being closed to automobile traffic from 10 to 4 on weekdays and all day on the weekends. You can usually find someone to run with during the daylight hours.

Running along the East River in New York City is also pleasant and popular, as is running on the West Side of Manhattan along the Hudson. Chicago's lakefront is a magnificent place to run. I always had a good time too in Washington, D.C.'s Rock Creek Park, on either bank of the Potomac, and on the Mall, which is flat, beautiful to look at, and usually chockablock with runners. Then there are the hills of San Francisco. If you take it easy going up and coming down, that can be a most exhilarating trip in terms of "I did it, I did it!" and the spectacular views. I have made that crossing several times. If you travel and plan your schedule in advance, you can have experiences like these, too, and not disrupt your training.

Some Training Specifics

Aerobic Exercise

In the 1960s, Dr. Kenneth Cooper developed the modern concept of "aerobic exercise" and popularized the term. "Aerobic" muscular exercise is fueled by oxygen in breathed-in air, in an amount that is significantly greater than the muscles are ordinarily using. The term means more than simply using oxygen to support the muscular activity involved, because that is the case for nonaerobic exercise as well. Nonaerobic exercise is any physical activity above that of the normal resting state involving one or more major muscle groups that is sustained, but not so intensely as to cause a significant increase in oxygen uptake by the muscles. In aerobic exercise, your muscles are "taking up," or using, *a significantly increased amount of oxygen* over what they normally do. The measure of this consumption is termed the "volume of oxygen uptake," or "VO 2."

There is a third category of exercise, anaerobic. The energy source for it is a chemical already inside the muscles. Anaerobic exercise, such as that practiced by sprinters, can be done very fast but not for very long. Aerobic exercise can be done for very long periods of time, but not nearly as fast. Exercising aerobically on a regular basis leads to improvement in musculoskeletal and cardiovascular fitness. Nonaerobic exercise can lead to an improvement in musculoskeletal fitness and general health, but only aerobic exercise fully benefits the health of the heart over the long run.

There are no little meters (at least not yet) that we can wear to measure VO 2. However, for the healthy person without heart disease, the heart rate is a simple substitute measure of the extent to which any exercise is aerobic. Research in exercise physiology has determined that when your heart rate rises above a certain level, you are doing aerobic exercise. A variety of formulae for using the heart rate to measure the level of aerobic activity—that is, significantly increased oxygen uptake by the muscles—has been worked out over time. They've come with varying levels of complexity. I still use the first that was widely accepted. Although it is not considered accurate for the highly conditioned athlete, it is reasonably accurate for the recreational distance athlete. It goes as follows.

Extensive research in exercise and cardiac physiology shows that your "theoretical maximum" heart rate—the top rate at which your heart can beat safely—is the number 220 minus your age. Using this formula, it is now generally considered that if your heart rate reaches a level of 60 percent of that figure (0.6 [220 – your age]), you are exercising aerobically (see Table 5.1 for the minimum aerobic heart rates for selected ages). The "aerobic range" is 60 to 85 percent of the theoretical maximum heart rate—that is, 60 to 85 percent of 220 minus your age. For the exercise to be aerobic, you want your heart rate to be in that range. In addition, your breathing should increase in depth and frequency, indicating that your heart rate increase does indeed reflect increased O_2 uptake by your muscles. The major factor determining the effectiveness of the BAFP and the TFOMTP for you is the amount of time you spend exercising energetically enough to boost your heart rate into the aerobic range while at the same time you are breathing harder.

Measuring Your Heart Rate

In order to measure your heart rate, you need a stopwatch and you need to know how to take your own pulse. The latter can be found by placing the tips of the index and middle fingers of one hand in the slight depression on the outer aspect (thumb side) of the opposite wrist (palm up) just about where your watch strap comes across. You can also find it in your neck about halfway up from its base, between your windpipe and the front edge of the major group of neck muscles. The latter is easier to do for most people (including me) than taking it on the wrist, but you must not take it on both sides at the same time—if you do, you could cause yourself to pass out. Once having found your pulse, count it for 6 seconds and multiply by 10 (or count it for 12 seconds and

Table 5.1

Minimum Aerobic Heart Rates for Selected Ages
(60 percent of theoretical maximum heart rate)

Age	Heart Rate
21	119
25	117
30	114
35	111
40	108
45	105
50	102
55	99
60	96
65	93
70	90
75	87
80	84
85	81
90	78

multiply by 5). That will give you your heart rate in beats per minute.

An alternate way of keeping track of your heart rate is to use a modern device called the heart rate monitor. Around your chest you wear a strap containing an electronic chip that you locate over your heart. The chip registers the flow of electricity over your heart that occurs with every beat. It then transmits a signal for each beat to a device with a specialized tiny receiver that you wear like a wristwatch. It presents the heart rate information to you, usually on an LCD display. These devices range in complexity from simple—telling you your heart rate and that's it—to complex: providing aerobic ranges, alarms, computer-downloadable information, and the like. You can check out the range of available types at your local pro bike or running-shoe shop, on the Web, and in major mail-order catalogs. The "standard text" for using a heart-rate monitor is Sally Edwards's *Heart Rate Monitor Guidebook* (see Appendix II and www.heartzone.com).

Breathing in Training

It is easy to make jokes about breathing: "Can't live without it" and "Breathing is essential to running" are typical. It is valuable, however, to recognize that certain breathing patterns are more helpful than others for comfort and performance. We can fill our lungs with air by expanding the rib cage and by lowering the diaphragm. It is important to be able to do both. And it is good to remember that both inhalation and exhalation are also important. The former brings fresh oxygen into the lungs from which it passes into the bloodstream through the millions of alveoli (tiny air sacs) that form the lungs. The alveoli also clear from the blood the carbon dioxide (CO_2) that is produced by your body's cells when they use oxygen for energy. The more you expand your lungs while breathing in, the more of those little sacs open up to be available for O_2 transfer in and CO_2 removal out. The more fully you exhale, the more surface area will be cleared of CO_2 so that more O_2 can be absorbed into the bloodstream on the next inhalation.

Many people find that breathing exercises done at rest are beneficial for physical and psychological reasons. One approach to stress management is through breathing exercises, beginning with the old admonition to "take a deep breath" before responding to a suddenly stressful situation. I do not use formal breathing exercises myself, although I do try to remember to fully inflate my lungs and clear them out several times a day by alternately expanding my upper rib cage, raising my shoulders, then depressing my diaphragm, and expanding my waist.

Breathing while working out is a different matter. In swimming, rhythmic breathing is obviously necessary. Any good swimming book will give you advice on that (see Appendix II). In running and bicycling, breathing depends upon how hard you are working. After twenty-five years of running, I find that when I am doing my usual workout, running $10\frac{1}{2}$ to $11\frac{1}{2}$ minutes per mile, my heart rate is up into the low end of my aerobic range but my breathing is still loose and easy, with no particular pattern. If

I go faster and increase my oxygen intake, I like to breathe in a regular pattern, taking four or six steps for a full inhalation-exhalation cycle.

When I get tired, I find that a few cycles of breathing out as slowly and fully as I can—"exhaling deeply," as it were—can often pick me right up. This is presumably because I am fully cleaning those alveolar surfaces in my lungs, getting rid of excess CO_2 that may have accumulated there. Not everyone will use rhythmic breathing. It is important to develop your own patterns, recognize them, and use them appropriately. One absolute no-no for everyone at any time is breath holding, an easy habit to fall into. Breath holding, even for a short interval, slows down O_2/CO_2-waste exchange in the lungs and unnecessarily increases blood pressure. Neither is beneficial.

Hills

For any distance athlete who trains on the road, hills are a fact of life unless you happen to live out on the Great Plains. Even in swimming, you can encounter the equivalent of hills when going into an adverse current or tide. Psychologically, there are two approaches to hills. You can love 'em or you can hate 'em. Because I live in a hilly area and must train on them, it is easy for me to say this, but you will be much better off if you learn to love, or at least like, them, or—okay—at least tolerate them. Whatever you do, do not get angry or irritated with them. You cannot make them go away, and those sorts of feelings will make going up them much more difficult. It happens that hill training is beneficial, not only for climbing hills in the races but for speed and endurance.

I find that "attacking the hills" is a useful approach. In running, you shorten your stride, lean forward a bit, actively use your upper body—swinging your arms at your sides, not across your chest—and breathe rhythmically and deeply. With some practice, you can actually glide up hills. I usually accelerate a bit going up shorter hills, although for the long ones I try to pace myself, accelerating only when the top is clearly within my reach. Coming downhill in running can create problems if you go too fast and pound too much. Running on the flat is certainly preferable.

However, for cycling I find that because I train on hills, I would rather race on a course that has at least some hills than one that is entirely flat. On a hilly bike course, you do have to work going up, but then you have the downs to look forward to. On an entirely flat bike course, you are pedaling all the time.

On the hills in cycling, you drop into a lower gear, increase your cadence, thrust the pedals forward, and stand up in the saddle when you need more power and cannot easily downshift because of mechanical pressure on the derailleurs. Whenever possible, make sure that you downshift *before* you get onto the hill, or at least do so near the beginning of it. If you get stuck in too high a gear on the hill, your quads will be burning and you may not be able to move the shift levers. Or, as you try to downshift the front derailleur, the chain may slip over the smaller ring and come off. Not fun, I can tell you! In cycling and running on steep hills, as previously noted, I find visualization useful. As you wind your way up, think about being on the top, what it will feel like, how relaxing the downhill will be. Look up the hill. In your mind's eye, see yourself at the crest. This approach helps me. It may help you too.

Weight Lifting and Training

The thinking on this subject has changed radically for all sports since I started out. Weight training is now considered by most coaches and other authorities to be an essential part of anyone's program. Weight training can be done as a primary activity of your off-season (it is of mine) and/or during your training season. For most of my time in triathlon/duathlon, I have lifted during the winter as my principal off-season activity (see "Winter Training," page 114), but not during the season. In 2005, I added a limited amount of in-season lifting to my workout schedule. Twice a week I do a 20- to 30-minute pre-run or -bike workout featuring stretching and a short weight-lifting circuit on my multi-station gym. Many of us do not have gyms in our homes, but you can use exercise rubber bands, Swiss balls, Pilates, and self-resistance exercises such as push-ups and abdominal crunches to accomplish the same ends.

There is a wide variety of weight-training equipment available for home use or at the gym/health club: free weights (barbells and dumbbells); circuit training on machines designed for the purpose, such as Nautilus; the above-mentioned rubber bands, and so on. However, as with all of your training, the most important consideration should be what your goals are. I spent my first weight-lifting winter many years ago with barbells and dumbbells in a gym. The fantasy life can be rich as images of Mr. Universe pop into your head. Men and women with bulging biceps and huge shoulders will surround you. However, bulk is not beneficial for the triathlete, and muscle definition, although very nice, is not a prerequisite to triathloning success. Most beneficial for you are building strength, endurance, and flexibility. There are numerous sources of information on how to go about doing this: books, magazines, the Web (see Appendix II), coaches, and of course athletic trainers at the gyms and on a private basis.

Comparing free-weight lifting with circuit training, the former will build more strength in a given amount of time than the standard circuit-training routine, and that result may be desirable for you. A free-weight-lifting workout does require more time than does circuit-training, although with the waiting time at a crowded gym's circuit factored in, the total time required for each may be about the same. Free-weight lifting does have to be well supervised to be effective as well as safe. Which exercises, what weights, how many repetitions, and what the progressions should be over time do have to be specified, for free weights or circuit training. It is a good idea to engage a sports trainer to help you get started and develop the right program for you. However, once you get going, constant attendance by a trainer is not necessary.

Finally, while you are weight training, regularity and consistency are as much a requirement as they are for sport-specific training, whether you lift year-round or just during the off-season. Most important for you is to choose or design a program that you are comfortable with and you will do consistently and regularly. You are not bodybuilding. As long as you do not injure yourself, and you keep your focus on strength, endurance, and flexibility, anything is better than nothing.

Stretching

When I started out, stretching was considered to be an important part of the warm-up and cooldown of every workout, if not something you would do for an extended session on its own. Now it has become a subject of controversy. There are still reputable authorities who believe that it is important for performance and injury prevention; but there are others, with studies to back them up, that hold to the view that it does little if anything for either. My own view is that it cannot hurt you and will certainly improve your flexibility, whether that has any objective benefit or not, so if you are comfortable stretching—better yet like to do it—do it. Stretching is a regular part of my winter training program (see below). Although I must admit that in the past I have done little of it during the racing season, now it is a regular part at least of the during-the-season pre-workout weight-training sessions that I try to do twice a week. There are a number of good stretching books on the market, beginning with the granddaddy of them all, Bob Anderson's. A beginning set of stretches, courtesy of the American Running Association/American Medical Athletic Association, which happen to be the ones that I use, is shown on pages 116–17. By the way, if you do not do an organized set of stretching exercises after working out, at least you should walk around and cool down some before jumping into the shower.

Winter Training

When winter is upon us in most parts of the country, that means cold, wind, snow, ice, wetness, grayness, general discomfort. To be sure, in the South and Southwest some conventional races are run throughout most of the wintertime. In the colder parts of the country, too, some hardy souls engage in one or more winter-type duathlons/triathlons. These include two or more of the following: skiing (downhill and/or cross-country), snowshoeing, ice-skating, running, mountain biking, and what have you. However, for most of us, as the weather turns colder, the multi-sport racing season draws to a close. Outdoor training is difficult and uncomfortable, if not plain impossible. What to do for the winter?

There is a range of approaches to the off-season. A few hardy souls take off completely for the winter. I say "hardy" in this context because shutting down completely means that you could have a fairly long road back the next spring. It takes a hardy soul to even contemplate that, much less do it. At the other end of the spectrum are those who maintain a pretty full program throughout the winter. They comprise a different set of hardy souls. Most people swim-train during the season in indoor pools. The year-round trainers just keep up their regular swimming program. If you like running in cold weather (I PaceWalk on a regular basis throughout the winter) and are careful about your footing (I once broke my ankle running on an icy day), you do not have to cut back on your running either. As for cycling, a few very hardy souls bike through the cold weather as long as the roads are clear. I used to do that too. I stress *used to*!

I do not recommend either "hardy soul" approach to winter training—unless, of course, you like the winter-type multi-sport racing, which I do not cover in this book because I have limited experience with it. If you *do* like it, I say, go for it! With the first (taking off completely), you have too far to come back. With the second (maintaining a full training program), you do not give your body or your mind much rest. In my view, your body needs some time off to decrease the risk of injury and let your muscles rest up. Your mind needs some time off to decrease the risk of burnout, and to deal with the boredom that can build up in regular training even for the most enthusiastic triathlete or duathlete. Thus, I suggest the happy medium approach to winter training, the one I use myself.

If you are considering the matter of winter training, I assume that you have already established your aerobic base, even if you have not yet done a triathlon or duathlon. You are coming off a season of regular training, whether or not you were racing. You have put in some hard work and you want to give yourself a reward for doing so. On the other hand, you do not want to lose ground. Can these seemingly contrary objectives be met in one program? The answer is yes. You can stay in shape while giving your body a well-deserved rest, and you can do that with activities that will enhance next season's performance. The key here is

Hold each stretch to the point of relaxation, approximately 10 to 15 seconds, and the rest for 5 to 10 seconds. Repeat for a total of three times.

1. Quadriceps (front of thigh)

Stand up straight. Bend one knee and bring the heel toward your buttocks. Reach your hand back and grab your foot or ankle. If you can't reach either, loop a towel around your ankle and hold the towel. Maintain a neutral pelvic tilt (hips are neither forward nor backward) and keep your knees side by side, with your hips squared off. Repeat with other leg.

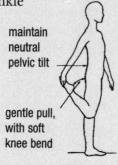

maintain neutral pelvic tilt

gentle pull, with soft knee bend

2. Calves

Place your hands against a wall or fence (about two steps away). To stretch the upper part of the calf, step forward with one leg and keep your heels flat on the ground. Lean your hips toward the wall while keeping your back straight. Repeat with the back leg slightly bent to stretch the lower part of your calf muscle. Repeat with other leg.

3. Upper Back

Place your hands shoulder width apart on a fence or something of similar height. Slowly lower your upper body while keeping your knees slightly bent and your feet shoulder width apart. Focus on the ground and keep your neck relaxed. Different areas of the upper back can be targeted by varying the height of the supporting object. Be sure to always bend your knees when coming out of the stretch to avoid lower back strain.

4. Hamstrings (back of thigh)

Stand about an arm's length away from a fence or other stationary object; choose an object whose height is consistent with the current level of your hamstring flexibility. Place your foot on the object and lean forward from your hips, trying not to round your upper back. Slightly bend the knee of the supporting leg. Repeat on the other side. To increase the intensity of the stretch, flex your foot and push through your heel.

5. Inner Thigh/Groin

While sitting, place the soles of your feet together with your heels a comfortable distance from your groin. Hold your feet, place your elbows on your legs, and slowly bend forward from your hips (try not to round your upper back) until you feel a mild pull in the groin area. If this stretch feels easier over time, gently add pressure to the legs with your elbows to increase the intensity of the stretch.

6. Chest

Stand straight, relax your shoulders, and reach behind your back with both arms. Interlock your fingers and squeeze your shoulder blades together. If you cannot bring your hands together, hold a towel between them.

7. Iliotibial Band (hip/thigh)

Lean toward a wall or fence with your arm extended. Place the foot closest to the wall behind the other foot. Gently bend the knee of the leg in front and lean closer to the wall. You should fell the stretch in the hip closest to the wall. Repeat on the other side.

8. Piriformis (lower back)

Lie flat on your back (A). Grab behind one knee with both hands and pull toward your chest (B). Using your hands, move your knee over the opposite hip, rotating the hip inward (C). As you move your knee, gently straighten the leg and point the toes toward the floor (D).

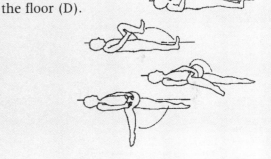

doing the 2½ to 3 hours per week that Dr. Cooper says is necessary for maintaining your aerobic base. That should be your primary goal for the winter. You may also decide to spend some time dealing with areas of athletic weakness, through activities that can be done mainly indoors.

As the leaves fall from the trees, I pretty much shut down for a 2- to 4-week period after my last race of the fall, which in my younger days, was usually the New York City Marathon; now it is usually the much-more-fun Central Park (New York City) Biathlon. Studies have shown that if you are in good aerobic shape, you will not lose too much if you stop training for up to a couple of months. I find it difficult to stop working out completely because of how it affects my mood, but I limit myself to a couple of easy PaceWalks a week for 2 to 3 weeks. After that period of renewal, I start up a reduced training program.

In considering winter training, the first question to ask is "how much?" Next is "what kind?" I aim at the recommended $2\frac{1}{2}$ to 3 hours of aerobic exercise per week—sometimes a bit more, sometimes a bit less depending on time and just how aerobic it is. Then next spring the 13 weeks of the TFOMTP gets me back into whatever shape I need to be in for the racing season.

I look for variety in my winter training, as you already know. Variety is good for the body and mind. As I have said, I am fortunate to have a small gym in my basement with a multi-station weight-lifting machine—a Tuff Stuff CFM 555, which requires no cable changes between stations (a great convenience). I also have a Giant Bicycles indoor bike trainer (made for triathletes, it even

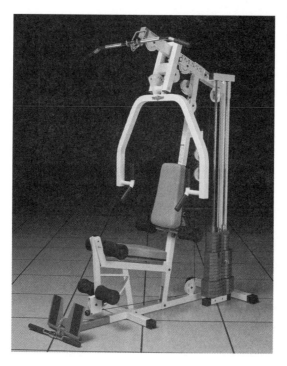

The Tuff Stuff CFM 555 multi-station weight machine. *Photo courtesy of Tuff Stuff Fitness Equipment, Inc.*

Skier's Edge All Mountain Master machine. *Photo courtesy of The Skier's Edge Company*

comes with aero bars), a Skier's Edge All Mountain Master lateral motion downhill ski trainer, a TimeWorks stepper with an upper-body rotation feature, an Abworks abdominal cruncher by NordicTrack, a Reebok Swiss ball, and a Power Block Personal Dumbbell System. I have a routine lasting about 60 to 75 minutes that I do two or three times per week.

For your winter program the most important criterion in deciding what to do is not the equipment or the specific exercises, or even the amount of time you spend. As with anything else you set out to do, in multi-sport racing or life in general, the most important questions to ask yourself are these: What are my goals? What do I want to accomplish and why? How do I define success? Is what I am doing in the winter related to what I am doing the rest of the year? These are the most important factors to think about. If you take some time doing so, you will come up with answers that will work for you.

In terms of triathlon and duathlon specifically, here are some sport-specific questions to think about, the answers to which will help you to design a beneficial winter training program. For the next season, what kinds and what lengths of races am I thinking about doing? How many races? Certainly the winter training requirements for doing a few short duathlons or Sprint triathlons are different from those for doing six to ten Olympic-distance tri's. For the former, you will likely focus just on maintaining your aerobic base; for the latter perhaps on building up your muscular strength and endurance. Whatever winter training program you follow, it should be designed to fit what *you* like to do in triathlon and duathlon and what you reasonably *can* do. It should not be some arbitrary one-size-fits-all or my-approach-works-for-me-and-therefore-it-will-work-for-you formula. I have found that a winter program that works for me and helps me to meet the goals I have set for myself is the one that is best for me.

Overtraining and Injury Prevention

I am sure that by now you are well aware of my views on this subject. I think that overtraining is more of a problem for the recreational triathlete than is undertraining. Assuming that you start the TFOMTP with your aerobic base well established and you train consistently and regularly, if you undertrain by even 25 percent you will still very likely finish, only quite slowly and probably with some discomfort. If you overtrain by 25 percent, you will not significantly increase your speed but you will have significantly increased your risk of training injury and psychological stress.

Overtraining means not only not enough rest but workouts that are too long and/or too fast and too frequent. It is easy to find triathlon training programs that have mega-time/mega-mileage requirements. They appear in the sports books and magazines all the time. However, they are usually written by elite athletes, for people who aspire to that level. These folks also are usually (although not always) young, have a low percentage of body fat, and have been athletic most of their lives. For them, triathlon training programs that provide for the equivalent of 60 to 100 miles of running per week may be suitable. If you are not in this category, you have to think of what is suitable for you and what kind of training you need to accomplish your goals—goals that are realistic for you as a whole person.

Since I first started exercising regularly, my ability to handle stress has improved a great deal. One of the goals shared by many recreational distance athletes is managing stress better, all around. Worrying about your race time and cutting into the rest of your life to increase training time, worrying about where you are going to finish in your age-group, will *increase* your stress level, not *reduce* it. Relax, enjoy. Run your training. Do not let it run you.

What you do in the race is not only a product of your training and how you run the race itself, it is also your genetic endowment, your natural abilities. The point is that extra training does not necessarily mean better performance. Extra training may well mean worse performance or nonperformance.

Certainly, the more you train, the more you risk injury. Exercise-related injuries can be classified into two groups: "intrinsic" and "extrinsic." Intrinsic (also called "overuse") injuries usually result from overdoing the sport. Examples include shin splints, swimmer's shoulder, biker's knee, tennis elbow, and stress fracture of the leg or foot. Extrinsic injury results from a collision with an obstacle or other physical object, such as an automobile, a pothole, a dangling tree branch, another exerciser, an animal (pet or otherwise), or a pedestrian. The most important element in intrinsic injury *prevention* is to avoid overtraining; for the extrinsic injuries, it is to be constantly aware of your surroundings and what is going on in them. Proper equipment (see Chapter 8) is also a major element in injury prevention. Number one in this regard is to *always* wear your helmet when you are on your bicycle.

Intrinsic injuries are more likely to occur while you are running. Extrinsic injuries are more likely to occur while cycling. I have had both types of injuries. Neither is fun. The good news is that you can make a full recovery from most injuries that you might incur while training or racing. The first order of business in dealing with an injury is to be aware of the possibility that you might be injured. You will be familiar with the customary muscular aches and pains that accompany regular working out, especially when you are getting started for the first time or at the beginning of a new season. If you develop a pain, an ache, or a discomfort that seems to be different from your usual ones, certainly if you suffer a traumatic injury, seek medical advice sooner rather than later.

By now you may feel that I have really hit you over the head on this overtraining issue (although it is the one hit on the head that does *not* cause an injury!). However, I have done it for a reason. Articles about the dangers of overtraining appear with regularity in the distance-sports magazines. Yet many people persist in overtraining. One reason is that alongside those cautions against overtraining are articles on an Olympic marathoner and his/her 100-plus miles per week, or an Olympic triathlete and his/her 40-plus hours of training per week. The point is that few of us are in that category. Olympians need that training time to do what they do. Triathletes and duathletes aiming to finish at the top of their respective age-groups at the national championships do not need that much, but they need significantly more than you or I do. You and I do not need mega-time or mega-miles to do what we do or want to do. If your goal is to comfortably participate and finish, to be there and have fun, do not overtrain. I cannot repeat that advice too often.

Rest and Downtime

On this important subject, let's listen to what some nationally known experts have to say. Tom Bassler, MD, has been active with the American Medical Athletic Association for many years. He is an outspoken advocate of slow, slow, slow—fun, fun, fun. He said, "Plan your rest periods with the same care that you plan your workouts! It only takes 4 hours of training per week to become a marathoner."

David Oja, a former coach of the Syracuse Chargers Track Club women's team, actually devised a program for resting (see left).

In following the TFOMTP for nearly twenty-five years in multi-sport racing, I have followed these Rules of Rest, which are built into it, and are built into my approach to year-round training as discussed in "Winter Training," page 114.

David Oja's "Six Rules of Rest"

1. Plan your rest as seriously as you plan your running.
2. Plan your rest according to your needs: how you feel, how injury prone you are, how long you've been running, what your goals are. [Sound familiar?]
3. Take days off on a regular basis.
4. Plan cutback weeks and don't be afraid to take unplanned cutback weeks if necessary. [I do both and find them enormously beneficial.]
5. Plan to take at least one month of downtime each year.
6. When judging how much rest you should have, if you err, err on the side of too much.

Training the Mind

A final thought—on training the mind. George Sheehan said that the first 30 minutes of a workout is for your body;

the balance is for your mind. A great deal of what I have been talking about in this chapter is mind training rather than body training. In fact, the two go together. The mind has to be conditioned if the body is to be properly conditioned. You must know what is realistic for you as a goal in relation to your physical skills, your athletic experience, and, most importantly, the balance of your life. This is mental work, not physical. I trained my mind to enable me to complete Olympic-distance triathlons, but I did not train it to propel me to place in my age-group (that is, until my age-group drastically diminished in size as I got older). I set a doable goal for myself—reasonable in the context of the rest of my life—and I achieved it. As I continue in the sports, my goals change. Slower is okay—just as long as I still finish and, most important, *still have fun*, which I do in almost every race. Being consistent and regular, and sticking pretty well to your schedule while at the same time not overtraining, are mind matters. The essence of happy multi-sport racing over an extended period of time is finding and maintaining that happy medium. Doing too much or too little is a function of the mind, not the body. Even the keys to successful hill climbing and useful breathing are found in the mind.

Distance sports are not cerebral in the sense that my other two sports, skiing and sailing, are. In those, the mind is constantly accumulating and processing data on wind, surface conditions, weather, rate of speed, direction, other moving objects, duration of light, steepness of slope on a hill or down a wave, and so forth. The mind then makes decisions controlling forward progress. Distance sports are also not cerebral in the same sense that team sports are. In the latter, the mind is constantly concerned with the player's role and responsibility, the rules, the current tactical and strategic position of his or her team, what the other team is doing, and how it can be countered.

The long-distance racer generally does not have a lot of split-second decision making to do except from time to time on the bike. However, in training and in racing, the mind is central for discipline and determination. In the races you must be able to estimate pace and remaining energy stores in order to appropriately regulate speed. When you are flagging a bit, it is your mind that will get you back into it and remind you of why you are out there and how you will feel when you cross the finish line. Thus, to be successful in distance sports, at whatever level you are competing, you must train your mind as well as your body.

Conclusion

The "Ten Rules of Running" (below), the thoughts on training of Rod Dixon, the New Zealander who won the 1983 New York Marathon in a dramatic finish, are a bookend for Bill Bowerman's "Ten Principles," which I shared with you at the beginning of this chapter. I think the Ten Rules apply equally well to triathlon training and are in accord with the Basic Principles of the TFOMTP, whether you are fast or slow, a potential age-group winner or a person like me whose continuous goal is to finish the race happily and healthily and, yes, having fun. Some of these rules are at the philosophical level, and some are practical. However, the main message is consistency, regularity, and wholeness. Rod can have the rule "Don't run when you don't feel up to it," because he knew that skipping a day now and then did not mean that he gave up training. Training was a major part of his life.

If you decide to engage in triathlon/duathlon racing on a regular basis—doing three or more events per year—it will become, or already is, an important part of your life. Obviously, you will not train the way Rod Dixon did, but then your goals are not the same as his were when he was a world-class marathoner. Training, if you follow my suggestions, will become important to you. At the same

Rod Dixon's Ten Rules of Running

1. Emphasize consistency in your training program.
2. Train in an environment that promotes a concentrated effort.
3. Maintain a strong commitment to being fit.
4. Realize that good, successful training is the best source of self-confidence.
5. Rest sufficiently after a race to restore energy levels.
6. Don't run when you don't feel up to it.
7. Enhance performance by going into a race with peace of mind.
8. Identify your nutritional needs as an athlete and nourish yourself properly.
9. Avoid injury by discarding shoes that are worn out beyond 75 percent of their "life."
10. Do not consider any one aspect of training more important than another. Each is integral to the total running program.

time, it will not, certainly it need not, and indeed it certainly should not, take over your life, pushing out everything else. As long as you follow the consistency/regularity rule, you can maintain a balanced approach to training, placing limits on it, making it additive to, not dominant of, your life.

STARTING FROM SCRATCH:
THE BASIC AEROBIC
FITNESS PROGRAM

This chapter begins with the same premise the last one did: you have decided to do your first triathlon or duathlon. However, in this case you have not yet established the aerobic base, that prerequisite for commencing the Triathloning for Ordinary Mortals Training Program (TFOMTP). In that case, this chapter, which presents my Basic Aerobic Fitness Program, the BAFP, is for you. Starting from absolute scratch, presently doing no regular exercise whatsoever, you can train to successfully complete a Sprint or Olympic-distance triathlon or a short-course duathlon in from 4 to 6 months to 1 year from the day you make the big decision. The length of time that you will need to get there depends upon such factors as noted in Chapter 5: your age, health status, present general physical shape and weight, your skill levels in the three sports, the amount of time you have to devote to training, and your eagerness level.

The most important element in making this journey a successful one is training your mind, along the lines that I discussed in the last chapter: to be realistic in defining success for yourself, to spend some significant amount of time on goal setting, to make sure that your life priorities are in balance, to be regular and consistent in your training, and to recognize that becoming a regular exerciser, then a multi-sport racer, is as much a matter of training your mind as it is of training your body.

For an Olympic-distance triathlon, you need to achieve a level of fitness that will enable you to exercise aerobically for up to 4 to 5 consecutive hours. For a Sprint-distance triathlon or a short-course duathlon, you need to be able to go for up to 2 to 3 hours. (Because, as you already know, the overwhelming majority of duathlons are of the short-course variety, from here on I simply use the term "duathlon" to refer to this type of race.) Assuming that you will be doing a conventional triathlon, you need to be able to, or learn how to run, bike, and swim. All of this may seem rather overwhelming. But believe me, based on the experience of many beginner triathletes who have used this program, all these goals and objectives are achievable for you, within a year, and for some in considerably less time than that.

As discussed in Chapter 5, my program is set out in minutes per day and days per week, not miles per day or per week. It obviously can be undertaken using any of the sports. Once you have become comfortable mentally and physically with exercising regularly, as long as you exercise vigorously enough to get your heart rate up into the aerobic range, you can use any of the sports in any of the workouts. Nevertheless, I suggest that in the beginning you concentrate on running. Running is technically the easiest of the three sports. It is also the simplest in terms of access, place to do it, time of day, weather, season of the year, and so forth. Of the three sports, it is the most demanding on the body. However, in order to be a successful triathlete, you must get used to the trials and tribulations of running, as well as to its joys.

The combination BAFP and TFOMTP takes up to one year from scratch to triathlon/duathlon completion. It may take you a year. It may take you considerably less. As you get into it, you will get a feel for just how much time it will take *you*. If you want to take a year, feeling you need a year to be comfortable in your mind and body with what you plan to do, I provide a year's worth of training programs for you. Overall, the combined program is divided into three phases. Phases I and II are covered in this chapter. Phase I is 13 weeks long. With a walk/run program, you start on the road to becoming a regular exerciser and achieving aerobic fitness. Then you arrive at the threshold of doing that. Phase II lasts for up to 26 weeks, depending upon your previous experience with regular exercise, and how you adapt, develop, feel, and just plain get into it. In Phase II, you will firmly establish your aerobic base. You also introduce swimming and biking into your exercise program. Phase II provides you with the time to do any learning and skill training in one or both of those sports. Phase III is the Triathloning for Ordinary Mortals Training Program (TFOMTP), presented in the next chapter.

If you are not starting from absolute scratch, or if you are but feel that you can move along quickly, you can hop into Phase I or Phase II at any point that you think will work for you. Just make sure to do it at a pace that will minimize muscular pain and the risk of musculoskeletal injury, and will not get you overanxious about the whole enterprise. I believe that unless you are in pretty good shape now, it will be useful for you to have put in 2 to 6 months of work at the aerobic base, $2\frac{1}{2}$ to 3 hours per week, before starting the TFOMTP. Nevertheless, this starting-from-scratch program can certainly be compressed even further, should you find yourself comfortable, physically and mentally, with doing so.

Medical Considerations

When starting out on an aerobic exercise program, it is probably a good idea to pay a visit to your physician, even if you are in good health. I especially recommend this if you are 40 and over. A medical evaluation may include a graded exercise or stress test (GXT). It comprises working out on a treadmill while your heart rate, heartbeat pattern (as measured by an electrocardiogram), and blood pressure are measured; and several tests of your lung function. Not everyone needs a GXT. A qualified cardiologist or sports-medicine physician can evaluate you and advise you appropriately on this matter.

Because there is some expense involved (it can be substantial if a GXT is included), if you do not have insurance coverage for the work-up, you may not want to undergo a medical evaluation until you have become a regular exerciser at the entry level and are convinced that you will stick with it. There is some risk involved in taking this approach, of course, although for at least the first 13 weeks of the full BAFP you may be walking only. When I started on the pathway to becoming a regular exerciser, I was in decent health, except I lived a sedentary lifestyle and was modestly overweight. But I had never smoked cigarettes, of the other recreational drugs used only alcohol on occasion, practiced safe sex, used my automobile seat belt, and so on. (Twenty-five years later, I am in much better health than I was back then, because I am a regular exerciser and am considerably lighter and considerably less fat.) I also had excellent health insurance coverage (and still do, lucky me). Nevertheless, I was over 40. Despite that latter circumstance, I did not undergo a health evaluation (which included a GXT) until I had been working out for about four months.

For an initial medical evaluation, you will probably want to consult your own physician. However, many physicians do not know very much about sports medicine or fitness and exercise. These subjects are taught in few medical schools and residency programs. Some misguided physicians are actually anti-exercise (although their number is declining. It is now well established that a sedentary lifestyle is a risk factor for premature mortality. Most physicians are aware of that fact.) Even more are anti-running, because they do not

---

Risk Factors Suggesting Need for Medical Evaluation

If you follow my advice and become a regular aerobic exerciser in a gradual, paced fashion, there is little health danger at the beginning, and a medical examination usually can be safely put off for a bit. However, if you are 40 or over, or if at any age any of the following apply to you, it is a good idea to be checked out sooner rather than later.

1. You have high blood pressure.
2. You have high serum cholesterol.
3. You are a cigarette smoker.
4. Upon exertion, you feel pain or pressure in your chest or experience severe shortness of breath.
5. You have previously had a heart attack (which is not necessarily a disqualifier).
6. There is a history of heart disease in your immediate family (parents, siblings).
7. You are more than 20 pounds overweight.
8. You have led a pretty sedentary lifestyle in recent years.
9. You have a history of lung problems.
10. You use prescribed medication on a regular basis.
11. You have a history of abuse of alcohol or other drugs.
12. You have any chronic problems with your bones or joints, or other limitations of your musculoskeletal system.
13. You have any other chronic illness, such as diabetes.

understand the sport and do not know how it can be done safely and beneficially. If you are not satisfied with the levels of knowledge and skill and the attitude of your physician regarding exercise, you should politely, nicely, but firmly ask for a referral to someone with competence in sports medicine or health and fitness.

Alternatively, you may want to go directly to a cardio-fitness center or similar establishment. They can be found in association with private physicians' offices and hospitals. They are usually staffed by knowledgeable medical professionals and are equipped to provide sophisticated medical evaluations. Upon your request, they will send a complete report of their findings to your primary care physician, thus keeping him or her happy and informed.

Getting Started

There are several different useful approaches to starting from scratch. When I started running in 1980, I used the walk/run method, then and still advocated by Bob Glover (see Appendix II). Bob's "Run Easy" program certainly worked well for me then and should work well for you now. In my view, walk/run is the safest way to begin a running program, and it is the best route to becoming a regular exerciser, en route to becoming a multi-sport racer.

Some people go out on their first day of planned running—not having run for any distance for a long time, if ever—and try to do it for 10 or 15 or 20 minutes straight. Unless you are very unusual, if you do this you will stop your workout short, gasping for breath and feeling very uncomfortable. The next morning you will likely ache all over and be so stiff that you may hardly be able to get out of bed. In contrast, unless you are severely out of shape, the walk/run method will almost certainly enable you to avoid gasping for breath at any time during your workouts, from that first day onward. This approach will also minimize the aches and pains, although for the first few weeks you will probably experience them to some degree.

There are two major variants of the walk/run method. One is to walk until you feel that you are ready to run, then run until your body and your breathing tell you that it is time to walk again, and so on, for the total time assigned for the particular workout. (You will find below a whole set of workout schedules, all in minutes.) The second variant is to walk for 2 minutes, run for 2 minutes, and so on, again for the assigned time for that session. You can then gradually increase the running minutes and decrease the walking minutes as you proceed through the schedule of workouts. A variant of walk/run, which can be fun, is counting steps for walking, then running, then back to walking, and so on, again for the minutes scheduled for that day. Yet another is going for a set distance, alternating walking and running, on the track, a road with utility poles spaced at regular intervals, or a city street evenly divided into blocks. The underlying principle of all of these methods is the same: to gradually ease yourself into running. As I have said before, do not try jumping in with both feet even if they are shod with shiny new top-of-the-line running shoes. For most of us, that approach simply does not work over the long run.

A second approach to starting from scratch is to walk only. This will provide a slow, easy, gradual introduction to running. It will also enable you to focus on the hard part of regular exercise, which as you know by now is the regular, not the exercise. In this plan, using the same tables (see pages 134–35), you begin with walking only, on a regular workout schedule, into the third month. In that month, introduce a small dose of jogging only. You will then develop your running skills over a second 3-month period. This is a very gradual program. Many people do not need to start out quite as slowly and gradually as provided for in this approach. However, if you think that it will work for you, do it. You can always speed up, in progressing through the program and in the rate of speed in your workouts. But if you go out too fast in either sense, hurt a lot, get frustrated, lose your regularity, possibly get injured, and then quit, it may be quite some time before you are ready to try it again.

With any of the above methods, you will eventually get to the level where you are running, or jogging, through your entire workout. The difference between jogging and running, by the way, is nothing but rate of speed, and that happens to be relative.

One person's run is another's jog. In my early days of racing, a friend of mine who consistently won our age-group in 10k races talked about "jogging" when he was doing a 7:30 mile. For me, that speed was about the fastest that I could do, and I could sustain it for only about 4 miles. (At my present age, I could not come anywhere close to that speed, even for 1 mile!) The great philosopher of running, George Sheehan, put the difference another way: "The difference between a runner and a jogger is a race entry-blank." The starting-from-scratch program that I set forth below has you doing up to 2½ hours per week of jogging/running by the end of the third month. However, for some people, the slower introduction described above may be "just what the doctor ordered." For some others it may indeed be just what *their* doctor orders for them!

Starting from Scratch: Phase I

In the realm of designing exercise programs, originality is no longer possible. I certainly make no claim to it. Many others have laid out beginning running programs, and were doing so well before I did the work back in the mid-1980s that led to the design of my own program. Mine draws heavily upon them. The basic precepts of all of them are the same: walk/run to begin, consistency, regularity, days off, hard/easy. Mine is simply tailored to the needs of the future multi-sport athlete, as I see them and have experienced them. When, back in 1983, I first developed what became the TFOMTP, it was pretty much in tune with the popular introduction-to-the-marathon regimens of the day. As you know, with minor variations I have stayed with the TFOMTP ever since. I have found it to work for me on a continuing basis, enabling me to achieve my primary goal in the sport of finishing my triathlons and duathlons happily and healthily and having fun doing so. I have also found it to be consistently doable over the 24-plus years that I have been a multi-sport racer.

If you have looked ahead at the TFOMTP, you will have noted that in two of the three variants, workouts are scheduled on five days per week, with two rest days. The third has one rest day. (As mentioned in the previous chapter, there are few training experts today who would argue that scheduled rest is not a necessary part of training.) Phase I requires only four rather than five workouts per week (see Tables 6.1 to 6.4). This sort of gradual approach is helpful in the beginning, to ease you into it. For those who are employed on a Monday to Friday schedule, I suggest that workouts be done on Tuesday, Thursday, Saturday, and Sunday. (If you have a different work schedule, you can obviously change the days on which you work out.) The relatively long workout each week is scheduled for Sunday, to help you get into the pattern that many distance athletes follow on a regular basis (and that is followed in the TFOMTPs). However, do not regard this suggested pattern as being carved in stone. Virtually any combination of days and minutes adding up to the weekly totals will do, just as long as you do not cram it all into less than three days per week.

To avoid musculoskeletal problems and to develop aerobic fitness, you must work out at least three days a week. Ideally these days will be evenly spaced, but if your schedule limits you to one weekday and Saturday/Sunday, it is better to start with that than not start at all. For each workout day, I have designated the number of minutes to be done. Note that through Phase I there is a gradual progression from a total of 1½ hours to a total of 2½ hours per week, but it is done in waves, following the Bowerman hard/easy principle on the "macro level" (the overall pattern of workouts from week to week). The hard/easy principle is also followed within each week, at the "micro level" (the pattern of workouts within each week).

I have divided Phase I into four sets totaling 13 weeks. In the first set of 3 weeks (Table 6.1), you should concentrate on walking, at a brisk pace, with a little running thrown in. As mentioned above, you may decide to use walking all the way through this phase. If you plan to start running fairly early on, I don't think that it is necessary to specify in detail how the time should be divided. You can find a pattern that suits you. As an example, assuming that you are doing timed segments, in the first week of 20-minute workouts you might do a 6-minute walk, a 2-minute run twice, concluding with walk 2 minutes and run 2 minutes. In the second week, you could go to walk 5, run 3, followed by walk 2, run 2, and so forth. As you come to the end of this set, you may find yourself running more and walking less than that. That is

Table 6.1. Getting Started

Phase I—Set 1, Mostly Walking

(Times in minutes per day)

Day	M	T	W	Th	F	S	S	Total
Week								
1	Off	20	Off	20	Off	20	30	90
2	Off	20	Off	25	Off	20	35	100
3	Off	20	Off	30	Off	25	35	110
							Grand Total	**300**
							(100 minutes per week)	

okay. Work out a comfortable pattern for yourself, just as long as you gradually increase your running minutes and decrease your walking minutes. At the end of the set, different folks will have arrived at different distributions of time between walking and running. At this point—getting started—you should not be focusing on speed but rather on the fact that you are working out on a regular schedule, you have kept your speed and distance under control so you have not been injured, you are running to some extent, and you are having fun.

In Set 2 (Table 6.2), you will begin to change the balance toward running. A typical 25-minute workout in this set might be run 4, walk 3 three times, concluding with a 4-minute run. The 40-minute workout could consist of five sets of run 5, walk 3. But don't overdo it. You are still new to this sport. You want to continue in it for some time, maybe for the rest of your life. Your muscles are still getting used to doing tasks that they have not been called upon to do in years, if ever. It is better to err on the side of doing too little rather than too much. More often than not, quitting after 2 to 6 months of trying to become a regular exerciser is related to nothing more than overdoing it: excess post-workout pain and/or morning stiffness, injury, stress, frustration, and boredom from lack of variation. By the way, to help deal with boredom, if you started out on the track, at this stage you should begin varying your routes by going out on the street or road once or twice a week.

Table 6.2. Getting Started

Phase I—Set 2, Walking/Running

(Times in minutes per day)

Day	M	T	W	Th	F	S	S	Total
Week								
4	Off	20	Off	25	Off	20	35	100
5	Off	20	Off	30	Off	25	35	110
6	Off	25	Off	30	Off	25	40	120
							Grand Total	**330**
							(110 minutes per week)	

In Set 3 (Table 6.3), the balance definitively starts shifting to running. At the beginning of the set, you may be putting three or four 2-minute walks into each workout. By the end of the set, you will probably be putting only one 2- to 3-minute walk in the middle of each run, if that. Notice that this set lasts for 4 weeks, long enough to let you ease into the final transition from walker to runner. Finally, in Set 4 of Phase I (Table 6.4), you will become a full-time runner. For the most part, the workouts are still fairly short. At least they will feel fairly short when you get to them, even if they do not look short to you right now, as you contem-

Table 6.3. Getting Started

Phase I—Set 3, Running/Walking

(Times in minutes per day)

Day	M	T	W	Th	F	S	S	Total
Week								
7	Off	20	Off	30	Off	25	35	110
8	Off	25	Off	30	Off	25	40	120
9	Off	25	Off	30	Off	35	40	130
10	Off	30	35	Off	30	Off	45	140
							Grand Total	**500**
							(125 minutes per week)	

Table 6.4. Getting Started

Phase I—Set 4, Running

(Times in minutes per day)

Day	M	T	W	Th	F	S	S	Total
Week								
11	Off	25	30	Off	35	Off	40	130
12	Off	30	35	Off	30	Off	45	140
13	Off	30	35	Off	35	Off	50	150
							Grand Total	**420**
							(140 minutes per week)	
						13-Week Total 1,550	(120 minutes per week)	

plate starting to run. By Set 4, you should be ready to drop the walk portion of each workout. You still should be checking your heart rate now and then to make sure that you are exercising in the aerobic range. You should be going neither too fast nor too slow. A good rule of thumb for not going too fast is that you should be able to talk to yourself or a partner while running. At the end of this set, you will be equipped to go to the next step: establishing the aerobic base that you will need when you start out on the TFOMTP itself: 2½ hours per week.

Congratulations! You did it, and I'll bet that it didn't seem so difficult. You walked and ran for a total of 56 days over a 13-week period—1,550 minutes total. You averaged about 28 minutes per day overall. By Set 4, you were averaging 35 minutes per day. You are now ready to commence Phase II, firmly establishing your aerobic base. In it, you will average about 35 minutes per day, and increase the number of workouts per week from four to five. You will also add cycling and swimming to your training program. At the end of this phase, you will be well on your way to becoming a triathlete.

Starting from Scratch: Phase II

In Phase II, you will average 2¾ hours of aerobic exercise per week for up to 26 weeks. Just make sure to treat this as a guidepost, not a set of milestones that you must achieve. You should adapt the workout schedules offered in this phase to your needs and predilections. How fast are you moving along? Are you pretty much running all the time? Are you working in cycling and—if planning for a triathlon—swimming as well? What do you like to do? What do you think will better keep you on track with your training? Treat this phase flexibly in terms of how long you stay in it and just what sports you do in it.

In the beginning, with the increase in the number of workouts per week from four to five, the number of minutes per workout will decline well below what you were doing per workout at the end of Phase I. The full Phase II is divided into two parts, each one containing an 8-week set and a 5-week set. Just as in Phase I, in each set there is a buildup in weekly minutes to a peak, with the next set beginning below that peak and building to a higher one. There is a similar changing pattern of increasing and decreasing minutes within each week. Thus, as in Phase I, Bill Bowerman's hard/easy principle is followed at the macro and micro levels.

In Set 1 of Phase II (Table 6.5), you will gradually work up to 3 hours per week, surpassing your previous high of 2½ hours

Table 6.5. Establishing the Aerobic Base

Phase II—Set 1, Building Up to 3 Hours per Week
(Times in minutes per day)

Day	M	T	W	Th	F	S	S	Total
Week								
1	Off	20	20	Off	20	20	40	120
2	Off	20	20	Off	20	20	40	120
3	Off	25	20	Off	20	25	40	130
4	Off	25	30	Off	25	25	45	150
5	Off	20	30	Off	30	20	50	150
6	Off	25	30	Off	30	25	50	160
7	Off	20	35	Off	30	40	45	170
8	Off	25	35	Off	30	40	50	180

Grand Total 1,180

(147.5 minutes per week)

achieved at the end of Phase I. Five workouts per week will come easily to you. You will begin to experience more and more the benefits of regular aerobic exercise for mind and body. In Phase II, Set 2 (Table 6.6), you drop back down, then build up once again to 3 hours. You are confirming your progress. By the end of this set, you will have been exercising aerobically for 6 months. The 6-month plateau is considered significant by many running authorities. You will have overcome the aches, pains, and minor injuries that some beginning runners experience. You will have trained your heart and lungs to function aerobically. You will have accustomed and then trained your mind to a pattern of regular exercise. You and your family will have recognized that regular exercise has become a regular part of your life. Once you pass the 6-month point, the likelihood that you will stop diminishes rapidly and markedly. In addition, once you reach this milestone, you are ready for another important experience: rest.

If you plan to do a Sprint triathlon or a duathlon for your first race, if you feel ready and you want to, at this point you can safely proceed to the TFOMTP variant that you will use to prepare for that first one. However, you may not want to push things, in which case you will go on to Set 3 of Phase II (Table 6.7). At the beginning of this set, there is a complete break. One week of rest is followed by one very light week. You will not lose your aerobic

Table 6.6. Establishing the Aerobic Base

Phase II—Set 2, Confirming 3 Hours per Week
(Times in minutes per day)

Day	M	T	W	Th	F	S	S	Total
Week								
9	Off	25	20	Off	25	30	40	140
10	Off	25	20	Off	25	35	45	150
11	Off	25	30	Off	25	30	50	160
12	Off	20	20	Off	30	40	60	170
13	Off	25	20	Off	30	45	60	180

Grand Total 800
(160 minutes per week)

Table 6.7. Establishing the Aerobic Base

Phase II—Set 3, Rest and Take Off

(Times in minutes per day)

Day	M	T	W	Th	F	S	S	Total
Week								
14	Off	Off	Off	Off	Off	Off	Off	0
15	Off	20	Off	20	Off	20	Off	60
16	Off	20	20	Off	20	20	40	120
17	Off	25	30	Off	25	30	45	155
18	Off	20	35	Off	30	40	45	170
19	Off	25	35	Off	35	40	50	185
20	Off	20	40	Off	35	50	60	205
21	Off	35	40	Off	40	50	60	225

Grand Total 1,120

(140 minutes per week)

base during this time. You will afford your body and mind some time off, a chance to consolidate their gains and recover from the new experiences that you have been putting them through. This rest period is important to prepare you for the challenges to come. It is not a good idea to skip it.

After the rest, in Phase II, Set 3, you will once again engage in building up your aerobic minutes, surpassing your previous weekly high a little more than halfway through the set. Phase II, Sets 3 and 4 (Tables 6.7. and 6.8), are designed to bring you up to the level of aerobic fitness needed to comfortably begin and comfortably complete the Olympic-distance preparation variant of the TFOMTP. As noted above, if you are aiming for a Sprint or a duathlon to start with, you certainly can go into the TFOMTP variant that you will be following directly from Phase II, Set 2. In Phase II, Set 4, however, the weekly workout pattern changes. The longest workout is now done on Saturday rather than Sunday, in the manner of the TFOMTP itself. A final note here. Let us say that you are reading this book and already exercising at a minimum at the aerobic base level, $2^1/_2$ to 3 hours per week, have been doing so for at least 6 months, and do not need to carry out

Table 6.8. Establishing the Aerobic Base

Phase II—Set 4, Getting Ready for the TFOMTP

(Times in minutes per day)

Day	M	T	W	Th	F	S	S	Total
Week								
22	Off	30	40	Off	35	50	45	200
23	Off	30	40	Off	40	60	50	220
24	Off	35	40	Off	45	65	55	240
25	Off	45	35	Off	50	70	60	260
26	Off	45	40	Off	50	75	60	270

Grand Total 1,190

(240 minutes per week. This is the Sprint-distance training program requirement.)

any of the earlier parts of the program. Nevertheless, it is still probably a good idea to do Set 4 of Phase II or some semblance of it before starting the TFOMTP.

Introducing Cycling and Swimming in Phase II

The organization of Phase II of the BAFP allows you to introduce cycling and swimming into your aerobic exercise program at a rate that suits you. Remember that the basis of my whole approach to triathloning is to first develop aerobic fitness. Expertise and excellence in one or more of the sports, although desirable, are not necessary to achieve your major goal: completing your first chosen multi-sport race happily and healthily. Thus, it is the total aerobic minutes done that counts, not the sports in which they are done.

At the same time, you must do enough of each sport to be comfortable doing it in a race. It is also helpful for performance and musculoskeletal comfort to have had some resistance training for the several muscle groups specific to each sport. For safety's sake, future triathletes must be able to swim well enough to go the required distance. Once again, the distribution of the times among the three sports is not critical during Phase II. Assuming that you know how to swim and ride a bicycle, you can start substituting swim and bike workouts for run workouts in any pattern that is comfortable for you. Some weeks you may not run at all. You must simply be certain that you are doing your chosen sport fast enough to get your heart rate into the aerobic range.

As noted above, if you do not know how to swim or ride a bike quickly and efficiently, Phase II offers you the opportunity to learn. You may count time spent in swimming lessons as a workout as long as you spend it swimming at the aerobic pace. Non-swimmers would do well to commence lessons early in Phase II (if not during Phase I once you know that you will proceed). Then you can schedule the lessons for 20- and 25-minute days. It will be easy to get the lesson and the workout in at the same time. If you are a novice cyclist, you can also use those short workouts to get a feel for your machine, learn how to sit on a racing saddle, become comfortable using toe clips with your running shoes or cleats and clip-in pedals with bike shoes (see Chapter 8). If you need to work on spinning (see Chapter 4) and riding in the proper gear, practice these skills in the short workouts. Continue to devote the long ones to running. Later in the phase, as you become more competent in the water and on the bike, you can cut back further on running and devote some of the longer sessions to the other sports.

As you come to the end of Phase II, you will have significantly elevated your level of aerobic fitness and solidified your aerobic base. You will also be comfortable doing the two or three sports that you will need for your first race. You are ready to begin Phase III, the TFOMTP itself.

THE TRIATHLONING FOR ORDINARY MORTALS TRAINING PROGRAM

Dream, Believe, Achieve. —seen on the back of a T-shirt on the bike segment of the Long Island Gold Coast Triathlon, Hempstead Harbor, New York, June 19, 2005

You are now ready to begin specific training for the first triathlon or duathlon that you have your eye on. You have started from scratch and have completed Phases I and II of the Basic Aerobic Fitness Program, described in the last chapter, or you are an already established recreational endurance athlete and have been working out aerobically in your sport for at least 2½ to 3 hours per week on a consistent basis for 2 to 6 months, depending upon what kind of shape you were in at the outset. For the past 5 to 6 weeks, you have gradually increased your workout time. If you are planning to do an Olympic-distance triathlon, you have averaged 3 to 4 hours per week over that stretch. For the Sprint/duathlon option, 2½ to 3 hours per week is just fine. You have achieved a reasonable, comfortable level of technical competence in running and biking and—if you are going to do a triathlon—swimming as well. You have clearly established your goal for your first race: to finish, happily and healthily. You will not be concerned with speed, although you certainly will be pleased if you happen to go faster than expected.

You are comfortable with the minutes rather than the miles approach to working out. You realize that the faster you go in your workouts, the more miles you will cover. This kind of workout will naturally produce a faster race performance. However, you will not push yourself to go faster in your workouts than is comfortable for you, risking injury and breakdown just to try to improve your race time. You know that the key to being on the racecourse for a certain number of minutes is not how fast you have gone in training but for how many minutes you have spent training aerobically. You will be able to keep your mind firmly fixed on what you need to do to achieve your goal: finishing your chosen race in a time that is right for *you, your* body, *your* mind, *your* experience, and *your* level of training. Therefore, you have cast yourself as an Ordinary Mortal in the world of triathloning and duathloning, at least to get started. You are ready to undertake the variant of the Triathloning for Ordinary Mortals Training Program, the TFOMTP, that will prepare you for your chosen race.

In this chapter, I offer you three variants of the original TFOMTP for the Olympic-distance event, which I have developed over the years for myself. In addition, there are two new shorter versions of the TFOMTP that will get you ready to start with (and perhaps stay with) the now common Sprint-distance races and duathlons. Each variant of the TFOMTP covers 13 weeks. If followed to the minute, for an Olympic-distance triathlon you will have worked out in the three sports for 3,900 minutes, or 65 hours—an average of 5 hours per week for that 13-week period. For the Sprint triathlon or duathlon, you will have worked for 2,730 minutes, or 45$^1/_2$ hours—an average of 3$^1/_2$ hours per week for 13 weeks. Although I recommend doing the full program, you can safely miss up to 10 percent of whichever one you choose and still do just fine in the race. I know. I have done that. In addition, the individual workouts do not have to be done to the minute each time. You can go a modest amount over on some, under on others. You can get behind a bit one week and make it up the next. Assuming that you work out at least four times a week, while maintaining your consistency and regularity, it is the total number of aerobic minutes that you do over the 13 weeks that counts.

How did I originally arrive at that 3,900-minute figure for the Olympic-distance, you might ask. How did I know that it would work? As I have noted earlier, I first developed the program for myself back in 1983, starting from the approach that Ardy Friedberg laid out in his seminal work, *How to Run Your First Marathon.* Ardy's program was designed to take an aspiring marathoner from being totally sedentary to being at the starting line of the Big One in 26 weeks. I modified his program to make it suitable, or so I thought, for triathloning. In the thirteenth week before marathon day in Ardy's program (which totals 26 weeks from scratch to marathon day), the runner is working out for 4 hours. Over the remaining 13 weeks, there is a total of 3,270 minutes of workout time—4 hours and 10 minutes per week on the average. I was dealing with someone (myself) who was already working out for about 4 hours per week. Figuring on having to train in three sports instead of just one, and liking nice, round numbers, I arbitrarily upped the average weekly workout to 5 hours. I adopted the same hard/easy flow at the micro (weekly) and macro (total program) levels that Ardy used, the one recommended by Bill Bowerman and many others.

I tried out this program for my own first triathlon. Lo and behold, it worked for me. And it has continued to work for me over the many years that I have been doing the sport. Closing in on my twenty-fifth season, I am using pretty much the same program that I designed when I started out, then modified some for this book. I have also continued to maintain a clear vision of what is doable for me in the world of triathloning: finishing happily and healthily, being comfortable on the course and after the race, just going out and having a good time, almost every time. In the subsequent years since I designed the program, I have discovered that there is quite a bit of support in the literature for the 5-hours-per-week plan (plus or minus an hour or so) for first-time Olympic-distance triathletes. I have put a few personal wrinkles in it (which I will not share with you here because I do not want you to be overloaded with alternatives. In the last chapter I share with you the version of the TFOMTP that I currently use in my March-to-October racing season.) You, of course, can put in your own wrinkles. The main point is this: the TFOMTP has worked for me over the years, just as it has worked for many, many readers of the first edition and the 1999 update of this book. Therefore, it can surely work for you too.

The TFOMTP for the Olympic-Distance

Over the years, I have developed three variations on the 13-week, 3,900-minute, 5-hours-per-week theme: six workouts over 5 days, five workouts over 5 days, and six workouts over 6 days. At one time or another I have used all of them myself. I currently favor the six-workouts-over-5-days version, but the other two work just as well. Simply pick the one that you think will fit in best with your schedule and other time commitments. For each of the variants, only the scheduled minutes of workout time are given. You decide how you want to distribute the total time each week among the three sports, although most people will not do more than one swim workout per week. To achieve the goal of the TFOMTP, it is not necessary to do more than one, unless you need to in order to make sure that your confidence level for the swim in the race is where it should be. Between running and cycling, you can decide which sport you want to do more of.

Each of the three TFOMTP variants is laid out in three sets. For the Olympic-distance event, the first set builds slowly over a 5-week period from almost 5 hours per week to almost 6. At the beginning of the second set, you drop back sharply to $2^1/_2$ hours, then build up to a peak at close to 8 hours a week before the end of this 6-week block. In the last set, you taper down for the last 2 weeks before your race. Notice that the hard/easy, buildup/taper-down pattern is followed over the 13-week span as well as within each week's workout schedule.

The first variant of the TFOMTP provides for a total of six workouts per week in all three sports (Table 7.1). You do them over 5 days, with two workouts on the same day once each week. For me, having two days completely off each week works best because it gives my body the intra-training rest that I have come to know that it needs. It also provides for training-schedule flexibility within each week, when my weeks get busy with other things. I have scheduled the days with two workouts on Tuesdays,

Table 7.1. The TFOMTP for the Olympic-Distance Triathlon

Six Workouts over 5 Days per Week

(Times in minutes; average of 5 hours per week for 13 weeks)

Day	M	T	W	Th	F	S	S	Total
Week								
Set 1								
1	Off	40/35	45	Off	45	65	60	290
2	Off	40/40	50	Off	45	70	65	310
3	Off	45/40	55	Off	50	75	70	335
4	Off	45/45	50	Off	55	75	65	335
5	Off	50/45	55	Off	65	75	60	350
Set 2								
6	Off	40	30	Off	25	35	25	155
7	Off	30	40	Off	35	45	55	205
8	Off	55/50	70	Off	65	80	70	390
9	Off	55/50	60	Off	75	80	75	395
10	Off	65/60	75	Off	75	90	100*	465
11	Off	45/45	50	Off	55	45	150*	390
Set 3								
12	Off	45	Off	60	Off	70	45	220
13	Off	20	20	20	20	Race		

* These two workouts should be combined (bike/run or walk), so you can get some experience changing your clothing and doing two sports consecutively.

after a rest day, but they can be done on any day that is convenient for you. I suggest pairing cycling and swimming on this day, because these sports involve less total body wear and tear than does running. In addition, for the two-workout days as set out in the program, the scheduled time for each workout is generally at the low end, relatively, for the week in question.

The two other variants of the TFOMTP are designed for those who do not like having a two-workout day each week in their lives. The total training time is the same, but in one variant it is distributed over five workouts on 5 days per week (Table 7.2), and the other variant has six workouts over 6 days (Table 7.3). In the first, obviously each session is slightly longer than in the standard

Table 7.2. The TFOMTP for the Olympic-Distance Triathlon

Five Workouts over 5 Days per Week

(Times in minutes; average of 5 hours per week for 13 weeks)

Day	M	T	W	Th	F	S	S	Total
Week								
Set 1								
1	Off	45	55	Off	55	70	65	290
2	Off	45	55	Off	55	80	75	310
3	Off	55	65	Off	60	80	75	335
4	Off	55	65	Off	60	80	75	335
5	Off	60	65	Off	75	80	70	350
Set 2								
6	Off	40	30	Off	25	35	25	155
7	Off	30	40	Off	35	45	55	205
8	Off	65	80	Off	75	90	80	390
9	Off	65	70	Off	75	100	85	395
10	Off	75	85	Off	85	100	120*	465
11	Off	65	60	Off	55	60	150*	390
Set 3								
12	Off	45	Off	60	Off	70	45	220
13	Off	20	20	20	20	Race		

* These two workouts should be combined (bike/run or walk), so you can get some experience changing your clothing and doing two sports consecutively.

six-workout/5-day program; in the latter, the sessions are just about the same length as they are in the first version. Other than 1 versus 2 days off, the essential features are the same. In each variant, there is a buildup in weekly training time through the first 5 weeks, a cutback in Weeks 6 and 7, a buildup again to a higher level through Week 11, then a taper back down to race week.

Over the 13-week duration of each of the three variants of the program, there are two combined bike/runs, one for 2 hours, the other for 2½ hours. You will note that this is your longest workout, even though you may be racing for 4-plus hours. Believe me, this approach works. To go 4-plus hours in a race, you do not

Table 7.3. The TFOMTP for the Olympic-Distance Triathlon

Six Workouts over 6 Days per Week

(Times in minutes; average of 5 hours per week for 13 weeks)

Day	M	T	W	Th	F	S	S	Total
Week								
Set 1								
1	40	35	45	Off	45	65	60	290
2	40	40	50	Off	45	70	65	310
3	40	45	55	Off	50	75	70	335
4	45	45	50	Off	55	75	65	335
5	45	50	55	Off	65	75	60	350
Set 2								
6	Off	40	30	Off	25	35	25	155
7	Off	30	40	Off	35	45	55	205
8	50	55	70	Off	65	80	70	390
9	50	55	60	Off	65	90	75	395
10	60	55	75	Off	75	90	100*	455
11	55	45	45	Off	50	45	150*	390
Set 3								
12	Off	45	Off	60	Off	70	45	220
13	Off	20	20	20	20	Race		

* These two workouts should be combined (bike/run or walk), so you can get some experience changing your clothing and doing two sports consecutively.

have to go more than 2½ hours in training. In preparing for an Olympic-distance triathlon, I have never gone more than 2½ hours in training. How can a training program be effective that has no workout longer than 2½ hours? Well, as I have said, it has worked for me. But more importantly, it works because of the *total* amount of time you have spent in your training. As long as you keep your race pace under control and do not exhaust yourself (see Chapter 9), *it is the total amount of swimming, cycling, and running that you have done in your training that determines how far you will be able to go, not the length of your longest individual workouts.* You should be able to do the race distances individually, however. The scheduled longer workouts provide you with the opportunity to do that in each sport.

Training for their first triathlon, some people do all of the race distances consecutively in a workout, sometimes more than once. They are setting about convincing themselves that they will be able to make it. Now, I can assure you that doing so is not necessary. I can tell you that I have never done that, not even when preparing for an ironman-distance event (see Chapter 10). But if you think that you *will feel better* on race day knowing that you have covered the race distances consecutively, do so. However, make sure that you do that extralong workout no less than two weeks before race day. You do not want to interfere with the scheduled pre-race taper.

The Pattern in Some Detail

In Table 7.1 of the TFOMTP, you start out doing just 20 minutes more, total, in the first week than you did in the last week of Phase II, Set 4. Having built up slowly, steadily, and consistently in Phase II (or your own base-building/maintenance version of it), you can easily move into this somewhat more demanding schedule. You can also easily add one workout a week, going from four workouts per week to five. Please do not regard this schedule as being carved in stone, however. You can vary the pattern even from week to week if necessary to fit your life schedule, as long as you generally follow the overall guidelines and do the scheduled minutes.

You begin Set 2 by dropping your workout time back sharply for two weeks. This gives your body a chance to rest, recuperate, and firmly consolidate its gains in preparation for the additional buildup. In the first two weeks of this set, you not only cut back on minutes per workout, drop back to five workouts per week in the standard program of six workouts over 5 days. Then, beginning with Week 8, you go into the most demanding segment, building up to almost 8 hours of training in Week 10. In the last week of the set, Week 11, you cut down on total minutes and find that the weekday workouts are relatively short. However, you conclude that week, and this hardest four-week segment of your whole training program, with your 2½-hour bike/run session (called a "brick" in triathlon parlance). I always look at Weeks 8 to 11 as the really challenging part of my own training. I know that once I get through them I am home free and ready to race. Note that although you do have one week of almost 8 hours of work and three weeks of 6½ hours, you still are averaging only 5½ hours per week in this set.

In Set 3, you taper down to the race. In Week 12, you still have two fairly long workouts, but only four workouts total. If you find yourself significantly behind on total minutes coming into this week, you may add an extra workout or two and/or add minutes to one of the scheduled workouts. However, do not jam any extra minutes into the last week. Your body and mind are facing a big challenge on the upcoming weekend, possibly the biggest sports/athletics challenge they have ever faced. You need physical rest and mental preparation time. Those last three 20-minute workouts should be done at a leisurely pace to keep you loose. You do not want to risk injury at this stage of the game.

The Sprint and Duathlon TFOMTP

There were few Sprints or duathlons around when I started out in the sport. However, as it has matured—and many race organizers and directors have made a conscious effort to make multi-sport racing more accessible, acceptable, and attractive—there are more and more Sprints and duathlons on the race calendar. They are ideal for getting into the sport. Although many people start off with an Olympic-distance event, many others find those distances intimidating, or they find the prospect of swimming a mile intimidating, or they find the prospect of swimming at all intimidating. So they get into multi-sport racing via a shorter triathlon or a duathlon. It turns out that, for many folks, the Sprint-distance triathlon and/or duathlon alternatives are what they stay with. Earlier in my racing career, I did numerous Olympic-distance triathlons and some longer ones too. As I have gotten older, although I occasionally do an Olympic-distance triathlon, most of my racing is at the Sprint/duathlon level. I am comfy and having fun, and I usually am on the course for no more than two hours.

As noted previously, neither the Sprint-distance triathlon nor the entry-level duathlon distances are standardized, as is the Olympic-distance triathlon. For the Sprints, usually the swim is in the ¼- to ½-mile range, followed by a 10- to 18-mile bike and a 3- to 5-mile run. For the duathlon, there is customarily a 2- to 3-mile run, followed by a 10- to 15-mile bike, with a second run on the same course as the first. For all of these distances, a program requiring 3½ hours per week over 13 weeks (again, after you establish your aerobic base following the recommendations in Chapter 6) works very well. It need not be fine-tuned up or down for longer or shorter races in the Sprint/duathlon category. It will carry you through the longer-distance races and have you trained a bit extra for the shorter ones.

The Sprint-distance training program is presented in Table 7.4 and the duathlon training program in Table 7.5. Note how each

Table 7.4. The TFOMTP for the Sprint-Distance Triathlon

Five Workouts over 5 Days per Week

(Times in minutes; average of 3.5 hours per week for 13 weeks)

Day	M	T	W	Th	F	S	S	Total
Week								
1	Off	20	20	45	Off	55	60	200
2	Off	20	20	45	Off	60	65	210
3	Off	25	20	55	Off	60	65	225
4	Off	25	20	55	Off	60	70	230
5	Off	25	25	60	Off	60	65	235
6	Off	30	Off	25	Off	30	20	105
7	Off	25	Off	35	Off	35	50	145
8	Off	25	30	65	Off	60	70	250
9	Off	25	30	65	Off	80	75	275
10	Off	30	35	75	Off	70	90*	300
11	Off	30	35	55	Off	55	120*	295
12	Off	20	25	50	Off	60	40	190
13	Off	30	25	20	Off	Race		

* These two workouts should be combined (bike/run or walk), so you can get some experience changing your clothing and doing two sports consecutively.

Table 7.5. The TFOMTP for the Entry-Level Duathlon

Four Workouts over 4 Days per Week

(Times in minutes; average of 3.5 hours per week for 13 weeks)

Day	M	T	W	Th	F	S	S	Total
Week								
1	Off	40	Off	45	Off	55	60	200
2	Off	40	Off	45	Off	60	65	210
3	Off	45	Off	50	Off	65	65	225
4	Off	45	Off	55	Off	60	70	230
5	Off	50	Off	65	Off	60	60	235
6	Off	30	Off	25	Off	25	20	100
7	Off	25	Off	35	Off	35	50	145
8	Off	55	Off	65	Off	60	70	250
9	Off	55	Off	65	Off	80	75	275
10	Off	60	Off	70	Off	80	90*	300
11	Off	55	Off	65	Off	55	120*	295
12	Off	40	Off	50	Off	60	40	190
13	Off	30	25	20	Off	Race		

* These two workouts should be combined (bike/run or walk), so you can get some experience changing your clothing and doing two sports consecutively.

follows the same pattern of buildup, ease back, further buildup, then taper that the Olympic-distance program has. The difference is that you spend less time for the former than the latter. Just as with the Olympic-distance program, the Sprint and duathlon training programs provide you with the endurance you need to cover the distances, just as long as you keep your race paces under control. The faster you go in your training, the more total distance you will cover and the faster you will go in the races. But the key to having fun in the race is not attempting to exceed the level of your training.

How the Principles Apply to the TFOMTPs

By now I am sure that you know the principles of my approach to training and the keys to making them work for you: consistency, regularity, hard/easy, scheduled rest, balanced training, not overtraining, and, most importantly, a clear concept—with which you are entirely comfortable—of the goal that you are trying to achieve, happily and healthily: completing your first triathlon or duathlon at your chosen distance. Bearing the principles in mind, and following the TFOMTP variant most suited to you, your needs, your life schedule, and your abilities, you will be able to achieve that goal.

As you know, the minutes-not-miles approach is central to my philosophy of race training/preparation. Just to reiterate: as long as you put in pretty close to the required minutes—training for the most part in your aerobic range, regardless of speed—and you race at speeds that are comfortable for you this first time around, you will be able to finish happily and healthily. At my training speeds, I am doing the equivalent in the three sports of 25 to 30 miles of running per week, on the average. However, in three of the four heavy weeks of Set 2, I am doing the equivalent of more than 35 miles of running, and in Week 10 I am doing the equivalent of more than 40 miles. If you train at faster speeds than I do, your mileage will of course be higher. But whatever your speed, I say again, do not worry. Do not pick up your training pace just to add miles. Once again, you have to train in each sport at a pace just fast enough to get your heart rate over that aerobic threshold of 60 percent of your theoretical maximum heart rate, which is 220 minus your age (see page 109).

Fluids

I cannot overemphasize the importance of proper hydration for the bike and the run, in your training as well as your racing. For any bike segments over 12 miles, I recommend carrying two water bottles. Personal fluid replacement requirements do differ, but on the bike I use a minimum of one bottle per hour, or every 15 miles or so, and it is always better to have too much water available than too little. Then when you come in from the bike on the two-sport workouts, just as you will in the races, if you have water left, you can take a big swig before you start out on the run. For the runs, it is a good idea to carry a water bottle in a water-bottle belt. I recommend not carrying it in your hand. Doing so can unbalance your body just a little bit, and that little bit of imbalance can be harmful to your back, shoulders, or legs.

Preference in fluids varies. Until my twenty-first season, I stuck to water only, but then I started using one of the "energy replacement" drinks during my run and bike workouts. Like many other endurance athletes who use energy drinks, I have experienced a difference in my perceived level of performance, both in training and at the races. See which approach works best for you.

Getting into the Swim of Things

If you will be doing triathlons, you need to feel sure that you can make it through the swim. Even though in every well-run race there are plenty of swim monitors on the course who can give you a hand (literally) if you need it, if you are afraid that you might not make it, you will have a tough time even getting into the water. If the race swim distance is 1,500 meters or less, in the swim workouts it is not necessary to swim for more than 45 minutes—or the time it takes you to cover that distance, whichever is less—unless you like swimming and want to.

Regardless of what the race instructions say the water temperature will be, it is a good idea to get used to cold water. You should know that the actual race water temperature is sometimes lower than advertised. On more than one occasion, I saw people start into a cold-water swim with no wet suit, only to see them turn around before they got very wet. For water temperatures of 70°F and below, you may want to wear a wet suit, especially if you have low body fat. Wet suits are not inexpensive. Entry-level suits are in the $200 range (see Chapter 8). Thus, for your first race you might borrow or rent one (some of the better pro bike shops and dive shops have them for rent). Correct fit is important (see Chapter 8), so if you borrow a wet suit, make sure it fits reasonably well.

If the race is in salt water, you must get used to saltwater buoyancy. It is a help, not a hindrance, because it keeps you higher in the water than you would be in fresh water. However, especially if you are wearing a wet suit, which magnifies buoyancy, you should experience that effect before the race.

Way at the back of the pack, having fun, at the finish of the USA Triathlon Age-Group National Championships, St. Joseph, Missouri, 1999. *Photo courtesy of USA Triathlon; Peacock Photography*

Open water, whether salt or fresh, presents challenges of its own. You may well encounter waves, short chop, surf, currents, and tides in salt water. I know of at least one excellent swimmer who trained well in the pool but did no open-water training swims; he panicked at the open-water-swim start of his first triathlon, and did not even begin the race. So if your chosen first race has an open-water swim, schedule at least three of your swim workouts in open water.

Conclusion

The TFOMTP variants are simple, straightforward, and designed to give you enough training so that you can finish your chosen race happily and healthily. As I have said, if you want to exceed the scheduled times, by all means do so (even though you do not have to), as long as you do not feel tired and logy and bored and/or pressured with the training. As for doing less than the scheduled times, as I said above, that's okay too. I would not do that by more than 10 percent, however. Although not every training session will be fun, the session lengths and periodicity are designed so that the overall program will be fun, and you will see it not only as a means to an end, but as a rewarding experience in itself. I obviously love to race. However, if I did not enjoy the training too—most of the time—I am sure that I would not still be in the sport.

8

EQUIPMENT

It will be obvious to you by now that equipment is an important element of multi-sport racing. Not that you need a great deal of it or have to spend a great deal of money on it to have a great deal of fun in the sport. Super equipment will not make a winner out of somebody who ordinarily runs 9 to 11 minutes per mile, rides 14 to 16 mph, and swims 35- to 45-minute miles. However, good equipment can make the sport significantly more comfortable, safe, healthy, and enjoyable. And if, like me, you are a "stuff person," you can really get into it in this sport. There is lots of "stuff" to be had.

Because triathlon and duathlon require buying and maintaining a bike, likely owning a wet suit, and paying not insignificant race-registration fees and travel costs to participate in the races even at the entry level, they are not the cheapest of sports. However, compare them to downhill skiing (which happens to be my winter sport). The basic equipment package for it easily costs as much as a good entry-level bike. Then you have to pay $200 a day and up for lodging and lift ticket, plus travel, meals, possibly a car rental, et cetera. Worse yet, compare multi-sport racing to sailing (my summer sport for ten years from the mid-1970s, before I got into triathloning). The cost of the central piece of equipment alone can run into the tens of thousands of dollars. In this context, triathlon/duathlon can hardly be considered expensive.

Starting from scratch, you can get into multi-sport racing with a decent bike for about $1,400 to about $2,500 (2005 prices) (see Table 8.1). A large chunk of that cost is for the bicycle and related equipment, and a wet suit. The list may seem a bit overwhelming at first, but if you acquire the equipment one piece at a time, it will prove not to be. Furthermore, you may already own major pieces of what you need and/or be able to borrow some of it from friends or family, saving a considerable amount on your initial investment.

Where to Buy

As a "stuff guy" myself, I have had what seems like tons of equipment during my years in the sports. Nevertheless, my most useful advice on the "what to buy" aspect of equipment is to locate the best bicycle shop and the best running-shoe store in your area, before you buy anything. A good bike and a good pair of running shoes are the two central pieces of equipment that you will need. The staff at the better shops for both should take into account your interests, where you are in the sport(s), what your skill levels are, and your expressed needs, as well as their own desire to make a sale.

A good running-shoe store will be owned and/or staffed by runners. It will carry a limited number of running-shoe brands, and not every model in every line. The staff will have carefully evaluated the myriad number of makes and models of shoes on the market and will have preselected a good range from which you can choose. They will make sure that the shoes fit, and will stand behind their products. They will also be knowledgeable about clothing, socks, and other accessories.

Likewise, a good bicycle shop will be owned and/or staffed by cyclists. I strongly suggest that you do not buy your bike in a department store or a sports superstore. The prices may be attractive, but choosing on this basis alone is being penny-wise and pound-foolish. Such stores generally carry only lower-end equip-

Table 8.1. A Basic Triathlon/Duathlon Equipment Budget

(2005 prices)

General		Bike shirt, shorts, and socks	$75
Warm-up suit, nylon or fleece	$75–100	Bike shoes (for clipless pedals)	$75–250
Waterproof digital watch	$25–50	and pedals	
Subtotal	$100–150	Jacket, long-sleeved shirt, tights (for cool-weather training and racing)	$75–150
Swimming			
Swimsuits (2)	$20–75	*Subtotal*	$865–1,425
Goggles	$10-50		
Earplugs	$5	**Running**	
Antifog solution	$5	Shoes	$60–120
Wet suit	$150–450	Shorts, liner shorts, singlets, T-shirts	$75–100
Subtotal	$190–585	Socks (4 pairs)	$15–40
		Sweatbands (2)	$12
Cycling		Polypropylene underwear (1 set)	$35
Bicycle, good quality, entry level	$500–600	Cap, woolen hat	$15
Bicycle computer; pumps (full size and frame fit), water bottles, gloves, other accessories	$100–150	Athletic supporters, compression shorts, support bras	$15–50
		Subtotal	$227–372
Bike helmet	$40–200	*Grand total*	$1,382–2,532

ment, are not equipped to handle ongoing service, and rarely have knowledgeable salespeople. By the same token, note that all bicycle shops are not the same. Not all salespeople know what makes a good bike good and a better bike better, especially for triathlon/duathlon racing.

One way to judge a bicycle shop is by the most expensive bike it carries. As noted in Table 8.1, a decent bicycle for the beginning triathlete/duathlete costs around $500 to $600 (2005 prices). If a $600 model is the most expensive one in the shop you first visit, look elsewhere. Really good bikes cost $1,000 and up. A really good bike shop, often referred to as a "pro shop," will carry at least a few bikes of that type. It will also be staffed by bike racers or tourers or triathletes who can speak to you from experience about the bike you are buying. Even though I strongly discourage buying a triathlon-specific bike (see page 166) for your first one, if the shop carries an array of them, all the better. The mechanics in the shop you patronize should also be knowledgeable and willing to spend time talking with you.

There is a large mail- and Web-order business for running and cycling gear. The prices are usually lower than those found in the stores. The reputable mail- and Web-order sellers make returning items as painless as possible. I do a certain amount of mail (and occasionally Web site) ordering for some of my equipment, especially clothing. You may also be able to buy running shoes through the mail/Web if you settle on one brand and know your proper size. Nevertheless, although I have used the mail-/Web-order business for years, I feel that it must be used with care.

That said, you should not make your first purchases through the mail or on the Web. Although you can find attractive mail-/Web-ordering prices for the most costly piece of equipment, the bike, it needs to be fitted. Furthermore, as when you buy a new car, it is a good idea to test-ride several different makes and models. So unless you know exactly what you are looking for and have ridden it, know somebody who can put it together for you or be confident that you can assemble it correctly yourself (mail-order bicycles come in a number of pieces, in a box), and do not care about getting after-sale service from a dealer who has an investment in you and your repeat business, buying a bike at a distance is not a good idea. I have never done it, and never will, no matter how good those prices look. I value my relationship with my bike shop and its owners too much.

Find those good, local shops. Develop good relationships with the owner, the salespeople, and the mechanics. Get educated. Buy your first round of equipment from them. After you become somewhat knowledgeable, then you can intelligently buy some of your equipment by mail or on the Web. But continue to spend money locally, especially on major items, even if the cost is a bit higher. Personal advice and counsel and continuing personal service are invaluable, and you do want those shops to stay in busi-

ness. Further, the mail-order/Web site equipment sources cannot make adjustments to your equipment, cannot give you advice on how to use it, cannot take care of warranty repairs, and cannot be there for you in case of an equipment emergency, especially one that occurs the day before a race.

Running Gear

Shoes

The most important part of running equipment is, of course, the shoes. For bicycling, shoes are the second-most-important piece of equipment. Not that the right shoe will convert an ordinary athlete into a superstar, as some shoe ads would have you believe. However, using the feet is central to the physical action of both duathlon sports and two of the three triathlon sports. Thus, when you make contact with the pavement or pedal, the correct foot container can make the difference between feeling good and avoiding injury, and experiencing just the opposite.

There are several characteristics shared by good shoes for any sport. First, the shoe must fit well. What does "good fit" mean? Simply put, the shoe should touch your foot in as many places as possible except over the toes. For the toes, the toe box should be roomy—forward, laterally, and vertically. In other words, a good

The most recent model that I use of my longtime shoe: New Balance. *Photo courtesy of New Balance Athletic Shoe*

sport shoe should fit your foot the way the right-size glove (with no fingers) fits your hand.

Second, the shoe must be comfortable. Although your foot should fit snugly in the shoe, it should not be pinched, squeezed, or squashed at any point. The shoe should not cause any kind of pain, whether you are standing still or moving. Third, people who overpronate (that is, roll their ankle too far in when they land on each step—there are many of us) should get shoes specifically designed to counteract overpronation. Overpronation is a common cause of injury farther up the leg. A knowledgeable sport-shoe salesperson can tell if you are an overpronator.

For injury prevention, it is important to keep track of shoe wear. It is best to discard a pair of shoes too soon rather than too late—that is, after you've got the shin splints or the sprained knee that can result from using an overworn pair of shoes. How do you know when your shoes are worn out? Most good-quality running shoes have what is called a midsole. It is the material that runs the length of the shoe between the outside tread and the bottom of the foot compartment. Midsole material has to be somewhat compressible, for comfort. The midsoles in most running shoes quickly develop little horizontal lines as they are used.

Take a look at those lines periodically. Too many (and just what "too many" is you have to learn from experience with, perhaps, some help from your friendly running-shoe-store salesperson) means that the insole has become overcompressed. When that happens, the shoe is thrown out of balance. And so is your foot strike. That can easily lead to injury. As a rule of thumb, if you are doing 2 to 3 hours per week of running, assuming that you have a good pair of shoes, after about 3 months of wear you should start looking at those midsoles. If there are lots of lines, or if the shoe appears to be developing a tilt to one side when looked at from the back, it's time to pay a visit to the running-shoe store to have them checked out.

Racing-bike shoes have stiff, inflexible bottoms with a cleat mounted externally, under the ball of the foot. You cannot walk in them easily, but they provide you with the most leverage on the pedal—traditional or clipless (see page 174). The rules for good fit are the same as for running shoes. As far as comfort is concerned, you will not be walking in them much, but when you are on the bike, they should feel comfortable, applying the same criteria that you do for comfort in running shoes.

There is no one best brand for running or cycling shoes. The best shoe for you is simply the one that is best for you. It must fit and be comfortable, and for running provide good cushioning and good stability for the forefoot (the flat part behind the toes) and the rear foot (heel). For running shoes bought at a running-shoe store, you should count on spending at least $60 for a decent pair; for bike shoes, you will spend about the same amount for an entry-level pair. I would not spend much less than that; I customarily spend considerably more. Because I happen to have very flat feet that pronate quite a bit, I need a running shoe with very good pronation control. They are not cheap. However, for comfort and injury prevention they are worth every penny.

Running shoes come in a wide variety of colors, but any one model usually comes in only one color. The uppers on the better shoes are usually made of nylon and suede. Look for at least some mesh material in the upper; it will help keep your feet cool. A molded inner sole is helpful for cushioning and stability. If your foot has a very high or a very low arch; if you overpronate, as I do; or if you frequently get shin splints, knee pain, or minor nagging aches in your feet or legs, you may need custom-made inserts called orthotics. Consult a well-recommended sports podiatrist or orthopedist.

Running-shoe technology is always advancing. New cushioning and stabilizing materials and combinations of materials are being developed all the time. The major shoe companies spend a great deal of money doing research. The best way to keep up with their progress is by keeping up with magazine articles on running shoes (see Appendix II).

Socks and Clothing

The most important part of running equipment after shoes is socks. Invest in several pairs of good-quality running socks. They will help to keep your feet cool and protect against blisters. As far as clothing is concerned, the most important rule is to wear as little as possible for any given temperature. In winter, if you are warm before the start of a run, you have too much clothing on. On summer mornings, if you are slightly chilly in nylon running shorts and singlet before starting out, that is good. You will get warm quickly enough.

For year-round running, you will need the following clothing items: nylon running or compression shorts (the latter look like shorter bike shorts without the seat pad inside), singlets (those tops cut like men's undershirts that racers wear), T-shirts (because most races give you one, you will accumulate these rapidly as you race), athletic supporter/support bra, sweatbands, warm-up suit, insulating long underwear, a woolen hat, and gloves. In winter, if it is too cold to be comfortable after running for a mile or so in anything more than a set of athletic long underwear, shorts, and possibly a fleece under an insulated windbreaker warm-up suit, plus woolen hat and gloves, it is probably too cold to be running. In really cold weather, even if most of your body warms up, you still risk frostbite, penile-tip irritation, nipple burn, and other assorted nuisance ailments. For a little more protection from the cold and a lot more protection from the rain (if you like running in the wet stuff), you can purchase a Gore-Tex or similar fabric suit. Their breathable fabric makes for very nice running gear. However, the suits made from it are considerably more expensive than the conventional nylon ones.

It will not take you long to work out clothing combinations that are right for you in various temperature and weather conditions. I find that having an outdoor thermometer mounted outside my bedroom window is helpful in making the correct clothing selection for a workout. Remember, unless you will be out for more than an hour, you will always be better off if you are a bit underdressed rather than a bit overdressed.

Cycling: The Bike

As noted, the most important piece of equipment is the bike. A great deal has been (and will continue to be) written about selecting the right bike. Articles on this subject appear with regularity in cycling and triathloning magazines. You can also gather infor-

mation from experienced cyclists and pro bike shop staff. I offer you some helpful hints based on my own experience.

The Bike Frame

The frame of the classic dropped-handlebar road-racing bike, with or without aero bars (see page 169), that most people ride in triathlons is made of one of four types of material. In current order of popularity, they are aluminum, carbon fiber, titanium/steel alloy, and the traditional "chromoly"/steel alloy. As bike prices go up, frame weights go down, but not by that much. For the beginner, I do not consider it necessary to spend an extra $500 to $2,000 or more to save a pound or even two pounds of weight on the frame. If you are concerned with weight, at the beginning of your triathlon/duathlon career it is much cheaper and healthier for you to lose that weight from your body than to pay for an expensive bike in order to save a pound in weight. If you become a regular multi-sport athlete and learn enough about riding to appreciate a bike that is lighter and "stiffer" than the entry-level variety usually is, then it does make sense to spend the money. (You will have plenty of choices and will be able to spend plenty of money—up to $10,000—if you choose to do so. Yes, those are four zeros you see there!) "Stiffer" means that more of the thrust that you apply to the pedals is converted into forward motion rather than into twisting the bike's frame. Stiffness can also mean discomfort, of course, but the better bike frames are designed to provide both stiffness and comfort.

If you do happen to be concerned about the weight of the bike at the entry-level price range, the most important place to save it is on the wheels. At the edge of any rolling circle, weight is multiplied by centrifugal force. Thus, small weight excesses at the wheel rims are magnified in terms of an increase in the rolling resistance of the wheel and tire to the road. Because aluminum is considerably lighter than steel, I recommend that the bike you buy—even your first one—have aluminum alloy wheel rims. With correctly tightened spokes, an aluminum rim is just as strong as a steel one. If you want to upgrade your first bike in any significant way, for a relatively small extra expenditure you can buy aluminum alloy rims that are significantly better than the ones that usually come standard on an entry-level model; they are lighter, have fewer spokes, and are actually stronger than a conventional wheel.

Fit

Frames come in different sizes, measured in the length (inches or centimeters) of the seat tube (the one connecting the post on which the seat is mounted to the bottom bracket—the transverse tube through which the short axle runs. This is the axle on which the pedals are mounted). See the bike diagram on page 84. A good first test for a good frame fit is that, when straddling the bike, wearing bike shoes, you have at least an inch (2 inches is even better) of clearance between you and the top tube—the tube that connects the seat tube to the head tube (see just below). Other parameters of bike fit that are important for efficiency, safety, and comfort include seat height and angle, handlebar height, and stem length. The stem is the short L-shaped bracket to which the handlebars are attached. They are connected by the stem through the head tube of the bike to the fork—the two vertical arms to which the front wheel is attached. These variables are best chosen and adjusted for you at the time you buy your bike. Again, the fact that there are all of these bits and pieces, and adjustments to be made, provide a good reason for buying your bike from a top-drawer pro bike store—like mine, Carl Hart Bicycles, in Middle Island, New York. In such stores, the people you are dealing with on the sales floor and in the service department know what they are doing, and are happy to share their skills and knowledge with you.

Configuration: Road and Triathlon Bike Variants

Frames for the traditional road bike come in a variety of configurations. They are generally denominated by the seat and head angles and the length of the wheelbase. (The seat angle is the acute angle made between a line drawn through the seat tube and the ground. The head angle is the acute angle made between a line drawn through the head tube and the ground.) Differences between various configurations are quantitatively small and may

The dropped-handlebar road-racing bike: a Klein 2006 Q Pro XV. *Photo courtesy of Klein Bicycles*

not be apparent to the untrained eye. However, these small quantitative differences make for big qualitative differences. Bikes designed for racing in tightly packed groups (criterium racing) tend to have moderately steep seat and head angles, in the 74- to 75-degree range, and a relatively short wheelbase, less than 39 inches. Touring bikes have slacker angles, in the 71- to 72-degree range, and a longer wheelbase, 40 inches or more. Triathlon-specific bikes have very steep angles, in the 78-degree range, and a shorter wheelbase. The differences in ride and handling characteristics between racing and touring and triathlon bikes are definitely noticeable, even to the neophyte. For example, racing bikes are designed for peloton (pack) riding in criterium races. They respond quickly to steering changes but thus can be somewhat skittish on the open road, which can be a disadvantage in the single-bike, you-against-the-clock (time-trialing), no-drafting-permitted racing of triathlon/duathlon.

As bicycle design developed with the growth of the sport, two types of bike were given the label of triathlon bike (also entirely suitable for the duathlon). The first was similar in many respects to what had originally been called the sport-tourer bicycle, now more often called the road racer. Its dimensions fall between those of the criterium bicycle-racing bike and the classic tourer. Thus, it will give you a reasonably comfortable ride over a fairly long period of time but will also give you a reasonable degree of maneuverability and stiffness.

The second-generation triathlon bike is specifically designed to accept aero bars (see page 169) as standard equipment, as a substitute for or as an add-on to the conventional dropped handlebars. In addition, its seat angle is often even steeper than that of a high-performance road-racing bike, to put the rider in a more forward position so that he/she can comfortably get over those bars. I strongly discourage starting out your triathlon career with one of these bikes, because it takes some time to learn how to use it safely, and the riding position is not the most comfortable in the world. However, if you get into the sport and begin looking for speed, you surely will want one.

Configuration: Mountain Bikes and Combis

Given that there are few design rules for the bike in triathlon, you can use a mountain bike or a combi. When you are starting out, you may want to consider both. (A combi is a cross between a road bike and a mountain bike, also sometimes called a hybrid. It features a mountain-bike type of design, without all of the latter's bells and whistles, and lighter wheels and tires.)

You should equip any mountain bike you use in a triathlon or duathlon with the street tires that come standard on most combis, as contrasted with off-the-road tires that come standard on mountain bikes. On a mountain bike or a combi, you will go more slowly than you would on a dropped-handlebar road bike. This is primarily because in the more upright riding position used on both types, you present more resistance to the wind. The bikes are also heavier than road bikes. However, you will also have a more comfortable seat and generally find the bike easier to control and handle. Higher-end mountain bikes have forward handlebar extensions that allow you to get over the bars some to reduce wind resistance.

Aero Bars

The aero bar (there are several different designs) is a device mounted perpendicular to the regular handlebar that extends forward from it. It allows you to bend over at the waist and move your hands off the conventional handlebars to a position directly in front of them, pointing forward. This effectively narrows your body shape in relation to the air mass that you have to push out of the way as you ride. Aero bars come in a variety of designs. All of them give the rider quite a time advantage—around 3 minutes over a 25-mile bike segment—although you have to be going almost 20 miles per hour before that aerodynamic advantage kicks in. Three minutes does not seem like much time, but at 20 mph, that is a mile.

I do not recommend aero bars for the beginner triathlete. To stay in balance on the bike and keep it under control, the bars

The "tri-bike," this one (a Trek Equinox 11) with integrally mounted aero bars.
Photo courtesy of Trek Bicycle Corporation

take some getting used to. Riding with bars still feels too wobbly for my taste. Then again, I do not go fast enough to gain much of an additional advantage from them, so the motivation to learn is not there. I am sure that with practice I could get used to them if I really wanted to. If you become a fast rider, then you should consider them. The clip-on version can be added to an existing set of handlebars. More sophisticated handlebar/aero bar one-piece combinations come on the higher-end tri-bikes. Most of them can also be bought separately for upgrading your present bike. Again, be sure to consult with a professional at your bike shop.

Tires

There are two types of bicycle tires: clinchers and tubulars (also called sew-ups). Clinchers are like old-fashioned automobile tires. They are U-shaped in cross section, attach snugly inside the wheel rim with a bead, and contain an inner tube. It takes some doing to remove and reinstall clinchers. Nevertheless, once the tire and tube are off the rim, the punctured tube can be replaced quickly, or a patch repair can be made easily. And newer types of tire irons make it easier to remove and reinstall clinchers and their tubes than was the case in the past.

Tubular tires have the two longitudinal edges sewn together to form an endless circular tube (hence the name) that encases an inner tube. Tubulars, which have come down in price compared to the clincher-tube combinations, are relatively easy to get on and off the rim, to which they are attached with a rubber-cement-like glue. Changing a flatted tubular tire is thus easier than changing a flatted clincher. You just take the whole flatted tire-tube assembly off the rim and replace it with a fresh one. However, if the inflatable inner tube of a tubular is punctured, it is quite difficult to get at. Thus, when a tubular is flatted on the road, the whole assembly needs to be replaced, which means carrying one or more spare tire-tube combos. So, over time, tubulars can be an expensive proposition. In addition, if you run out of replacement sets while on the road, you have also run out of options for getting home other than walking or catching a lift.

Nevertheless, in the past, tubulars were popular with higher-end racers. Being lighter and offering less rolling resistance, they performed better than clinchers. However, in recent years clincher tires have gotten better and better in terms of performance and—since the introduction of Kevlar belts and other improvements in tire design—in terms of puncture resistance too. Thus, in my view it is unnecessary for the beginner or the recreational triathlete to use tubular tires.

Crank Sets and Gearing

The crank set is the whole apparatus to which the pedals are attached. I explained front (chain ring) and rear cogs, gearing, and gear ratios in Chapter 4. The standard triathlon bike, whether of the road-racer or triathlon-specific type, generally has two chain rings, usually with 52 and 39 teeth, respectively. Back in 1998, I installed a Shimano triple crank set (three chain rings—found on all mountain bikes) on my top-of-the-line Klein Quantum Race bike to make hill climbing easier. I was one of the first generation of riders to do that. The one significant development in crank sets in recent years is that you can now get a factory-installed triple on road-racer (although not triathlon-specific) bikes even at the higher end. I use the third, small (30-tooth) ring up front only infrequently. But when you have to go up a really steep hill in the middle of a race, it is nice to be able to drop down to a very low gear and just spin up that hill without wearing out your quadriceps.

The number of cogs available on the rear wheel has expanded steadily over the years, from the formerly standard five (combined with two chain rings to make the "10-speed") to up to ten on some of the higher-priced derailleur systems. This feature provides many more available "speeds" (gear ratios)—up to 30! However, you will likely find that most of the time on most terrain you will use a fairly small set of gear ratios. It is not the number of available gear ratios as much as the increased range that makes biking better with derailleur systems having more rear cogs.

Derailleurs and Shifters

Since I wrote the first edition of this book, there have been two major advances in derailleur/shifter design. Virtually all bikes have the first, and all but the truly low-end bikes have the second as well. The first to appear was "indexed" shifting for the rear-wheel cogs. Formerly, when shifting, you had to feel your way with the shift lever when—through the derailleur—moving the chain from one rear cog to the next, easing it over gently lest you go too far and jump two or three steps at a time. Now as you shift you experience a positive "click" when moving the chain up or down from one rear cog to the next, just as you did with the 3- and 4-speed Sturmey-Archer hub shift systems found on the old English Raleighs and Rudges (of my childhood). Some front derailleur systems also have a version of indexed shifting. More recent has been the integration of the shift levers with the brake handles. The Japanese bicycle components manufacturer Shimano, first on the block with this kind of device, calls theirs the "Shimano Total Integration" (STI) system. The world's other major shifter-brake-derailleur manufacturer, the legendary Italian company Campagnolo, makes a similar system, as do several other smaller manufacturers. This is a marvelous advance, for in order to shift you never have to move your hands off the handlebars to the down tube where the shifters were previously located. In addition, when coming to a stop, you can brake and downshift at the same time, if necessary.

Brakes

There are two types of bicycle brakes, which have changed little over the years. "Sidepull" brakes are generally found on all the varieties of road bikes; "center-pull" or "cantilever linear pull" brakes are generally found on combis and mountain bikes. Virtually any bike in the price range we are talking about will have decent brakes, whatever the design. By the way, if you happen to buy a bike with auxiliary brake handles (they are a second pair, mounted under the handlebars, found only on lower-end bikes), I recommend you get rid of them at once. They do not provide the same stopping power as the regular brake handles. They can also be distracting and thus dangerous. Just learn how to ride using the regular brake handles from the beginning. (An exception to this is the high-tech auxiliary handlebar braking system found on high-end cyclo-cross bikes. If you get into the off-road "Xterra" class of multi-sport racing, not considered in this book because I have never done one, you will want to give this kind of bike a look.)

Saddles

Like running shoes, the best saddle (seat) is the one that fits you best and provides the most comfort. No saddle will keep your bottom from getting sore forever, but some do a better job of it than others. Do not be fooled by appearance. Some uncomfortable-looking saddles can be quite comfortable. So try out several, especially if you do not like the one that comes with the bike you have selected. Saddles can be changed easily. In addition, putting a good lightweight pad/cover on a saddle that is initially uncomfortable can help the fit and feel (for years I have used one made by Quintana Roo). As of 2005, the evidence purporting to show that bike riding causes impotence in men was still under question in terms of its biostatistical/epidemiological standards of validity. Nevertheless, if you find that one of the newer saddles designed with the existence of your genitalia—male or female—in mind is more comfortable for you, by all means get it.

Conclusion

Just as with running shoes, the bike that fits you best is the best bike for you. If you are buying a new bike for your great triathlon/duathlon adventure, there is a certain minimum amount of money you should spend to ensure that the bike you buy will be of decent quality and will last you for more than one season of racing. Even more than with running shoes, it pays to spend some time talking with knowledgeable friends and reading cycling books and magazines on equipment. However, if you buy your first tri-/du bike from a reputable pro shop like Carl Hart Bicycles—a bike that at a minimum has an aluminum frame and aluminum-alloy rims for the wheels and is the proper size for you, with a price in the $500 to $600 range—you will be getting a machine very suitable for entry into the marvelous world of multi-sport. Further, if you cannot afford that amount right now, then get something comfortable that you can have fun riding.

After all, at the outset all you really need to be able to do is get around the course safely and enjoyably, without worrying about speed. If you do get into the sport, you will have plenty of time to get a better bike.

Cycling: Clothing, Shoes, and Accessories

Clothing

Your basic bike wardrobe will be simple. Cycling shorts have long legs to prevent thigh chafe, and are usually elasticized for a close fit. To provide some additional cushioning, there is a seat pad in the crotch, made of chamois leather or, much more commonly, a synthetic material. Bike shirts are generally made of form-fitting Lycra or one of a variety of looser synthetic "breathable" materials. They usually have two or three pockets on the back at the waist that can be used for carrying a variety of paraphernalia. For additional comfort, using a pair of padded bike gloves is also a good idea. For cold-weather riding, many types of wind-shielding/heat-conserving outfits are available. For some comments on race clothing, see Chapter 9.

Pedals and Shoes

The traditional pedal design, found on bikes at the lower end of the triathlon entry-level bike range, consists of a flat pedal with a toe clip attached to its leading edge. The toe clip is an open cage with an adjustable strap at its after rim into which you can slip a traditional bike shoe (with a horizontal cleat on the bottom that grips the rear crossbar of the pedal) or a running shoe. The trailing edge of the toe-clip loop is then tightened down on the shoe with the strap. This whole arrangement provides for a firm connection between shoe and pedal. However, with a traditionally cleated bike shoe, the apparatus is cumbersome to adjust each time you stick your shoe into it and can be dicey to release when you need to do so in a hurry. So using a traditionally cleated bike shoe/pedal combination has become increasingly uncommon. However, a running shoe is usually safe and fairly easy to use with a toe clip, even when you tighten the strap.

The running-shoe-in-the-pedal-with-a-toe-clip system is a

common choice for beginning multi-sport racers. Many a duathlete will continue to use it even as they become more experienced. They thus avoid changing from the running shoe to the bike shoe and back to the running shoe, in transition a time-consuming process. In duathlons, not worrying about time, I still like to do the double switch so that when I am riding the bike, the shoe is firmly attached to the pedal (see the next paragraph). A third alternative, found on less expensive bikes, especially of the mountain or combi variety, is the plain flat pedal, on which you simply place your foot and push. You cannot pull up with the off pedal as you can with any cleat system, and your feet can flop around on the pedals, but you do just step onto them.

In place of the toe-clip/strap pedal system, over the past 20 years the "clipless" pedal system has become popular. It consists of a special bracket with its own spindle that is screwed into the crank (the arm attached to the front chain ring that turns it and through it moves the chain) in place of the standard pedal. A special cleat mounted on the bottom of the bike shoe connects it to the pedal. To attach the cleat to the clipless pedal, you just "click in" to the pedal, usually by pressing down and forward at the same time. To release, you simply twist your foot sideways. For most of us, it does take a bit of practice to learn how to use such a system. However, once you do, you will find it convenient, safe, and fast. It is a system designed to permit you to pull up firmly with one leg at the same time you are pushing down with the other.

There are several different cleat-pedal-bracket designs for use with the classic bike-racing shoe. There is also one setup designed for mountain bikes that can be used on road bikes as well. All the popular ones will be on display at your pro bike shop, and the salesperson will be able to fill you in on the advantages and disadvantages of each one. Although lower-end bikes come with toe-clip (or no-clip, just flat) pedals, the better bikes come without pedals. You can thus choose (at an additional cost, of course) just which clipless system you prefer. I highly recommend using the clipless pedal system. You can examine all of the common varieties of it at any good pro shop.

Riding in Running Shoes

Because there is no way to attach them, running shoes cannot be used with clipless pedals. As mentioned, I am still more comfortable using bike shoes on the bike segment of a race and do not mind spending the time it takes in transition to change shoes, even making the change twice in duathlons. If the terrain warrants it, however, I do on occasion use the running-shoe-in-the-pedal-with-the-toe-clip system. Another alternative that enables cycling while wearing running shoes is the platform system. This device has a cleat on the bottom of a shoe-shaped flat platform that attaches to a clipless pedal. On top of the platform there is a toe-strap loop and cage, as on a conventional pedal, but the platform extends under the full length of the running shoe, providing more support than does the conventional pedal. Although I have found the platform system cumbersome to get in and out of and do not use it, you might find a platform system attractive, so take a look at it also.

Helmets

All multi-sport races, USA-Triathlon sanctioned or not, for liability and safety reasons require that you wear a helmet, with the chin strap securely fastened. The helmet must be of a hard-shell design and have an adjustable rear-retention system. It must be made by one of the leading manufacturers. In this context, the term "leading manufacturer" is functionally defined by whether you find the helmet for sale either in a bike shop or through a Web/mail-order company. Because of liability issues, there are no substandard helmets available for sale from any reputable commercial source.

A couple of words of caution in buying, maintaining, and using your helmet(s). Microfractures can occur in the foam protective material or even the hard shell of the best helmet if it hits the ground with your head in it. Thus never buy a used helmet (for you cannot be certain of its history), and always replace a helmet that has hit the ground with your head in it even once. Further, the industry now advises that helmets be replaced every three years, for the protective material can dry out and become less resilient. I firmly believe that because serious head injuries occur close to 10 times more frequently in bike riders without helmets than in riders with helmets, you should *never* get on your bike without putting on your helmet first. Helmet design has improved considerably over the years, providing increased safety and increased comfort. When buying a helmet, as with running shoes and bicycles, first and foremost get one that fits you and, with the straps properly adjusted, is secure on your head. Your bike shop personnel should be qualified to help in this regard.

Accessories

Carrying at least one water bottle is a must for both training and racing. Virtually any bike in the price range I am talking about will have brackets on the frame for two water bottles to keep them firmly in place when you are under way while at the same time allowing for easy removal and replacement. Water bottles are made of flexible plastic, with a nipple you can pull open with your teeth that allows you to drink easily while riding and then close the bottle easily as well.

Water bottles come in two sizes, the old standard size and a new larger size that, although fitting into a standard bracket, holds about 50 percent more fluid. Unless you are really concerned about a few ounces of frame weight (and you should not be as a beginner/recreational triathlete), consider getting the larger-size bottle. As discussed elsewhere, maintaining your hydration is a must for happy cycling. For your shorter training rides, one bottle will often suffice. In the races, unless the bike segment is short, I always carry two of the larger-size bottles. Better too much water on board than too little. If you start going for longer and/or more intense rides, or want the utmost in convenience in taking on fluids while you are under way, you could look into a hydration pack system. They all have some variation of a water-filled bladder, in a backpack, with a strawlike tube that is positioned next to your mouth for the utmost ease of access.

You should always carry a frame-mounted air pump in case you get a flat and have to change tubes. Several designs are available. For quick pumping up there are miniature CO_2 cylinders with special valve adaptors. Check all of them out at your pro shop. You will want to have some kind of under-the-seat fitted bag in which to carry at least one spare tube (in the longer races I carry two), a patch kit, the CO_2 cylinder(s), and a small tool kit.

A Few Final Thoughts on Bike Equipment

Shock-absorbing handlebar padding is a nice, inexpensive extra. The modern Shimano or Campagnolo combined shifter-brake handles almost invariably come with their own padding. I use a rearview mirror (two, actually) even on my relatively high-priced bikes. It is a genuine safety item, useful to see motor vehicles coming up behind you on the road when training, and to see who is overtaking you (important for me in multiple-loop courses) when racing.

I highly recommend that you buy an electronic speedometer/computer. Most models give your speed, elapsed time, total distance covered, and average speed on a given ride or race segment, and a few other bits of information. An important one for me provided by some bike computers is "cadence"—that is, how many times per minute you are turning the pedals through the full circle. Maintaining your cadence in a fairly narrow range at a reasonably high rate is helpful in keeping a comfortable and energy-efficient pace. I try to stay in the 80 to 95 rpm range, and I use the monitor built into my bike computer to do so. Although most computers are hooked up to their sensors by wires, you can now get wireless versions that declutter your bike's frame. However, avoid getting a computer that has many more features than you would ever use. Speaking from experience, I can tell you that such a computer can be a bear to reset if you accidentally press the wrong button. Some of those instruction manuals are not the easiest pieces of text to decipher.

Swim Equipment

Suits

Except for the wet suit (see below), swim equipment is by far the simplest and cheapest of the three types to acquire and maintain. For pool swimming, a regular bathing suit is just fine. I use a men's tank suit, not a bikini. For racing, briefs for men and a one- or two-piece racing (not sunning) suit for women is all you absolutely need. In most cases, you will wear the suit throughout the race. If you use a wet suit, you do not necessarily need to wear a swimsuit under it. Other than when wearing a "tri-suit" (also called a "skin-suit," see page 182), I wear lightweight bike liner shorts, which I keep on throughout the race. After the swim, I put on lightweight bike shorts over them and wear them for the run as well. The modern suits and liner shorts dry quickly and provide good support for both sexes. Although the faster racers use just their suits for the whole race, for comfort on the bike and run legs I recommend putting on the appropriate specialized clothing over your swimsuit.

Goggles and Nose Clips

Goggles are a necessity for swimming. You must be able to see clearly at all times, for safety in relation to other swimmers and to make sure that you are on course. Inexpensive swim goggles ($5 to $10) work reasonably well in keeping water out of your eyes but can become painful after 20 to 30 minutes. An investment of $25 in a pair of padded goggles is well worth it. If you prefer not to have your nose open in the water, you will also need to wear a nose clip. If you are in the latter category and are a slow swimmer like me, so that slightly increased drag would not be an issue, try out a pair of light dive or snorkeling goggles. They cover nose and eyes and are much more comfortable on the face than any kind of racing goggles. I have used dive goggles in my racing and training for years.

Wet Suits

The major advance—and major new expense—in triathlon equipment that has appeared since I wrote the first edition of this book is the wet suit designed specifically for swimming on the surface of the water, not for diving. Triathlon-specific wet suits were first used to provide protection against the chill of cold-water swims. However, it was quickly learned that their most important advantage for the triathlete was to provide flotation and reduce friction, thus increasing speed and making the swim less demanding. The material from which triathlon wet suits are now made is thinner and slicker than that found in the standard dive suit but still pro-

2005 International Triathlon Union World Cup Champion and top U.S. male finisher at the Athens (2004) Olympics, Hunter Kemper, in his Aquaman full suit. *Photo courtesy of Hunter Kemper and Emmanuel Millet*

vides warmth and increases speed. As with bike and running-shoe technology, wet suit technology is advancing quickly.

There are three popular designs. The "full suit" covers your arms and legs as well as your torso. The "long john" is like the full suit but without sleeves; the "short john" covers only the torso and upper thighs. Prices range from approximately $150 for an entry-level mail-/Web-order short john to more than $400 for a top-of-the-line full suit. (I do not recommend buying a wet suit that you are not able to try on, so if you are buying through mail- or Web-order, make sure the suit is returnable.) You will obviously have to decide for yourself if you want/can afford to make the investment, then decide which design will best meet your needs.

If you are buying your suit in a store, make sure to try it on. It is obviously critical to get the best fit possible—as close to your skin as you can get. You will want it to fit snugly when dry (although not so snugly as to be constricting, especially to your breathing), because it will loosen up a bit when it gets wet. You can find triathlon wet suits in pro bike shops and running-shoe stores that cater to triathletes, and in certain dive shops. Some dive shops carry entry-level triathlon-specific full suits costing in the low $200 range. If you do buy a wet suit in a dive shop, make sure that you are getting a triathlon suit, not a dive suit. Renting is an alternative when you are starting out. Your area may have a bike shop or dive shop that rents triathlon wet suits.

Caps

The race organizers will provide you with a colored swim cap.

On Clothing

For training, the important factors are comfort and proper protection/adaptation for the temperature. For the bike, you need at a minimum a pair of shoes (and socks), a pair of liner shorts with or without seat padding, a pair of bike shorts with padding, and a shirt. I wear padded liner shorts under my padded bike shorts, and bike gloves. (As you know by now, I am into comfort!) As for the shirt, one of those bike jerseys with the pockets in the back is nice, but you can wear just a T-shirt. Again, if you are biking in cool weather, you will need to wear one or more layers of protective clothing—liner(s)/fleece(s) underneath, windbreaker on the outside—an earflap under your helmet, and warm gloves. For run training, again the most important item is the shoes. For running in warm weather, you will need shorts (of the boxer or the "compression" variety), liner shorts, and a top. For running in cooler weather, the drill is the same as for biking in cooler weather.

In the races, the clothing situation has altered in a major way since I entered the sport (see the next chapter). In the early days, some racers changed clothing completely between segments.

However, complete disrobing out in the open has been prohibited in triathlons since the mid-1980s, and I have not seen a changing tent since that time either. Unless you are wearing a tri-suit (see below), you will be wearing your bathing suit throughout the race (men may choose to wear lightweight bike shorts for the swim as well). For those who like a bit more comfort (guess who?), for the bike segment you can put on a pair of cycling shorts and a bike shirt or T-shirt over your suit. For the run, you can stay in your bike shorts (doffing the bike shirt), or you can switch to running shorts. You can also add a singlet or T-shirt for the run if you wish.

For speed through transition, the faster triathletes will skip wearing socks in their bike or run shoes, and will eschew gloves on the bike too. (After all, socks and gloves do take a few seconds to put on and get off.) As for me, you have guessed it again—I'm still into comfort. I put on a pair of bike shoe anklets that will also be comfortable in my running shoes. I also use bike gloves, putting them on for the bike and taking them off for the run. In transition, I now usually take a total of 8 to 10 minutes for both. Slow? Yes, very. Comfortable? Yes, very.

Tri-suits are now popular for triathlon and duathlon. They come in one- and matching two-piece versions. The top part has a zipper in the front for ease of getting it on and enabling you to cool off a bit during a hot race, and has one or more bike-shirt-like pockets on the back. The bottom part is a lightweight bike short with lightweight seat padding. A tri-suit is designed to be worn throughout the race, with the wet suit worn over it during the swim. If you do not wear a wet suit, or if in a particular race in warm water wet suits are prohibited, the whole tri-suit is designed to be worn in the swim as well. I use the one- and two-piece varieties of tri-suit, but usually put a regular bike shirt over the top for that segment, unless it is a very hot day.

Sunglasses

I strongly recommend them, for protection against glare and UV rays and on the bike for protection against flying objects. Anything from an inexpensive variety-store pair to a fancy curved bike-eyewear set will do for starters. I happen to wear bifocal glasses. I now have prescription sunglasses, made by tinting an old pair of glasses left over when I periodically change prescription as my visual acuity changes with aging. The correction provided by a prescription that is just slightly off is okay for training and racing, and then you do not have to bother with flip-ups. Of course, contacts have become evermore common; if you use them, you can simply wear sunglasses of one type or another over them. Another alternative that I also use is a pair of bike eyewear by Bolle, for which prescription inserts are available.

Conclusion

Good equipment helps to make training and racing fun. The budget/list of equipment given on page 159 is long and can get to be expensive if you buy everything brand new that you will need for racing. However, the only essentials other than a swimsuit and clothing to protect your modesty (and ensure that you are in compliance with USA-T rules) are a pair of running shoes that fit well, an effective, comfortable pair of swim goggles, a bike that works, a hard-shell helmet that meets current safety standards, and a pair of sunglasses. Many people can find much of what they need to get started in the dresser, the closet, and the garage or storage room, or at a friend's or family member's house. The most important thing to do when starting out is to assemble a set of equipment with which you are comfortable. Once you get into the sport, if you are so inclined and can afford it, you can obviously shop 'til you drop for new equipment and clothing. But the most important thing is the stuff of racing, not the stuff you race with.

THE RACE

*I advised him to set realistic goals, focus on enjoyment and
the health of the sport, and not focus at any time on
having to perform heroically.* —Dr. Don Ardell, known nationally
*as the "Dean of Wellness," and perennial world and national
age-group champion in triathlon and duathlon, speaking
to a newcomer to the sport*

You have completed your training. You have become aerobically fit. You have learned or relearned how to swim, bike, and run—for the duathlon, the latter two. You have acquired the equipment that you will need for "tryin' the tri" or "doin' the du." You have made sure that your overall health is fine, taken steps to prevent injury, and taken care if you have become injured. You have chosen a suitable race, entered it, and received your entry confirmation and race instructions (see Chapter 3). You have made any necessary travel plans and accommodation arrangements. You are ready to achieve the goal that you have been pointing toward for all of these weeks and months: completion of your first multi-sport race.

Competing in your first triathlon or duathlon will be a unique experience. It cannot be duplicated. There can never be another first time for you in multi-sport racing. Make sure that you remember the day (that will not be hard to do), because you will never experience another one like it for the rest of your life. As of the end of the 2005 season, I had done more than 100 triathlons and over 60 duathlons of various lengths. As you know, I did my first triathlon back in 1983. I have to say that I do not recall many details of many of my races, especially if I did a particular race more than once. It happens that I have done the Mighty Hamptons twelve times. I remember little of most of them. However, I surely do remember that very first one, at a level of detail I find remarkable (see pages 188–97).

If you are like most of the rest of us in the sport, you will likely be nervous before your first race. You will wonder if you really will be able to do it. Will you make it through the swim? Will you be able to ride your bike up all the hills? Will you be able to finish the run without walking, or indeed will you be able to simply finish it? Will the pain level be tolerable? Has all the time and energy that you put into training really been enough and really been worth it? Is this guy Jonas right?

If you have done the training program—not necessarily to the minute but necessarily following its basic principles (see Chapter 5)—the answer to all these questions is yes, you will finish; yes, you will do so happily and healthily. Following the principles and going through the training program will enable you to achieve your goal and ensure that you will be in for one of the great experiences of your life: the exhilaration, the high, and the feelings of self-worth, self-esteem, and accomplishment that come with the achievement of that goal. Believe me, the feelings are magnificent, worth every hour of your training.

Making It Through: Some Specifics

For triathlon, your first question is likely to be, will I make it through the swim? Yes, you will, for several reasons. In triathlon, as you know by now, the swim always comes first, for good reason. As I said before, of the three sports, it is potentially the most dangerous one. Because it is first, you and all the other triathletes will be at your freshest. Furthermore, having the swim first invariably spreads out the field, even more so if there is a wave start (see below), which is common in the larger races. (This is important when you get to the bike segment, for the course is usually on a fairly narrow road where crowding is not desirable.) If you are doing an Olympic-distance triathlon, you have been training to exercise aerobically for up to 5 hours straight the first time out. You will certainly have plenty of energy in storage to enable you to finish the swim.

As far as safety in the swim is concerned, the race organizers are just as interested in it as you are. You will be required to wear a brightly colored swim cap. You can expect the course to be well marked and well monitored. There will be people on a variety of small watercraft watching you all along the course. In many races, you will be permitted to rest in the water while holding onto a monitoring watercraft, as long as you do not try to move forward. If you have any fear at all, just make sure that you do not try to go too fast. If you do run out of breath, just turn over on your back for a blow.

As for the bike segment, the same thoughts apply for the tri and the du. Will you have to walk your bike up the hills? You most likely have become used to your bike (although I have met people at a race who are on only their second or third ride on their new bike—not recommended). I will assume, then, that you know how to shift and brake your bike, are able to maintain a proper cadence by selecting the correct gears, and feel comfortable and in control on the saddle. With the training you have had, you will do just fine on any hills on all but the toughest triathlon and duathlon courses. Remember, the key to successful long-distance cycling is riding in a gear that is low enough to permit you to pedal at 80 rpm or more regardless of incline. This will prevent knee strain and early energy exhaustion. Do it, and you will be okay.

Will you have to walk in the triathlon run leg? (In the duathlon, you will likely have a fine first run, when you are fresh. But your experience on the second run will likely be similar to that of triathletes on their run leg.) Of course, you may have chosen to fast-walk the run leg, and that is fine. Otherwise, unless you are fast and a potential top age-group finisher, or are going for a PR (personal record) that day, for beginners I recommend a different approach. I suggest a 2- to 6-minute planned, vigorous, purposeful walk at the beginning of the run leg in triathlon (the beginning of the second run leg in duathlon) in order to aid the bike-run transition. Otherwise, transitioning to the run can be wobbly, awkward, and disconcerting as you try to work out kinks in your legs that you have not encountered before (except possibly in your "brick" [bike-run] workouts in the TFOMTP). A second planned 2-minute walk at around the 12-minute mark can also be helpful in completing the transition and really getting your legs stretched out. Other than that, only if you have not paced yourself and have gone out too fast will you end up walking later in the run because you cannot run anymore and must walk. If, based on your training paces, you have accurately estimated the race paces of which you are capable and have stuck to them, you will be just fine. If you have a lot of energy left with a mile or two to go, you can pick up the pace then, pass some faltering folks in front of you, finish strong, and feel like even more of a hero than if you finish in a comfortable trot—at which time you will still feel like a hero!

How much will it hurt? It will hurt. You cannot do long-distance aerobic events and expect not to hurt unless you are a very unusual person. However, it should hurt no more than training did, even though you are going farther. It is conceivable that with your adrenaline level up, as it will be during the race, you will hurt less than you did in training—as long as you didn't try to overdo it and go too fast. In any case, if you do experience pain, the memory of it will fade quickly after you finish. You will remember the race, but not the hurting. I hurt at some point during most of my races. However, within a day or two, although I remember the course, the race anecdotes, the old friends I saw, the weather, the finish, and how I felt overall out there, in the golden glow of accomplishment I have forgotten the specifics of any pain that I might have suffered.

You must continue to keep your objectives in mind: to finish, to have fun, and to feel good. As I mentioned in Chapter 1, at a meeting of the Big Apple Triathlon Club in New York City on June 6, 1984, Dave Horning, then-elite triathlete and then and now race organizer, was talking about the 1984 Liberty to Liberty Triathlon. (This one required a 2-mile swim through New York Harbor to the Statue of Liberty, a 90-mile bike ride to the outskirts of Philadelphia, and a 10k run to Independence Hall. A slightly shorter, slightly easier version of the race was still being run as of 2005.) He said that his principal goal for the race was for everyone to have fun doing it. He encouraged the Ordinary Mortals in the audience who would be doing the race to treat the bike ride more like a tour or a rally than a road race. He welcomed the use of support crews. "Stop and have a picnic; enjoy yourselves," he suggested. He pointed out that although triathlons, at least the name races, are won by the elite athletes, the sport would not, and indeed could not, exist without the participation of the thousands of us Ordinary Mortals who contribute our sweat—and our entry fees—to it. He was correct then, and even though ours is now an Olympic sport, he still is.

Doing the 1983 Mighty Hamptons Triathlon

Because my name was not Dave or Mark or Scott (first or last), and my first triathlon was the 1983 Mighty Hamptons (MHT), I obviously had no chance to finish at or near the head of the men's division. The men's competition in the 1980s was dominated by just four triathletes: Dave Scott, Scott Tinley, Scott Molina, and Mark Allen. I think that two out of the three Scotts were in that race, although I am not sure which ones. I was 456th out of 489 finishers overall. I was 2 hours and 10 minutes behind the winner. However, I was 1 hour and 10 minutes ahead of the last person to finish, and he was younger than I was. Most importantly, I had a race and I had a wonderful time, with a finishing time that for me was fast. Most important to me, by the next day when I had physically recovered, I experienced feelings about myself and my abilities that I had never felt before. They were worth the whole nine yards.

Most articles that you read in the triathlon publications about races concern the winners and near winners. Most people like you and me will never win. Unless you happen to be in a small age-group cohort—as I am—you will most likely never even place in your age-group either. But we race too. Our view is just different from that of the fast folks. It is the view from the middle to the back of the pack. So, let me take you through my first race with me. I wrote the words in the next section more than twenty years ago. But believe me, I still remember many of the details of that first race as if I had done it just a couple of months ago, even though many details of other races are now gone from my memory.

The Night before the Race

I am registered and checked in. My bike is numbered. I am numbered. I have all the race paraphernalia loaded into the three plastic bags that each entrant was given, one bag each for swim, bike, and run gear. I have double-checked and triple-checked the bags and all my stuff to make sure that forgetful me (even back then) has not forgotten anything this time. By golly, it is all there—the several varieties of shoes, socks, shorts, shirts, headgear, glasses, gloves, undergarments, and watches that one needs (well, *I* seem to need) for triathloning. The race numbers are pinned on in the appropriate places. I really am an ATHLETE.

I eat well, very well, at the carbo-loading dinner. I feel so good that I break all the rules and have a big, rich, gooey hot-fudge sundae bought from a purveyor of homemade goodies on Main Street in Sag Harbor, New York, where the race is held. The sundae is wonderful. I worry a little bit about insulin overshoot and reactive hypoglycemia (although on race day I would suffer no ill effects). I go to my room and fall comfortably asleep.

The Morning of the Race

I arise early, intentionally. I am staying in a guesthouse with a shared bathroom. I am known to be slow in the morning, and I do not want to hold up anyone else. Feeling virtuous and considerate, I am out of the bathroom before anyone else awakens. I do not feel tired. My adrenaline level must already be up, because I have had less than seven hours of sleep. I eat my breakfast: pita bread, an apple, a banana, and Gatorade. (I eat a much simpler pre-race meal now: an energy bar and about a quart of orange juice.) I check out my equipment once more, hop in the car, and drive over to the race site. My bike is already there, having been left in its numbered stall in the transition area the night before under the watchful eye of the race organizers. As previously noted, the transition area is the place where we change from swim to bike and bike to run, the place where all competitors' bikes are racked, with enough room beside each for laying out equipment. For some races, such as the MHT of that time, you check in the day before and leave your bike overnight. However, for most races, even those that require day-before-the-race check-in, you bring your bike with you when you go to the race site in the morning.

I arrive early and get a good parking spot near the transition area. I bring my bike back to the car from where it had been parked for the night and top off the air in the tires with a little 12-volt air pump I have brought along (soon thereafter replaced in my kit by a full-size floor hand pump with a pressure gauge that *real* triathletes use). My tires are only $1\frac{1}{8}$-inch clinchers, not 1-inch sew-ups. But at least I have a 10-speed bike (a reasonable number of gears for the time). One of my fellow age-group members, Bill Crosby (whom I would meet a few years later at another Mighty Hamptons event, then see again at my twelfth Mighty Hamptons in 2005), is going to race on an almost-antique ladies' Raleigh with a 3-speed Sturmey-Archer gear shifter, a full steel chain case, and a wicker basket on the handlebars. Marvelous.

I put my bike back in its place, lay out and do a final check of my gear, and at the appropriate time start walking at a leisurely pace toward the start of the swim. The swim course is a point-to-point from a distant spot up the beach back to the transition area, so we have to walk a mile and a half to get to the start. (In most races these days, the swim is an out-and-back or a loop back to the start point.) I could have gone to the start on the bus, which was provided. But I thought that the walk would be a good way to stretch out and warm up. I was right. I recommend it. (If you are in a race such as this one, the race organizers will probably provide you with a numbered plastic bag to take to the swim start to hold your footgear and clothing used for the walk. The race organizers collect the bags and bring them back to the transition area.) As I reach the swim start, I am starting to relax.

The Swim Start

I am really going to do this, I keep telling myself. I go down to test the water, thankful for the pleasant temperature. (As I recall, no one wore a wet suit back then. I do not believe that the triathlon-specific wet suit had even been thought of, much less developed.

Now I would not do a race without one [see Chapter 8], unless wearing one is prohibited by the rules for a particular race.*) I stand toward the back of the assembled throng. I think about the swim. Based on my (minimal) swim training, I estimate that my pace will be about 50 minutes per mile. (I actually do 44 minutes. Race psychology is a powerful force.) I take off my shirt and deck shoes, place them in the numbered bag, and put on my goggles, earplugs, and swim cap. I am ready.

The Swim

The gun goes off. (It can be a horn or a whistle also.) For this race, there is a single mass start. The wave start, now common (see page 202), is still a thing of the future. The water is suddenly white with splashing and churning swimmers. I take seriously the admonition (now *my* admonition) to let the bulk of the traffic get out in front of me to avoid risking a kick in the face. I walk slowly to the water's edge and wade in. I look around for an open space, adjust my goggles, and dive in. I am racing.

The swimmer's world is a strangely isolated one. It is not quiet, but the only noise you hear is that of your own breathing and swimming motion. Goggles tend to fog quickly (the following winter I began using an antifog solution, a great help), so your world is really only you and the water. The beach is on the left and the course is laid out in a line along it. There are big red buoys marking the course. I swim from one to the next (that's still the most comfortable way to do the swim: going from one buoy to the next, not thinking about the finish until you have passed the last buoy on your way in to the beach). I am swimming for distance for only the eighth time in my life, over a $1\frac{1}{2}$-mile course.

I have convinced myself that I will make it if I just take it easy. And I do. I swim using a leisurely crawl stroke. When I need a blow, I just turn over and do a comfortable elementary back-

---

* For USA-Triathlon-sanctioned races, the rules state that wet suits may be worn without penalty for temperatures up to 78°F. With water temperatures between 78°F and 84°F, wet suits may be worn, but wearers are not prize-eligible. For temperatures above 84°F, wet suits are prohibited. That is for safety. You can get overheated when swimming in warm water. It has happened to me.

stroke. In the crawl, I happen to breathe on my right side. Some small waves are coming in from that side. Being a sailor and knowing something about wave action, I time my stroke so that I will breathe at the top of each wave. Fortunately, the wave pattern fits my swimming pattern. As I breathe to my right, I keep looking for other swimmers, and see none. Well, I think, I figured that I would be at the back and indeed I am. Finally, I look over to my left. It turns out that a fairly substantial number of swimmers are back there, some of them way back there. Because the lead swimmers seemed to be halfway to the finish line when I entered the water a minute or so after them, this turn of events gives my ego a big boost. I pick up the pace a bit.

The end of the swim is now in sight. I will make it. A swimmer is coming up on my right shoulder. I am not going to let her by, I decide. All of a sudden I am racing, not just finishing. I swim as fast as I can toward the finish line. She does not pass me. I make it. I did not drown. Indeed, in the swim I have my best relative time of the three events, finishing ahead of nearly a hundred people. I trot up the ramp toward the changing area. I am told to take it easy. I am handed a cup of Gatorade and am spritzed down with fresh water courtesy of the local volunteer fire department. Then I head for the transition area to change my clothes for the bike segment.

The First Change

The changes, taken together, turn out to be my slowest events, relatively speaking. They were then and they still are. In fact, in certain triathlon circles, Steve Jonas's ridiculously slow transition times are legendary. I am certain that no one took more time than I did: 23 minutes in toto. These days, top tri- and duathletes customarily spend a total of 90 to 150 *seconds* in transition. Ah well, what can I say? I like being comfy.

In that first transition in that first race, there is the matter of my earplugs. I am using a pair of flat-topped ones and cannot manage to extract the right one with my wet, water-ridged fingers. But standing near my bike is Dave Horning (of the Liberty to Liberty Triathlon), not racing that day in the Mighty Hamptons due to an injury. At the pre-race conference the night before,

Dave had seemed like a friendly fellow, so I try my luck. Can he help me with my earplug? He comes right over, with a big smile, and seconds later has deposited the offending rubber object in my hand. What a wonderful sport this is. In what other sport does the Ordinary Mortal play on the same field with the best (and in the longer races still does)? Not only that, in what other sport is the Ordinary Mortal able to enlist the personal assistance of a top athlete in solving an equipment problem? A memorable moment. (By the way, by my second season I was using those little pine-cone shaped earplugs with grippers, and I still do. They work better in keeping water out and are easy to remove from the ear.)

My pre-race plan included a complete change of outfit for each event. Feeling good about my swim performance, I stroll over to the changing tent. (When in the mid-1980s a national rule prohibiting disrobing in transition areas [done by the occasional immodest soul out in the open] took effect, the changing tents disappeared.) I note in passing that the changing tent is not busy, but that fact does not really register with me. I take off my boxer swim trunks (the equivalent in swimming, I find out later, of using a 3-speed bike) and put on a complete, fresh bike outfit. (I find out later that I am one of very few people to do this. I not only wear socks, which not everybody does, but I change my socks twice, using anklets for the bike and my then-customary over-the-calf support socks for the run.) At any rate, after a leisurely change, which affords me a nice rest and the opportunity to eat a banana, I walk over to my bike, buckle on my helmet, and set out on the bike leg.

The Bike

I am feeling good. It is not yet too hot, so the self-generated breeze of a brisk ride is enough to keep me cool. The first half of the course is hilly, but because I train on hills I am not too uncomfortable on them. By the time I get out on the course, the field is fairly well strung out. I pass an occasional cyclist. In turn, I am passed as well. On the whole, this segment is uneventful for me— until mile 22 or so of the 25-mile circuit. I am pedaling at a decent pace across a flat stretch of farmland heading toward what will be a fairly steep descent to the end of the bike leg. A petite woman wearing a smart red and black one-piece tri-suit overtakes me. As she passes me, she sings out gaily, "I like your form."

"What form or which form?" I think to myself. I have not been biking for very long and have had no coaching. She couldn't be referring to my cycling form, could she? Could it be my body? Back then, being more of an A shape than a V shape, I doubt that. I accelerate a bit and draw even with her. I see that the person who hailed me is a smiling little woman with muscular legs and sparkling eyes who looks to be in her mid-fifties. Perhaps she was referring to my biking form after all, or perhaps she likes younger men. At any rate, I begin talking with her.

We pedal along and engage in some pleasant chitchat about cycling. She has a very good bike (I do not), and she tells me that she has been cycling seriously for two to three years. I think, "I have been cycling seriously for a bit more than two to three months." The conversation lapses. Suddenly, she pulls ahead of me. I have been suckered, I think. I accelerate as fast as I can and go charging past her, calling out, "You are in a race, madam!" About half a minute later, a small red and black blur goes screaming by me just as we begin the descent to the bike-leg finish line. I pedal hard, but I do not see her again until the run.

The Second Change

Following the advice of the triathlon guidebooks I had read, I start slowing down about half a mile from the end of the bike leg and glide comfortably into the changing area. Again, I do a leisurely, complete change from bike to run outfit. My color coordination is perfect, but boy am I slow. How slow is indicated by the reaction of my 10-year-old son, who is standing with the rest of my family in the spectator area as I start out on the run. I am thrilled to see them. I run over to say hello, give and get kisses. Except from my boy, who is waving at me—no, no, don't stop, get out there, you are so far behind!

I later learn that my kids and their mom had arrived in time to see the race winners finish the whole event, before I came in from the bike segment. (That race pattern has held for me from that day to this, and I am still out there having a good time, even if my time is still not, by comparison, very good.) They see me come in from the bike (I do not see them at that point). But then they see people who arrived after me on the bike segment get out on the run before I do. My boy is impatient. I can imagine him saying, "Dawdling while dressing again, Daddy, just like you do in the morning!" (I discover—by later looking back at the recorded split times [the times spent in each race segment, including the two transitions]—that the next fifteen people who finished ahead of me in the race spent more time swimming, cycling, and running than I did, but less time in transition.) Regardless, I am reinvigorated by seeing my family, and I smartly trot onto the run course.

The Run

The run will prove to be the toughest event for me. It is 11:10 A.M. when I get going. It is by now very hot. I go slowly and am all right for the first mile or so. I pass the little cyclist in red and black. She is going even more slowly than I am. (Seven months later, I would meet her at the 1984 Long Island Half-Marathon and remind her of the episode. She would remember it well. She would tell me that her response to my "You are in a race, madam" challenge, which sent her speeding up for the last two miles of the bike, had ruined her for the run.)

Soon thereafter, however, the heat and the problems of the bike-run transition begin to get to me. I am suffering. But I keep on running, however slowly. Mistakenly, I believe that it is somehow wrong to stop running and walk. I do not learn—in this race at any rate—from the example of a woman walking near the beginning of the run leg. I pass her at that point, but later, running comfortably now, she overtakes me, then leaves me far behind.

Yes, it is hot. Water stops are adequate, but mile markers are not. Ten minutes apart I pass two people standing about a mile from each other who each gaily say to me: "Only six miles to go." I am struggling. Everything hurts. I am going very slowly. "I will never, never, never do a marathon," a little voice inside my head says. (I would do another triathlon three weeks later and my first marathon less than three months later.) With three miles to go I see some friends sitting on a shaded bench in downtown Sag Harbor. I sit down for a brief chat. Revitalized, I pick up my pace a bit and head for the finish.

With about two miles to go, I pass a man in my age-group. I get about 30 yards ahead of him, figuring that I have him. "Why are you racing when you said that all you wanted to do was finish?" the persistent little voice says. "Because I'm racing. Now keep quiet and concentrate," I retort. I keep going. With one mile to go, ignoring the wisdom of the great African-American baseball pitcher Satchel Paige, who said, "Don't look back; someone may be gaining on you," I do look back. Satchel was right. I am losing my lead, ever so slowly. I try to pick up my pace. I cannot. I have already given it everything I've got. I am running on empty. With about half a mile to go, I hear footsteps. I can do nothing about it.

I think about the experience I had had many times in sailboat racing going downwind, being blanketed from behind, hearing the splop-splop-splop of the little waves on the other boat's bow as she catches up and goes by, with me powerless to do anything about it in that case either. Here, in this race, with a quarter mile to go, with the finish line in sight, I am passed by the man I had passed before. I try once more, but I just cannot go any faster. Then, within another two minutes, as I cross the finish line myself, the thought of defeat is replaced with the overwhelming thought of victory—my victory for myself in finishing. I did it, I did it, I did it! Oh, what a feeling! As Nat King Cole used to tell us, "Unforgettable."

Aftermath

I am tired, sore, and stiff but absolutely flying. My family is there—a great feeling. I take it real easy. I strip off my sweat-soaked running gear very slowly. I drink—water, Gatorade—and drink some more. I pack up my things and walk to the car. We go over to the pool at the race headquarters motel. The kids go for a swim. I sit, reflect, bask in my own private glow. I did it, I really did it. I have seen a new me, and I really like what I see. When is the next race?

Little did I know how many "next races" and further mind- and body-expanding experiences there would be for me in the next 20-plus years, how participating in this sport would change my life in so many positive ways—a major one being the creation of this book. And now that we are talking about this book, let me turn from my first race to yours.

On Racing and the Races, for You

As you know for sure by now, I am neither a technical expert nor a fast triathlete. I am, however, "long." That is, I have been at it for a long time, with great enjoyment. One nice benefit of that for me is that I have finished in the top three in my age-group many times. That is because my race age-group cohort, never that big to begin with, especially in the New York metropolitan area where I live and work, has steadily shrunk in size. Thus most of the time when I have come home with a prize, beginning after I turned 60, it has been simply because there were three or fewer of us in my age-group.

Top-level technique, form, and speed are not my things. I do know something about racing in comfort and finishing happily and in good health. I also know something about maintaining a thoroughly enjoyable racing career over many years. I view the plaques and trophies that I have won as rewards for my longevity in doing triathlons and duathlons. In no particular order of importance, I share with you some of my observations and experiences in racing for all of these years that hopefully you will find helpful.

How Triathlons Are Usually Laid Out

For most triathlons and virtually all duathlons, the transition area is literally and figuratively at the center of the race. It is here that you place your bicycle on a bike rack, usually by looping the bottom of the brake handles over the rack's horizontal bar. The racks are usually numbered, and you must set up at the rack that is designated for your race number. You place your biking and running gear on the ground to one side of the bike's rear wheel, laying it out in some order of use that makes sense to you.

If the swim start is close to the transition area (meaning that it is an out-and-back or loop course, not a point-to-point), you get fully prepared for the swim in the transition area. In an occasional race (as in the Long Island Gold Coast Triathlon, mentioned at the beginning of Chapter 7), the swim is point-to-point, starting at some distance from the transition area and going back to its vicinity in a straight line. In this case, you have to walk to the swim start, or go to it on a bus if one is provided. If you are not wearing a wet suit, you usually wear a shirt to keep warm (triathlons generally start early in the morning) and shoes or sandals. In many cases, the race organizers have provided you with a numbered bag that they will pick up and bring back to the transition area. You may also want to carry, not wear right away, your goggles, cap, nose clip, and earplugs. However, it is a good idea to put on your wet suit, if you have one, in the transition area. A wet suit is much easier to get on when your skin is dry, and it just might be damp with sweat after a long walk on a warm summer morning. For comfort, you can leave the zipping-up until you get to the swim-start area on the beach. You will likely need help zipping up. Do not be afraid to ask for it.

The bike course will be an out-and-back, a single loop, or several laps on the same loop, all starting and finishing at the transition area. The run in the Olympic-distance and Sprint triathlons and the duathlons is usually a single loop or an out-and-back, although on occasion it, too, consists of laps. The overall race format is straightforward: swim, out-and-back or point-to-point; transition area, change to bike stuff; bike, single loop or laps; transition area, change to run stuff; run, out-and-back or single loop or laps; and finish.

In almost all races your finishing time is your total time from the start, changing time included. If you are concerned about your overall time, do a little transitioning practice. As you know, in that first race I spent 23 minutes changing my clothes. I looked great. I had a different outfit for each leg, and they were color coordinated. However, if I had dressed a little less stylishly and had spent only 13 minutes changing (the average changing time for people who finished toward the end, as I did), I would have moved up 23 places on the final results list.

Equipment and Checklist

I am compulsive and I have a poor memory. Thus I use a detailed checklist that I go over with care as I pack at home for a race.

Before leaving home, I check over my equipment bag(s) once again before I walk out the door. Whether I am staying in a motel at a distant race, or leaving for the race directly from home, I carefully lay out my stuff on a chair or a couch the night before the race. I do not want to be setting up my stuff in the transition area before a race and find that I left my swim goggles or bike helmet at home. My very detailed checklist appears in Table 9.1. Using it as a template, you can design a checklist that suits you. I strongly suggest that you do so. For some reason (wonder what it might be?), the older I get, the more I need to use the checklist before *every* race to try to ensure completeness in assembling and packing my equipment.

Table 9.1. The Checklist

General

Race directions, registration materials

Energy bars, food

Warm-up suit, long-sleeved T-shirt

Wear-to-the-race shoes and socks

Shoehorn

Waterproof digital watch with chronometer/timer

Felt-tipped pen (for doing your own triathlon
  body marking)

Glasses, sunglasses, "bike eyewear"

Sunscreen

Extra safety pins, plastic bags (2)

Towels

Bottles of water (for cleaning your feet)

Number belt

Keys, money pouch, belt

Fresh clothing (for after the race)

Alarm clock

Swim

Swimsuit

Cap

Goggles, antifog solution

Earplugs

Nose clip

Wet suit

Bike

Bicycle

Bicycle pump (full size)

Bicycle pump (frame fit)

Water bottles (2)

Seat bag w/spare tube

Bike computer

Bike shoes and socks

Bike helmet and gloves

Bike shirt, shorts, liner shorts (if not wearing a tri-suit)

Wind shell, long-sleeved bike shirt, tights (for cold days)

Run

Singlet, T-shirt, shorts (if not wearing a tri-suit)

Cap, sweatband

Running shoes, running socks (optional), orthotics
  (if you use them)

Wind shell, long-sleeved T-shirt

However, even with checklists, I have forgotten things. For example, during the 1998 season I managed to arrive at one race without the front wheel for my bike. Well, not to worry, my friend Dan Honig, president of the New York Triathlon Club, was short of volunteers that day. So I helped out and was thus able to turn a memory lapse into a good deed. Even with the checklist, I still occasionally manage to arrive at a race without one piece of equipment or another, but thankfully nothing as major as a missing bike wheel.

At your first race for sure, you will likely be nervous enough without having to worry about mislaid or missing equipment. So do use a checklist. The one I present in Table 9.1 may seem to contain a lot of stuff, but it's all essential or helpful, which you will come to realize after your first race. Furthermore, from the list you will easily be able to make up one that works for you, for yourself. It may be longer than mine, or shorter. But do make certain that you take everything that is on *your* list.

Pacing

Just as consistency is the way to successful training, it is also the key to successful racing. You should work out at a comfortable pace in each sport and get used to it, then estimate how long it should take you to complete each race segment at your comfortable pace. As you get into each segment, try to get onto your planned race pace and stick with it. The number-one rule of racing to finish is, do not go out too fast. If you overdo it in the swim and bike segments, you may end up walking for most of the run.

There are no split-distance markers for the swim. On an out-and-back course, you will of course know when you have reached the halfway mark. You have to feel what the proper pace is for you. For the bike segment, in some races there are intermediate-distance markers, but I find that the mini speedometer/timer/cadence-counter/distance-recorder computer that I have mounted on the handlebars on each of my bikes keeps me on track. In the run segment, except for the short ones, there are likely to be markers at every mile. Use them. In comparison with my training speeds, in the race I usually go a bit faster on the swim and the bike and a bit slower on the run. You may have a different pattern. However, once you find one that is right for you, stick to it.

Racing

Related to pacing is racing—that is competing directly with one or more fellow triathletes or duathletes in some portion of the event rather than competing solely with the clock. I raced for a short time in each segment of my first triathlon, as described above. I still do it from time to time. As you know, I am a truly slow runner now. I tend to be a fair cyclist by comparison, especially so in the entry-level duathlons and Sprint triathlons, which attract a lot of first-timers. They, because the races are relatively short, may not have trained that much (unless they have read this book!). In the entry-level duathlons and Sprints, then, for fun I count my "passes" on the bike. (However, I don't count the number of times I get passed back, on the run!) Most of the time I do not let racing take over, and I never let it wear me out. If on a particular day I am riding fast enough to get some passes, that's great. But I keep my eye on my main event: finishing the race, and having fun doing it.

Auto-timing

In an increasing number of races, the timing is done electronically, for your overall time and for your "splits" (the time you spend in each race segment and in each transition). As of 2005, two main technologies were in use. By the time you are reading this, there may be who knows how many more. The primary one was a version of the "Champion Chip."™ At check-in, each competitor is given a Velcro strap or a hospital-style snap-on plastic tie to which is attached a piece of plastic with a microchip inside. Each chip carries a unique identifying code, matched to your race number. You place the strap on your ankle, and at each transition point of the race, a device records that unique information and puts it into a computerized race record. You are required of course to turn in the chip-strap after the race, or mail it in if you forget to give it back then and there. If you do not turn it in, a credit card (for which you have provided the number at registration or check-in) will be charged a penalty fee.

A second system coming into use in 2005 consisted of a disposable antenna worn somewhere on your body. Just like the chips, the antenna contains a unique code that can be read by dedicated recording devices set up along the course. A major advantage of this system is that the antenna is cheap and disposable. You just throw it away after the race.

The Modern Swim Start

As previously noted, this is the one mass start you will be in. Even with a wave start, it can be a mess. For most races, you gather in a group on the beach. With the gun, everyone charges into the water, usually with some degree of noise. In a few races, you start in the water, treading water until the gun goes off. The start is more in slow motion here, but there is still plenty of clamor.

Whether you start on the beach or in the water, whether there is a single mass start or it is in waves, you will be asked to "seed" yourself (being more up front in the pack or farther back) by your expected time. The faster swimmers will be asked to move toward the front of the throng, the slower ones toward the back of it. Be smart and be honest with yourself. If you are not a fast swimmer and start too far up front, you will only be in the way. As swimmers climb over and go around you, you stand a good chance of being grabbed on the leg or kicked in the face, perhaps separating you from your goggles. If you are not sure of just the right spot for your pace, it is better to start too far back than too far forward. At the back, at least you are in full control of any passing situation.

An increasing number of races, especially the bigger ones, use the staggered, "wave," start system. This is a boon to the racers. You start in groups of 50 to 200 at 1- to 5-minute intervals, depending upon the distance (the longer the swim, the more time between waves). Your overall finish time is appropriately adjusted. The organizers place you in a given wave according to a predicted swim time that you put down on your entry blank, or by an age/sex grouping. There is still some clamor, confusion, and kicking at the start of each wave, but it is nothing like what happens in a total mass start.

As a first-time triathlete, you may want to use alternating

strokes in the swim. Although I now generally use the crawl all the way, in that first race I spent about a third of my time doing elementary backstroke. Breast, back crawl, and sidestroke are also used. There is no rule restricting the allowable stroke, but virtually all triathlons have a swim time limit or cutoff, for safety reasons during the swim itself and also because the organizers do not want people riding the bike segment miles behind everyone else. If you need to keep your head out of the water to manage your breathing—because the water is cold, or for psychological reasons—by all means do it. You will slow down a little bit (hopefully not *too* much), but you will feel more comfortable. For finishing happily and healthily, that is what counts.

It is important to stay on course and swim in a straight line. Because there are no lane markers on the water, this may take some doing. However, any deviation from the true course just adds unnecessary distance to your swim. Whatever your stroke, you need to get your head out of the water and look straight ahead from time to time. The breaststroke or lifesaving crawl is good for this. Most swim courses are marked by buoys or patrol boats or both. Buoys are the best. They stay in place, whereas boats can drift. You can also sight on the turning mark of an out-and-back course, and/or the finish line. Whatever the swim distance, I find it best not to think about the overall course length but rather to swim from buoy to buoy. As well as helping me stay on that straight line, I find it makes the whole swim segment go by faster.

In the swim, it is best to find a little niche for yourself with no one passing you and you passing no one. Once in the niche, get into a nice steady rhythm and stay there. It usually takes at least a quarter of the distance to do this; sometimes it takes me up to half the distance.

Salt water is a nuisance if you swallow some, but the added buoyancy is a plus. Lake swimming is nice because there are no tides, usually no waves of any consequence, and usually no currents. However, lake bottoms can be mucky, and swimming through aquatic grasses, which I have done on more than one occasion, can be a bit disconcerting.

In tidal salt water, the race organizers have probably worked out the timing of the start so that any tides or currents are going with you. However, if you have thought that "swimming uphill" is an impossibility, you should know that I have done it more than once, against an incoming tide and/or a current and/or a headwind with waves. Also, on a loop or parallel-with-the-shoreline swim course, you can find yourself swimming uphill in one direction (against a tide or current) and downhill (with it) in the other. If it happens to you, just go with the flow, literally. Ideally, the course is laid out so that you do the uphill segment first. Be patient—you should get quite a ride going the other way. You do occasionally get to ride a current just downhill in a point-to-point swim, as in the New York City Triathlon, where the swim is in the Hudson River. That is fun. Everyone has a wonderful ride and usually sets a swim personal record.

Some years ago, I gave up any attempts to go faster in the water and am entirely comfortable psychologically over the triathlon distances as long as I do not try to go fast. Therefore, I have given up any swim workouts except those that are long, slow, and steady, in the pool and—when the opportunity presents itself— open water. Furthermore, for many years now I have used the crawl stroke in combination with a frog kick, the so-called trudgeon crawl, exclusively. It is not particularly fast, but it is comfy. That is not to say that you *should not* do the training sets, of which I gave a few examples in Chapter 4, and so on, if you want to go faster, only that you *need not* do them if you are not too worried about your time.

The Swim-Bike Transition

When coming to the end of an open-water (nonpool) swim segment, before I stand up I generally swim in until my hand (doing the crawl stroke) touches the bottom. That way I do not have to push too much water out of the way with my whole body as I start to jog up to the beach. It is easier to do this than trying to wade quickly in waist-deep water. Coming out of the water, stay in line through the exit chute. Race officials must get your number and record your time, or your timing chip or race-number antenna must register with the recording device. If there is a traffic jam here, just be patient. You will be losing much less time than you think.

For saltwater races, a sprinkler rinse may be provided. Do not skip it if there is one. It is helpful to get the salt off your skin before the bike and the run. The shower also helps get any sand off your feet; for producing blisters, there is nothing quite like sand in your socks. For freshwater swims, showers are usually not provided. In this case a bucket pre-filled with water or a spare bike water bottle (which is what I have used for foot spritzing for many years now) back at your transition-area slot can be a big help should you need to get sand or mud off your feet. Otherwise, you must wipe off your feet with a towel, a time-consuming endeavor. However you plan to handle cleaning your feet, at the beach drink some water if it is available, then jog gently from the end of the swim chute through the transition area to your bike. I suggest not trying to run here. Your feet will be bare and the space is likely to be crowded. You do not want to get a foot stepped on at this point, or step on something like a water bottle lying around that could trip you, or—worse—something sharp. So you want to be able to see where you are going, without rushing.

Some people ride and run sockless. If every second counts for you, that's fine, but I like to protect my feet. After what was— even for me—a time-wasting experience using two different pairs of socks in my early racing days, for years now I have used one pair rather than two for the bike ride and the run. (I talked about race clothing in Chapter 8.) In triathlons, most people keep on for the whole race whatever they wore as their base layer during the swim. If you are wearing a one- or two-piece tri-suit, you will simply wear it for the whole race. If your base layer is your bathing suit, for the bike segment you may put on a pair of bike shorts and a bike shirt. Now that I regularly wear a tri-suit, I usu-ally wear a bike shirt over it for that segment. For the run, again if you are not wearing a tri-suit, you will likely switch to a singlet top (which you can also wear under your wet suit from the start). For a consideration of the shoe alternatives, see pages 161–63 and 174–76.

Make sure that you put your helmet on and securely fasten the strap. You will not be allowed on the bike course without it. I wear a sweatband under my helmet, to control the sweat that would otherwise drip into my eyes (I sweat a lot) and also to keep the helmet from slipping down over my eyes. I use bike gloves for comfort. Many racers do not, for speed of transition. Also, remember to put on your glasses or bike eyewear.

The Bike Ride

In most triathlons and duathlons, the bike segment is an almost pure time trial. You are out to cover the distance as quickly as you can, on your own. Drafting—that is, riding close behind one or more other racers to take advantage of the windbreak provided— is prohibited in all USAT-sanctioned races and most others as well. Thus, as noted, the pack riding and/or pace lines to facilitate drafting that are used in most bike races, from local club criteriums to the Tour de France, and that United States Cycling Federation–licensed bike racers are used to, generally do not appear in multi-sport racing.

Make sure that you carry at least one water bottle. If you have only one water bottle bracket on your bike, you can carry a second bottle in the pocket(s) on the back of your bike shirt, if you use one. It is very important to drink on the bike leg. Sometimes there are water-bottle exchange points where you can drop off an empty bottle and, slowing down of course, pick up a filled one while still under way. Your empty bottle is collected by a volunteer, but you are unlikely to see it again unless you spend a lot of time searching through a large pile of empty bottles at the end of the race. Therefore, if you know that there is a water-bottle exchange and you plan to use it, bring along a bottle you do not mind giving up. In addition, you never know what you might be given in exchange. I have on occasion picked up a neat new bottle as a souvenir.

Ride your own race. Try to get into that steady, smooth, regular cadence that you practiced in training. Spin your way up the hills in a low gear. Power your way down the hills. Downhills provide a good opportunity to pick up time. You should take advantage of them. However, if the road surface is not smooth, do not try to go too fast. A flat tire or an unexpected bump on a fast downhill could prematurely end your participation in the race as well as cause serious long-term injury. A minute or two off your time is not worth that risk. Keep bike safety firmly in mind throughout the race, for your own sake and that of your fellow competitors.

Bike-Run Transition

Some of the same clothing considerations apply here as in the swim-bike transition. Running shorts worn over your swimsuit are optional but can help limit chafe. The tri-suit leg extends down the thigh like that of a bike short (although usually not quite so far) and thus provides chafe protection during the run. Spend a few extra seconds to lace up your running shoes properly. No need to risk foot blisters now. This transition is easier than the swim-bike routine, because you do not have to dry off, remove sand, and put on socks. Move through this transition purposefully and methodically, but do not forget anything. I always put on a fresh sweatband here. I also change glasses if the ones I have worn on the bike are covered with sweat drippings.

The Run

At the beginning of this leg, you are likely to encounter the most difficult physical adjustments of your race. Your legs feel rubbery, your stride is short, you cannot get stretched out, you cannot get moving. This may last a mile or two, or more. In the 1983 Ricoh East Coast Championships, it took me about 45 minutes to painfully shuffle the first three miles. I finally stopped trying to run, walked about a quarter of a mile, got stretched out, and ran the last seven miles at a sub-9-minute pace.

I learned some lessons from that experience that have stayed with me since (although I have not done sub-9s in a long time). As I said at the beginning of this chapter, I suggest starting off the run with 2 to 6 minutes of purposeful walking. You may find that walking for another 2 minutes or so at the 12-minute mark is helpful. This routine helps get everything stretched out, making the run more comfortable and faster. You can also try static stretching before starting out on the run, in addition to or in place of the walking.

Fluid intake is ever so important on the run. If you are slow like I am, even in a triathlon with an early start time it is likely to be pretty hot by the time you get out on the run. However, even if it is cool, keeping yourself well hydrated is essential for finishing at this point. Remember the old but true adage of the long-distance runner: if you get to the point of feeling thirsty, it is already too late to catch up on water intake. Keep drinking enough so that you do not get thirsty. After trying the fortified drinks in several races, I found that water is the best drink for me. For you, a fortified drink may be best.

If it is hot, at each water stop on the run (likely to be every mile or so), pour a cup of water over your head, and splash another on your face. One poured down the back of your neck helps too. If spectators offer garden-hose rinses, take one, but make sure not to get your socks wet. Running in squishy socks feels distinctly uncomfortable. If I am in a hurry for one reason or another, I do drink on the run, but I take small sips to avoid swallowing air and developing that bloated, uncomfortable feeling. Belches always seem to come slowly when I am running. If I am taking it easy in a particular race, I will stop to drink water and to splash it liberally on my head, face, and neck. If there is shade on the run, go to it, even if it means crossing the road more than once. The temperature in the shade can be 10 to 15 degrees cooler than in direct sunlight. On an out-and-back course, running in the shade on one side of the road outbound may mean that you are running against inbound runners ahead of you. If so, just make sure that you stay out of their way, but stay in that shade.

If at some point during the run leg you must slow to a walk to recoup some energy, do it. Better to finish having walked than to persist in running to the point of getting sick and not being able to finish at all. However, "hitting the wall," as marathoners can do at the 20- to 22-mile mark—when they have to stop, or drop into the very slow "marathon shuffle"—can happen in multi-sport racing, although it seems relatively rare at the distances I am talking about. If you have eased into the run leg at the beginning and paced yourself properly during it, you may not find it necessary to engage in unplanned walking. Remember, your overall performance is the product of your training *and* how you run the race. It is both that will get you across that finish line, happily and healthily.

That Golden Glow

Wow! You did what you set out to do: finish your first triathlon or duathlon. Revel in that golden glow. I still do after almost every race. You are basking in your feelings of accomplishment. You deserve them. You feel really good about yourself, perhaps better than you have ever felt before. You are proud of what you have done, and you should be. Your mind and your body reflect your sense of pride. You have trained your mind to guide you to work out regularly, with discipline, on a schedule, as well as deal with all of the logistics of this fairly complicated sport, and then get through the race according to plan and under control. You have trained your cardiovascular and respiratory systems to work aerobically for an extended period of time. You have trained your musculoskeletal and nervous systems to do aerobic work in three different sports. You have done this with a training program that does not require you to turn the rest of your life upside down. Thus, while exploring the limits of your mind and body, you have kept your overall life priorities straight. Most importantly, you have achieved your principal goal of finishing the triathlon or duathlon of your choice, happily and healthily.

Recovery

Immediate Post-Race Doings

At the end of your first triathlon or duathlon, you will probably feel the way I did: very tired, rather stiff, but very proud of yourself. Take it easy at first. Drink. Get in the shade if you can. Get into some fresh clothes if possible. At least change your shoes and socks. Walk around a bit. Stretch out gently. Sit down and rest. Then carefully gather up all of your stuff, check the contents of your race bag to make sure that you have left nothing behind, collect your bike, and load the car. You will go home or back to your motel room for a much-deserved shower. If it is a motel, and you are doing a race that will have you finishing in late morning, see if your motel will give you a late checkout time. Many will. The next morning, go out for a light jog or an easy spin on the bike for 20 minutes or so. This will help get whatever pain and stiffness you are experiencing (if any) out of your muscles. But most of all, bask in the glory of self-satisfaction.

The Next Few Days

In my experience, and that of most other triathletes, recovery after the Sprint- and Olympic-distance-equivalent triathlon and the entry-level duathlon takes very little time. Usually within a day or two, you will feel just fine physically. (You will very likely have felt just fine mentally within minutes of finishing the race.) This is in marked contrast to the post-race experience of most people who do marathons. For myself, the good mental feelings of accomplishment post-marathon began right away, but physically it was another story. My muscles ached, a lot. I walked around rather stiffly for several days. Stair climbing and descending were hard on my thighs. In terms of post-marathon exercise, I found that I could not do anything more than 10 to 20 minutes of very easy jogging for 4 or 5 days after the race. Full physical recovery took me 2 to 4 weeks. This is a figure that you will hear commonly from marathoners.

Post-triathlon and -duathlon recovery is an entirely different matter. Unlike in marathoning, although you may be exercising at a demanding aerobic level for you for an extended period of time, you are using different muscle groups in the different segments of the race. Further, for about a fifth of the time in the triathlon, about 90 percent of your body weight is being supported by water, and in both the tri and the du you are sitting down while exercising for about half the time. Then there are the two mandatory breaks, the transitions. They may be short, but they are stops. All of this makes the multi-sport racing experience very different from that of the marathon, even if you are on the course for comparable amounts of time.

After my first triathlon, I felt fine physically by the next day. After almost every race, I still do. My mental state was a different matter. I was not just feeling fine; I was flying. Having done that first race early in September, and knowing that the triathlon season was not quite over, I immediately began casting around for another race. As I mentioned before, I found one, almost as long as the Mighty Hamptons Triathlon, and did it—3 weeks later. Again, I finished happily and healthily. In the interim, 2 weeks after the first race I did a 100k ("metric century," 62-mile) ride on my bike at close to race pace in an American Heart Association cyclethon. Eight weeks after that second triathlon, I ran my first marathon. Admittedly, I was quite a bit younger than I am now.

In my second season of triathloning, I did three races over a 4-week period, with 2 weeks between events. Again no problems. I viewed each race as a long workout to be done 2 weeks prior to the next race. Between races, I just maintained an easy 4 hours or so of aerobic work per week. I felt good in and after all three races and maintained a pretty consistent, if fairly slow, performance level throughout. Since that time, I have averaged about seven triathlons and duathlons per season—fewer in the mid-1990s for family reasons, but in the 2000s eight to ten per season (twelve in 2005!) with strong family support. Even when I was going long (see Chapter 10), I was able to maintain that frequency, with comfort. Although some runners comfortably do a number of marathons in one season, most do not. Multi-sport racing is quite different, for most people, in that regard.

The Next Race

After your first race, if it is early enough in the season and you feel like getting further into the sport, you can look around for one or more additional races to do. Occasionally I race on consecutive weekends, but most of the time I space out my races. Some folks do race every or every other weekend throughout the season. As for distance, assuming that you have used the TFOMTP as is, I would not try to do anything longer than an Olympic-distance tri right away. If you successfully completed a Sprint triathlon for your first event, you can certainly think about hopping into the TFOMTP at Week 8 and doing an Olympic-distance race for your next event.

If you decide to try a marathon after triathloning, I suggest that you make it your last event of the season. You should probably allow at least 6 weeks after your last triathlon before doing a marathon. For your training schedule, you can use the Generic Program of the TFOMTP (Table 7.1, page 146). You can still devote two of the scheduled training sessions per week to swimming or cycling in preparation for the marathon, just as long as those workouts are aerobic.

Next Steps

Once you get over the psychological hump of doing your first race, your horizons may expand rapidly. If you do not do another race that first season, you may, like me, find yourself looking forward to seeing race schedules for next season in the triathlon publications and on an increasing number of Web sites (see Appendix II). I plan my season very early. I also get my race applications in early, because the popular and well-run races tend to fill increasingly far in advance.

Although completing any triathlon or duathlon is a wonderful experience, you may look for new challenges. Just make sure that any goals you set for yourself are achievable for you, as you did in your first multi-sport race. Nothing turns off an endurance athlete faster than frustration. Because you set your own goals, you are entirely in control of your own frustration level.

The two types of challenges that you can consider are "going faster" and "going longer." If you want to go faster in a race, you have to go faster in your training. There are plenty of fine articles, books, and coaches around to advise you on how to do this. As you know, I do not and never have done speed/interval training. I am so much slower than the top people in my age-group—it takes me close to twice the time it does them to finish an Olympic-distance event—that there is simply no way I could ever get fast enough to compete with them, no matter how much speed work I did. So I don't waste my time and energy trying, and cannot offer you advice on doing so. However, going longer was something that I thought I could do. And I did. Having done that, I can help you with it. If at some point you would like to try, read on.

GOING LONG

I felt so good when I crossed the finish line. People who saw
me on TV thought I was spaced out. All I did was go
beyond [my previous] limit. —*Julie Moss, after the*
February 1982 Hawaii Ironman Triathlon

People have asked me, "Well, have you ever done a 'real'
triathlon?" By that, they invariably mean an ironman-
distance event (2.4-mile swim, 112-mile bike, 26.2-mile
run, which is a marathon). I invariably reply that over whatever
distance someone is doing a triathlon or duathlon, that race is
very "real" for him or her. Nevertheless, some authorities in the
world of triathlon try to make the ironman-distance races—especially those operated by the World Triathlon Corporation (WTC),
which runs the Ironman Triathlon World Championship race in
Kailua-Kona, Hawaii (otherwise known as the "Hawaii Ironman"), and numerous others around the world—the gold standard of triathlon. I strongly disagree with this formulation.

I believe that somehow treating ironman as *the* race in the
world of triathlon denigrates all the other individual accomplishments of all the other triathletes and, by extension, duathletes as
well. I deplore words such as "Tinman" (its use is fortunately
declining in popularity among race directors), which has been
used to refer to triathlons shorter than the ironman-distance. This
is not to say that doing an ironman is not an exceptional achievement. It surely is. However, in my mind, the ethic that says that

all the other distances stand in the shadow of the ironman-distance hurts the sport.

As I said in Chapter 1, the strong implication of the "ironman ethic" is that if you have not done an ironman, you are not a "real" triathlete. Most people who contemplate doing a triathlon or a duathlon of any distance, at least when they start out in the sport, would not think of doing an ironman, for a number of reasons. First and foremost, unless you are into the sport at all, just doing those distances consecutively is beyond your comprehension. "You've got to be totally nuts" is a common reaction to the suggestion. Three more practical reasons are lack of time for training, lack of money for equipment and travel, and just plain lack of interest in putting body and mind through the strain that going long requires. That going long can be a fantastic experience is true. It surely was for me. Nevertheless, it is hardly for everyone, or indeed for most people.

Not everyone is physically and/or mentally capable of doing an ironman. Moreover, not everyone *wants* to do it. In fact, most of us *would* think "Are you crazy?" (I surely did before I did my first. By the way, for a triathlete, do you know who a crazy triathlete is? One who has done a race that is longer than the longest one you have done.) Dr. Donald Ardell (who wrote the foreword to this book), an ofttimes age-group national and world champion, has never done and says he never will do an ironman. He believes that the wear and tear on his body of the training for ironman, and the race itself, at the speeds at which he would be naturally doing both, would interfere with his ability to be a winner at the Olympic-distance and shorter events, which he so loves doing.

To say that the folks who do the Sprints, the duathlons, and the Olympic-distance tri's are *not* doing the real thing can discourage people who would like to get into the sport from even trying, and can drive certain people to try to do more than they should—for the health of their body and/or their mind or their family situation or their employment. It can drive people to try to go long for the wrong reasons. It can take the fun out of doing the regular-distance races. I hope that this ethic will fade and we will get back to what triathlon was when I first got into it: every race was real and every competitor was real too.

This said, I have gone long myself for what I believed to be the right reasons. Going long worked for me. In fact, doing the ironman-distance, more than once, was one of the great experiences of my life. In the balance of this chapter, I share with you how I got there, how to decide if you should try "going long," and how you can train to do that—without turning your life upside down in the process. I then offer two workable training programs, one each for the half-ironman- and ironman-distances.

Why Go Long?

Suppose you get into triathlon and become comfortable doing Olympic-distance events. Although going long or longer was not on your agenda when you started out, it may end up there, as happened to me in a hurry in 1985. Who knows why. Because it's there, or training for one is a really good way to get in shape, or you've never done anything like it, or you want to do something that has been accomplished by only a tiny proportion of the world's population, or you want to feel the thrill of crossing a Long Course or an Ultra Course finish line, or you will grow in stature in the eyes of your kids, or your friends will say, "You did *what*?" Or because you will grow in stature in your own eyes.

If you are like me, you will go slowly in the race. If you are like many other first-timers who are faster than I am and perhaps have more time to train, unlike me you will likely finish with many people behind you. However, either way, if you work at it and focus during the race, you will finish. Then you will experience feelings unlike any others you have ever had, even those that you felt when you crossed the finish line of your first multi-sport race at any distance. Mind bending. I really did this? Life altering. I have been in a couple of tight mental spots since I did my first ironman and helped myself get through them by saying, "Self, you've done *an ironman*; you can get through this."

But do you *have* to "go long" in order to be a "real" triathlete? As I said at the beginning of this chapter, not at all. Any finisher of any triathlon or duathlon at any distance is a *real* triathlete or duathlete. It is just that some triathletes and duathletes go further than others do (and yes, for you nonswimmers who want to go long, there are long-course duathlons too).

I Decide to "Go Long"

I started triathloning with a great deal of enthusiasm in that September of 1983, once I found that indeed I could do the distances consecutively. As I noted in Chapter 2, at the time I had a winter sport, downhill skiing, that I loved and was reasonably good at, at least in terms of style. However, one skis for only a limited number of days a year. I had a summer sport, sailing, that I loved, too, and was also reasonably good at—in terms of seamanship if not making the boat go fast. However, sailing, except in those rarely experienced moments of pure panic, is not a physical sport. Rather it is a mental one. It is also one in which "working on the boat" is for many sailors (including myself) half the fun, and that is not a sport at all.

Now for the first time in my life I was into a truly physical sport, for which I was training five days a week, and could do for a long season (in the Northeast—starting with the early duathlons and finishing with the late ones—about seven months a year). And I loved it, just as I loved skiing and sailing. In my second season I did three triathlons and one of those new-fangled biathlons (as they were then called and still are by one of their earliest developers, the oft-mentioned Dan Honig of the New York Triathlon Club). In my third season, with a total of seven multi-sport races under my belt, I decided that for a new challenge I would try to go long.

Why did I, at that time? Who knows. Probably for the same reasons that got me started running, then got me into road racing, then into triathloning. I had the time to train. Sounded like a good challenge for me—one that I had a reasonably good chance of meeting, once I set my mind to it. I chose a race in southern Vermont (which sadly went out of existence just a few years later). It was called the Green Mountain Steelman. The race segments comprised a slightly stretched version of the standard half-ironman-distance (1.2-mile swim, 56-mile bike, and 13.1-mile run), with a semi-inverse order of events: 2.5-mile swim, 13-mile run, and 60-mile bike. Getting ever more comfortable in the distance sports, especially in the water, I thought that I could manage them.

I geared up for that event by going to the first World Corporate Games* (WCG), held that year in Toronto, Ontario, Canada. There was no triathlon in the games then. (Triathlon has been part of the games since the second ones, held in San Francisco, California, in 1988. I competed in that triathlon. On the bike segment in Golden Gate Park, we had to stop for cross traffic.) As part of my training for the Steelman, in the games I made up my own "triathlon over time." On consecutive days, I did half of the scheduled marathon—a 24-mile bike road race and a 5-kilometer swim. They were all fun, I found, and doing them was also part of my preparation for the Steelman. I had surmised that a 7½-hour-per-week training program for 13 weeks would do the trick for the longer distances if I went slowly in the race. I was right. At the end of the week that began in Toronto, I finished the race in southern Vermont in just under the 8½-hour time limit.

I Decide to Go Even Longer

At the end of the Steelman, I was on top of the world. I was tired and sore but flying at the same time. Here was this former nonathlete out on the water and the road for close to 8½ hours, clearing some monstrous hills on the bike in the bargain. As the last competitor on the course, for the last 50 miles of the 60-mile bike ride I had a local fire department ambulance with me. Every so often, the driver would ask me if I was going to finish. When I affirmed that I would, he duly radioed that information into race HQ, which kept the course open for me. He also lied a lot. As I topped each long hill on a very hilly course, he told me that it was the last hill I would encounter. It never was until the very last

* Over the years the WCG became the World Masters Games. Except for the team sports, which do have qualifiers, they are essentially an open-entry Olympics for veteran athletes in about twenty-five sports. The minimum entry age is determined by the international governing bodies for each sport. You simply register, pay your entry fees, and go. The games are now held regularly every four years—in the year following the Summer Olympics—in various places around the world.

one, but the benign deception he practiced did help me stay on the course and get through the race. The last hill on the bike course was steep. I was told later that it was so steep, in fact, that the winner of the race, Kenny Souza, had to walk about the last quarter of it. (Kenny went on to dominate the duathlon world from the late 1980s to the mid-1990s.) So I did not feel so bad when I walked the last half of that hill. I finished the race. I finished!

Two days later, for some reason, the "iron thought" zoomed into my head. I knew that a race called the Cape Cod (Massachusetts) Endurance Triathlon, an ironman event, was to be held in three weeks. I was in the best shape I had ever been in, and thought it unlikely that I would ever be in as good shape again (I was wrong). I had to try it. I entered the race. (By the way, for many ironman races now, you can hardly get in just three weeks ahead of time. The WTC Lake Placid, New York, ironman, for example, routinely sells out within not too many hours of opening up for entries on the Web, as do a number of other ironman-distance races. Certain very popular Olympic-distance races, such as St. Anthony's in Saint Petersburg, Florida, also sell out quickly via the Web.) I continued to train regularly, throwing in one century (100 miles) bike ride and two 16- to 18-mile runs.

Going at race paces that were comfortable for me, I had a great time throughout. Slightly ahead of my projected time on the bike leg, I even stopped for a hamburger-and-a-Coke lunch at a convenient fast-food place on Cape Cod's Route 6. I finished last overall, but happily and healthily, within the 17-hour time limit at 16:42. One of the era's four top male triathletes, Scott Tinley, finished that race in exactly half the time I did. In so doing, he set the then-world record for the distance. During the race I actually saw Scott pedaling south on Route 6 as I was pedaling north. I waved over to him and called out something like "Way to go, Scott." He waved back. There I was, out on the course on which the best in the world was competing. And he waved at me! "How about that," as Mel Allen would have said.

That race would not be my last at that distance. Between 1985 and 1994, I started five ironman-distance triathlons. I finished three of them (twice within the time limit, once well over it). On the other two, I made it about halfway on the marathon before running out of time and stopping. I have also started and finished three other half-ironman triathlons, all within the time limit. I was last in five of the six races that I finished, but in all but one I finished happily and healthily. By the way, if you like being noticed, it is far better to finish last than sixth from last. When you are last, everyone knows who you are. When you are sixth from last, you are completely anonymous.

How I Went Long

As with any multi-sport race at any distance—assuming that you have the time, the desire, and the determination to train up to the required endurance level—the key to success is setting a reasonable goal for yourself in relation to your true capabilities for speed. Suppose that, like me, you are inherently slow. However, suppose that, again like me, you are just fast enough to have a reasonable chance to make the distances of a given race within the time limit established for it. (Most Long and Ultra Course races have time limits for completion of the swim and bike legs, and for overall finish as well.) Then suppose that for your first long race you are thinking about doing a half-ironman with a time limit of $8^{1}/_{2}$ hours.

How would you figure out if you had a reasonable chance of finishing? Consider my calculations for doing the Hudson Valley (half-ironman) Triathlon in 1998. First, you realistically appraise your speed potential. I knew that I could swim a mile comfortably in about 40 minutes, for at least 2 miles. The 1.2-mile swim would thus take me around 48 minutes. I figured that I could comfortably average 14 mph over the hilly 60-mile bike segment, and so would need something over 4 hours for it. In that case, I would have about 3 hours left to do the half-marathon (13.1 miles), allowing me 13 minutes per mile (reasonable for me on a hot, hilly course). If I could achieve these times, I would have about 40 minutes for the transitions and a "wiggle-room" allowance.

In the event, I used up about half of my wiggle room. The swim took about 10 minutes longer than expected because a strong Hudson River current against us on the "out" leg caused an "uphill" swim for half the distance (although we had a nice ride "downhill" on the return). The bike segment was hillier than I had expected it to be, adding about 10 minutes there too. And a very hot day made my run even slower than contemplated. However, I finished the race in 8:25, five minutes under the time limit. Because there were only three of us in the 60 to 64 age-group, I picked up a top-3 finisher's plaque in the bargain. So, if you are interested in going long, make some preliminary calculations. If it seems feasible in terms of your own speed potential, then, *if you want to*, for yourself and no one else, you can apply yourself to do the necessary training.

At ages 48 and 51, respectively, following completion of my base program for the season, I did my first two ironman-distance events, both on Cape Cod, on $7\frac{1}{2}$ hours per week of training for 12 weeks or so. At the 1990 Vineman in the wine country of California (a race that is still held), I did not finish because it became clear upon approaching the halfway point of the marathon that I was not running fast enough to make the (shorter than usual) 16-hour time limit. I was going fast (for me) on the marathon, but because I had had a rather slow bike and had encountered some bowel difficulties at the bike-run transition, I was way behind the closest competitor. I had no crew, the volunteers would be going home when the course was officially closed, it was getting cold, the road was totally dark and totally lonely, and I was told that there might be a mountain lion or two in the area. Encountering one of these if, say, I had fallen into a ditch in the dark and broken an ankle was not my idea of fun. So I stopped and took the sweeper van back to the transition area.

When I set out to try the distance again at Martha's Vineyard, Massachusetts, in 1994, I increased my training time to 10 hours per week for 13 weeks, following the 13 weeks of the base program for the season. (That race, on a visually beautiful course, was held only once due to local opposition to it.) I also added several more long bike rides and more hill work to my training. I wanted to increase my relative speed by increasing my endurance. In this way I thought I would be able to maintain slightly faster paces over the full length of the bike and the run.

I did not finish that race either. I got close to halfway on the marathon. Even though I was slowing down, it still seemed by the clock that I had an outside chance of making the time limit, or being close enough to the end that I would be permitted to finish anyway. But then there was a downpour. Soaked and shivering, and with my own crew coming 'round in the car to be able to pick me up, I called it a night.

Six weeks later, still trained up, I entered the Great Floridian Triathlon, held in Clermont, Florida. (In 2005, the increasingly popular Great Floridian was the USA Triathlon Ultra Distance Championship event, the seventh consecutive year that it was so designated.) I finished, but way over the time limit. The organizers let me stay on the marathon segment, a well-lit loop going three times through the residential district that surrounds Lake Minneola, because I had crew with me. At about one o'clock in the morning, I was at the 20-mile mark. A young lady from the race committee came by and asked me if I was going to finish. "Oh yes," I said. An hour later, I had gone about 3 miles farther. She appeared again and asked the same question. I gave the same reply. "Okay," she said, "here's your finisher's T-shirt. I'm going to bed." She handed the shirt to my crew in the van.

I finished the race at 3:20 A.M., with a total elapsed time of 19 hours and 20 minutes. I felt really good the next day when a couple of 12-hour finishers said, "You were out on the course for *how* long? Man, now *that* is an achievement!"

If you want to go long, if you think that going long is something you can do, if you think that going long will bring some new joy to your life, if you just want to take up a new challenge and realistically have the time to train for it, then by all means go for it. I did and I am very happy that I did. But, please, don't do it for the wrong reasons, such as someone else challenging you, or you thinking that you will not have done the "real thing" until you go long. I have not done a long triathlon since I finished the Hudson Valley Triathlon, a half-ironman, in 1998. (I did do the Vermont Sun "Aqua-Bike," a swim-bike duathlon at the half-ironman distances, in August 2005.) Since that time, I have never felt that the Sprint- and Olympic-distance tri's and the duathlons that I have done were not "real." Shorter, surely, but just as real. "Long" is now defined for me by how long I can continue to race, not by the distances in any particular race.

Training for Going Long, for the Ordinary Mortal Triathlete

This section is based primarily on my own experience in the three ironman-distance races I finished, the two I didn't finish because I ran out of time, the three half-ironman races I started and finished, and the two long biathlons that I started and didn't finish because of weather conditions. As I mentioned above, my training for these races—7½ to 10 hours per week over 8 to 12 weeks after I had done the Olympic-distance TFOMTP—was modest by anyone's standards. Some authorities recommend as much as 20 hours per week of training as the minimum for an ironman-distance race. I do not think that you need nearly that much, if you determine in advance that you will go no faster in the race than is necessary to beat the time limit.

However, is the amount of training that I did back in those days sufficient? Again, it all depends upon you and how fast you can go *in the race*. Some years ago, Larry Kaiser wrote to me that at age 39 he had done the 1988 Cape Cod Endurance, spending just about the same amount of time training as I had: 7 to 8 hours per week over 3 months. I finished that race in 16:21 (sixth from last and thus totally anonymous, as I recall). Being inherently much faster than I am, he finished 189th out of 400-plus finishers. Not bad for 7 to 8 hours per week of training. In the September 1989 issue of *Triathlon Today!* it was reported that Ken Wiseman did *double* and *triple* ironman-distance races on a 14- to 15-hour-per-week training program. A triathlon "authority" once upon a time recommended 14 to 15 hours per week as the minimum time required to do an *Olympic*-distance triathlon without going particularly fast. So much for that.

Nevertheless, given my experience of just making it or not being able to get through the marathon in under the time limit and not finishing, I now recommend a somewhat more demanding training program than I used back then. If your estimate of the time it will take you to do the distances in each segment of your chosen race indicates that you can make the time limit, I think that, to be on the safe side, you should average 8 hours per week for 13 weeks to prepare for a half-ironman (see Table 10.1) and 12 hours per week for 13 weeks for an ironman-distance event

Table 10.1. The TFOMTP for the Half-Ironman-Distance Triathlon

(Times in minutes, average of 8 hours per week for 13 weeks, exclusive of race week)*

Day	M	T	W	Th	F	S	S	Total
Week								
1	30	Off	60	Off	60	90	120	360 (6)
2	45s	Off	90	Off	75	90	120	420 (7)
3	45s	Off	90	Off	75	90	120	420 (7)
4	45s	Off	90	Off	75	90	120	420 (7)
5	Off	60	60s	60	60	90	90	420 (7)
6	60s	60	60/30s	Off	60	Off	150	420 (7)
7	Off	90	60s	90	Off	120br	180	540 (9)
8	Off	90	60s	90	Off	120	180br	540 (9)
9	Off	90	60s	60	Off	120br	210b	540 (9)
10	Off	90	60s	90	Off	120	180r	540 (9)
11	Off	90	60s	60	Off	120br	210b	540 (9)
12	Off	90	60s	90	Off	120	180br	540 (9)
13	Off	90	60s	90	Off	120br	180r	540 (9)
14	This is the week before the race. Take it very easy; go at your own pace.							

* s = swim. You certainly can do more sessions if you want to: the noted ones are the minimum. br = brick, b = bike, r = run.

(see Table 10.2). It happens that these numbers are in the same range as several other published first-timer Long Course racing programs. Those time estimates again? Well, to make the standard 17-hour limit for an ironman, you would need to make these minimum times: the 2.4-mile swim in about 100 minutes, the 112-mile bike in 8 hours (that's an average speed of 14 mph), and the marathon in 6½ hours (15-minute miles). That would allow about 50 minutes for transitions plus some wiggle room.

Doing either of these programs takes commitment and dedication but will not turn your life upside down (except possibly during the last four weeks of the ironman program, which has a series of very long workouts on the weekends). As with the Sprint/duathlon and Olympic-distance TFOMTPs, these schedules are set down in times, not distances. On most days, you choose which sport(s) you do. For most weeks, I have assigned by type only the minimum number of swim workouts, and, in the later

Table 10.2. The TFOMTP for the Ironman-Distance Triathlon

(Times in minutes; average of 12 hours per week for 13 weeks, exclusive of race week)*

Day	M	T	W	Th	F	S	S	Total
Week								
1	30s	60	90	Off	90	90	120	480 (8)
2	45s	60	90	Off	90/30s	105	180	480 (8)
3	45s	60	90	Off	90/30s	105	180	480 (8)
4	60	30s	90	Off	90/30s	105	180	480 (8)
5	Off	90/60s	60	120/60s	Off	150br	180	720 (12)
6	60s	90/60s	60	120/60s	Off	150br	180	720 (12)
7	Off	90/60s	60	120/60s	Off	120br	210	720 (12)
8	Off	90/60s	60	120/60s	Off	120br	210r	720 (12)
9	Off	60/60s	60	60/60	Off	120	420b	720 (12)
10	Off	90/60s	90	90s/60	Off	180	270br	840 (14)
11	Off	60/60s	90	60/60	Off	90	420b	840 (14)
12	Off	90/60s	90	90s/60	Off	180	270r	840 (14)
13	Off	90/60s	90	90s/60	Off	180br	270b	840 (14)
14	This is the week before the race. Take it very easy; go at your own pace.							

* s = swim. You certainly can do more sessions if you want to: the noted ones are the minimum. br = brick, b = bike, r = run.

stages, the "brick" (bike-run), and long bike and long run workouts. For the ironman, there are two required long bike rides (7 hours; if you can cover more than 100 miles in that time, you can cut it back), and two required long (3 to 3½ hours) runs.

The long workouts are scheduled for the weekends; the two workouts per day are primarily during the week. Although you will not find the pattern variation among the weeks that occurs in the shorter TFOMTPs, each week is set up with a short-long rotation. The heavier set of weeks is designed with two off-days to give your body regular rest. You may use one of those days to "catch up" for a missed workout, but I would try to take off at least one day per week. Again, as in the Sprint/duathlon and Olympic-distance TFOMTPs, these programs are designed to get you through the race distances at speeds that you can manage, as long as you can manage them in your training. As with the shorter programs, the faster you go in your training, the faster you will go in the race. But at the paces designed to "make the time limit," this amount of training will get you there. I know. Taking a chance, more often than not I got there on rather less.

Choosing a Suitable Race

My advice on choosing your first race generally applies to choosing your first longer race. Let me emphasize a few points. If at all possible, for your first long race choose one that you can drive to (rather than fly to). If you drive, equipment handling will be much easier, and you do not have to worry about assembling/packing/unpacking/reassembling your bike. I also suggest choosing a race that has only one transition. Facing your first long-course race, you will have enough to concern you without having to think about how to handle a two-transition-area race. (My third race, the Vineman, had two transition areas, but by then I was somewhat experienced at the distance.) If there is only one transition area, you can handle all of the logistics of the race on your own, although having your own crew with a car helps in any long race in which you expect to be on the course for a long time. However, two-transition-area long-course races almost invariably require that you have crew to help you get set up in two locations, which will be some distance from each other. The crew may also need to help get you out to the first one, and have a car waiting at the finish, which will be at the second transition area.

Race Planning for the Long Run

To reduce your chances of being surprised, make sure that you know the nature of the course. For example, I don't think that I would ever try the Hawaii Ironman (even if I could get in through the lottery or, by some miracle, qualify in my age-group). Wet suits are prohibited for the swim, and there is a mass start (with 1,600 or so competitors). I could easily be run over at that start, no matter how careful I was. Furthermore, I can actually get seasick in rough water. If the water is rough, I have to swim sidestroke in order to keep my head out of the water. Sidestroke is a very slow stroke. If I had to use it at Hawaii, without a wet suit, I might not even make the swim cutoff time. Even if I could make that time cutoff, I doubt that I could make the bike segment time limit. The out leg of the out-and-back bike route to Hawi consists of an endless uphill. When you are riding the bike, a crosswind functions like a headwind. You feel it. For the Hawaii bike segment, there is more often than not a crosswind. Then there is all that heat with no shade. That is why I could not do Hawaii.

These are some of the factors to consider when you look into doing that first long-course triathlon: one transition area or two, water temperature, calm or potentially rough water, ambient temperature, wind potential, hills on the bike and the run, and shade on the bike and the run.

In addition, even with planning, there may still be surprises. On an oval course at Martha's Vineyard, there was a crosswind, meaning that I had a strong breeze in my face for about 85 percent of the bike leg. On the bike segment in the Great Floridian, I experienced a recurrent cramp in my right lower back that I had not had for a long time, necessitating a stop to stretch it out about every half hour in the last half of the bike leg. Plain old bowel problems cost quite a bit of time in transition (at the Vineman and at Martha's Vineyard).

You can also make mistakes in your pre-race planning. Mental preparation and visualization were very important for me for the long races. However, for the Vineman in California, I made the mistake of visualizing the Cape Cod course. Not only was the Vineman bike course much hillier, it was sunnier, because it was held earlier in the summer when the days were longer. Thus for me at Vineman, the marathon started in the hot late afternoon sun of an early August day, not in the cool of oncoming dusk, as it had at Cape Cod in late September. I had not thought about that.

If you do decide to go long, it is a good idea to do so a season ahead, so that you will have plenty of time to plan out your overall training schedule and race logistics. You can find the races listed in all of the major calendars in the magazines and on the Web. If you are thinking about doing one next year, you can get an idea of when they are held by looking at this year's calendars.

Just as with the Sprints, the Olympic-distance tri's, and the duathlons, established long-course races are generally held on the same calendar weekend each year.

If you have the inclination—no, the strong desire, I should say—and the requisite average of 8 to 12 hours per week over 13 weeks available for training, then go for it. Do not worry about going fast; just think about finishing. And think about using close to all of the available time. As I have often said, if I can go long in triathlon, virtually anyone who wants to (for the right reasons) can too. Just remember, the ironman-distance is not the gold standard of the multi-sport realm. The triathlon or duathlon that *you* do, that *you* have fun with, that makes *you* feel good about yourself, and feel that *you* have accomplished something special is the gold standard of our sport. Every triathlon is a significant challenge, and every triathlon finisher has accomplished something significant for him- or herself.

SOME FINAL THOUGHTS, NEARING A QUARTER-CENTURY IN THE SPORT

If I can do it, you can do it too!
—*Steve Jonas, from 1983 onward*

Now, dear reader, some final thoughts on my approach to, rather than the "how to," of multi-sport racing, gleaned from almost twenty-five years of experience, as of the time of this writing.

On Energy, Clarity, and Self-Esteem

At the beginning of Chapter 1, I noted that the late, great philosopher of running, Dr. George Sheehan, often talked about the "energy, clarity, and self-esteem" that are added to one's life when one engages in regular aerobic exercise. If you become a triathlete or duathlete, you will of course engage regularly in aerobic exercise. I can tell you that doing that, especially in the context of multi-sport racing, surely does add "energy, clarity, and self-esteem" to one's mental and physical well-being. During my time as a triathlete and duathlete, I have experienced major positive changes in my body and my mind. I have become fitter, and my body has become tighter and stronger. That happens for almost every regular aerobic exerciser. But beyond that, by entering this sport at my own level of competence and ability, I became a competitive athlete, in my own way, for the first time in my life, after the age of 40. What a benefit *that* was to my self-image, to my feelings about myself—yes, to my self-esteem.

As a preventive medicine specialist, I am very familiar with the data on the relationship between regular exercise and health. It is not that knowledge that motivates me to be a regular exerciser, however. Like so many others who engage in distance-sports racing, I have so much fun doing it that I train to race rather than racing because I happen to train. So the racing itself, especially the low-stress way in which I do it, benefits my physical and mental health—"energy, clarity, and self-esteem," as George loved to say.

Winning Plaques and Having Fun

As I have grown older (I was 68 during the 2005 racing season), I have more and more often received an award for being one of the top three finishers in my age-group. For example, in 2004 I came away with plaques in six out of my seven races. In the 2005 season, I won plaques in nine of the twelve races I entered. In fact, I have received plaques consistently since I turned 60. Why? Is it a result of suddenly becoming faster or more competitive as I get older? Hardly. Most often, I earned the award not for being fast but simply because I was still out there. I keep crossing the finish line as the number of other people in my age-group declines. Only a few times when I finished in the top three were there more than three of us in my age-group. Thus, I view my plaques as rewards for being there, for longevity in the sport, not as awards for speed. I am fond of saying, "I am not fast, but I am long." Finishing happily and healthily is still my focus; just having fun out there is still my primary goal. Getting a plaque as compared with not getting one does not make me happy; it simply makes me *happier*.

My Performance and Physical Condition over Time

In my training, I have been gradually slowing down as I get older. Even on a good day, I rarely run better than 10 to 11 minutes per mile. My bike speed has dropped probably about one mile per hour, and my swim speed by 3 to 4 minutes per mile. So on the average, I have slowed down by 10 to 15 percent since I got into the sport. I have experienced a similar drop-off in speed in the races. Why is this so? I am in much better physical condition than I was back in the mid-1980s. My weight and body fat proportion are down significantly. My total cholesterol is way down (thanks to medication), with the proportion of high-density ("good") blood-serum cholesterol up (in part thanks to regular exercise) and triglycerides down. My resting heart rate is down, and my heart rate while working out is lower than it used to be (and not due just to aging); I have (fortunately) always had low blood pressure. The drop-off in speed is due most likely to age. If slowing down as you get older happens to pro athletes, why should it not happen to me? My attitude about this fact? Isn't it nice that I am still racing at 69 (in 2006) and can notice that my speed is dropping because I am getting older.

How I Use the TFOMTP Now

In my own training and racing, I still use the TFOMTP pretty much as I laid it out in the first edition of this book in 1986, with just a couple of variations. My base program is the five-workouts-per-week variant. The minute allotments for each session within each of the weeks in the program have not changed. However, I have adapted the overall program to my season-long racing schedule. In mid- to late March of each year, after the end of my ski season, I begin with Week 1 and go through Week 12. By that time, I will usually have done at least three races in the New York Triathlon Club (NYTC) series: the "March Madness" Biathlon in New York City's Central Park in late March, the Queens Biathlon in Alley Park in mid-May, and the first of the New York Tri-/Biathlon Series in Harriman State Park in early June. (As you know, NYTC's Dan Honig still uses the term "biathlon" for the two-sport races.) I count the minutes I do in each of those races and any others I might do during those first twelve weeks toward meeting my training program requirements. Because I know that I will be racing regularly throughout the season and will not be going for speed in any of my races, I have dropped the "taper" week from my own training program.

After the first twelve weeks, I switch into a "two-four" pattern for the rest of the racing season. I do two "light weeks" (Weeks 6 and 7) and four "heavy" weeks (Weeks 8 to 11) on that rotation. I continue to count any race minutes toward meeting my scheduled requirements. This pattern has worked for me for a number of years now. It has the "hard-easy" element. It also has flexibility. As long as I stay pretty much in the "two-light, four-heavy" distribution over the course of the season, I sometimes flip the order of weeks if, for example, I go on vacation with my wife and my opportunity to train is significantly reduced. As I said, this approach works well for me. If you become a "regular"—doing a number of races each season—something like it might work for you too.

The Race: Pace and Goals

I have learned much in nearly twenty-five years of racing, and share some additional thoughts with you here. Even after you experience your first multi-sport race, there are other "firsts" that await you if you continue to do it: your first race of the other type, duathlon or triathlon as the case may be; your first race longer than your very first one; your possible first age-group top-three finisher's award if you stick with it and get faster or—like me—simply older. I cannot emphasize too much the importance of going slowly enough to stay comfortable and not run out of gas, especially in your first race. If you have speed potential, once you get into the sport there will be plenty of time to develop it, if you want to.

At many races, you will still see bikes with luggage racks and/or handlebar baskets and/or bells and/or 3- or 4-speed hub shifters. That's the spirit! If you are a first-timer, there is no reason not to pull that old 2-wheeler out from the storage room or the back of the garage, or go for it on your mountain bike or combi, or a bike you borrow from a friend or family member to try the sport out before investing big bucks in a modern road-racing or triathlon-specific bike.

As to race time goals, if I am doing a race that I have done before, I almost never look at my previous times before this year's race. Rather, for a given race I usually set my time goal for that day at some time *during* the race, usually on the bike segment. Then, based on the weather, the wind, course conditions (road surface, traffic, and so on), how I feel that day, and the like, I say to myself, Well, let's try for such-and-such a time. If I make it, great. If not, there is always the next race. When I get home, if it is a race that I have done before, I will then look at my records to see how I did in the past.

I actually ruined myself for that ironman-distance race on Martha's Vineyard that I entered in 1994 by being caught up in thinking about personal bests and possibly placing in my age-group. (If there had not been two walk-up-right-before-the-race last-minute entrants—now unheard of for an ironman, by the way—there would have been only three of us in my age-group.) I should have maintained my usual focus on simply finishing—hopefully within the time limit, but over it if I were slow and still permitted to be out there by the race marshals, and having a good time doing so. If in the course of doing that, were I to set a personal record or even get a plaque, great. But I needed to just let that stuff happen, not aim for it. But I had my head in the entirely wrong place in that race, even though competitors were permitted to stay on the course to the finish even if their time would not have been official, and I happened to have a personal crew with a car and fresh clothing were I to need it. I forgot that for me the best focus, indeed the only focus, should be on finishing. When there was that heavy rain shower at about mile 12 on the run segment, I got wet and quit.

The vital importance to me of having my head in the right place so that I can just go out and have a good time was brought home the next weekend. I did the short Yankee Trader Biathlon in my own neighborhood in my hometown of Port Jefferson, New York. I rode my mountain bike that day because for this point-to-point race with the start a bit distant from my home and a finish down the hill from it, it happened to be convenient to do so. I did not look at the entrants list. I had a slow but comfortable run and a fun ride on a familiar course. As I customarily do, I finished toward the back of the pack, but I was happy and healthy when I did so. Because I had many errands to do that Saturday, I skipped the awards ceremony. I found out later that I had finished first in my age-group. (Don't ask who was second!) I had won my first "first" ever, with a mind-set that I was just going out to have a good time, not a fast time. What an important lesson: have a good time, if at all possible.

Four weeks later, at the Great Floridian (ironman-distance) Triathlon in Clermont, Florida, I maintained my focus simply on finishing. As you know from the previous chapter, I did so. I was way over the official time limit but finished nevertheless. I had my head in the right place, and that is what counted. I felt just great. The lesson was repeated a few years later in 1998 in the early-season New York Triathlon Club Queens (New York) Biathlon. I was nursing a right groin pull and coming in very slowly, even for me. Going through lower Alley Park toward the end of the second run leg, I noticed an ice-cream truck pulling into a parking lot right next to the run course. Having a sudden urge for a chocolate éclair ice-cream-on-a-stick and money in the runner's wallet that I generally carry on the races, I bought one.

I crossed the finish line munching the last bits of the bar, albeit more than half an hour behind (because of the injury) even my customarily rather slow time for that early-season race. As I came in, my good friend and fellow (but fast) triathlete Odd Sangeslund (in 1998 he was a regular winner in the 65 to 69 age-group; in 2005 he was still racing and still a regular winner in the 75 to 79 age-group) ran up to me. "Did you finish?" he said. "Sure did," I responded. "Then you are third in your age-group," he happily told me. It had happened again. I had fun and got a plaque, without being concerned about the latter in any way.

On July 17, 2005, I did my 100th triathlon, the 9th annual Hudson Valley at Kingston, New York, sponsored appropriately enough by my good friend Dan Honig and his New York Triathlon Club. (Recall that I had been a member of the NYTC, or the Big Apple Triathlon Club, since I joined it at my second tri, back in 1983. In 2005 I had the second-lowest still-active member number.) The race was also my 159th multi-sport race overall, and I

July 17, 2005, my 100th triathlon. As usual, not too many bikes are still there when I get underway. *Photo by Chezna Newman*

would do my 160th five weeks later at the Central Park Triathlon in New York City.

It was an appropriate triathlon for my 100th. It was at the Olympic-distance. The swim was in the Hudson River; on that day there was an upriver current from an incoming tide (the Hudson is tidal as far north as Albany, New York). That meant swimming uphill on the two downstream legs of the triangular course, but getting a nice ride downhill on the upstream part. On land, the course was very hilly on the bike and the run legs. Furthermore, it rained intermittently, and I was caught in a heavy downpour for about half of the bike leg. Fortunately, I was on my combi bike because I came to the race from a week at tennis camp in Vermont, where Chezna and I also did some riding together. So I had a stable ride in the rain. Finishing that one gave me a special feeling of accomplishment, nice for my 100th tri.

Beyond the course and the weather was the fact that, as in my very first at Sag Harbor, I actually raced during the event, something I rarely do. This time, too, my racing partner was an athletic woman in her fifties. Just as in my very first triathlon it was a lady who came up on me toward the end of the bike segment. She passed me with about 5 miles to go. Once again I put the bit in my teeth and re-passed her. But this time, all the way in to the transition whenever I heard her coming up or saw her in my rearview mirror, I put the hammer down. I entered the transition a couple of minutes ahead of her. But I had to do my usual routine in transition, including a much-needed pit stop, and she got out on the run several hundred yards ahead of me. When the road was straight, she was in sight, but at first I thought, "Nah, she's too far ahead. Just run your race and enjoy yourself, especially because the rain has stopped and the sun is coming out." So I settled into a nice rhythm—not too fast, but comfy and moving. However, after about a mile, when I could see her up ahead, I noticed that I was beginning to close the gap. I stayed within myself, but I was reeling her in.

After the finish of the 2005 Hudson Valley Triathlon at Kingston, New York. Just behind me is my longtime friend Dan Honig, president of the NYTC, with three race volunteers.

Photo by Chezna Newman

About half a mile from the turnaround on the out-and-back run, I passed her, with an encouraging word to her to be sure. At that point, I picked it up a bit. After the turnaround, I was able to see her going out to it and confirmed that I had a decent lead. Every once in a while on those 3.1 miles back to the finish, I ignored Satchel Paige's admonition not to look back because "someone might be gaining on you." If, when I could see her back there, she seemed a bit closer, I did suck it up. I was determined this time *not* to have the same experience I had had at the end of the run at Sag Harbor those many years ago: passing someone but then simply not being able to pick it up again when he re-passed me. I kept the hammer down, gradually pulled away, and finished about 250 yards ahead of her. It did not matter to me that it took me more than twice as long to do the race as it took the winner, or that I was next to last overall. First of all, I had finished my 100th tri, on a tough course in tough conditions. Second, because I was the only one in my age-group, there was the Jonas-bonus of a plaque. And third, I had a race-within-a-race, and this time I won it! How nice.

Some of My Favorite Races

Like most tri/duathletes, I am region-centric. I do most of my races in the New York metropolitan region where I live. First among my favorite races are those of Dan Honig's NYTC, both the du's (Dan's biathlons) and the tri's. Dan's races are well organized and efficiently run and have an admirable safety record. There are lots of them. And I do lots of them. (In fact, more than one-half of my race total is made up of NYTC triathlons and biathlons.) I do the "March Madness" at a leisurely pace with plenty of warm clothing on and just a few workouts under my belt. But I would not miss it, and neither would the usual 600 other competitors who turn out that early in the season for a race that usually has a waiting list of another hundred folks. I almost always do the Queens Biathlon in May, as well as the New York City Biathlon in Central Park in September, finishing up with the Central Park Biathlon in October. On occasion I have done Don's Bronx Biathlon in late April.

My wife, Chezna, an exercise walker, and I have taken to doing the Spring Couples Relay, held in Central Park usually on the Saturday of Mother's Day weekend. Dan runs this relay for race director Nancy Klitsner of the New York City Parks and Recreation Department. This truly fun event consists of a 2-mile run/walk, which Chezna does, a 12-mile bike, which I do, then a 3/4-mile row around one of the Central Park lakes, in which I do the rowing and Chezna sits there looking pretty and telling me which way to go (with the boat). Entry for this popular and limited-number-of-entrants race closes early.

As for conventional NYTC triathlons, I generally do the first of two Sprints that Dan runs in New York's Harriman State Park. It's held in June and features one monster hill plus several more ordinary ones; it is reputedly the toughest triathlon mile for mile in the region. It can also be done as a biathlon. The Long Island Gold Coast Triathlon—a Sprint held on Hempstead Harbor in June to

After the finish of the 2005 Central Park Triathlon, my 160th multi-sport race overall. *Photo courtesy of Dot Photo/NY Triathlon Club*

benefit the United Community Fund of Great Neck and North New Hyde Park, and run by Dan as well—is by contrast almost entirely flat. Just a gas. I also usually do the Central Park Triathlon, run by Dan for NYC Parks and Recreation in mid-August. The swim is held in the Lasker lap swimming pool at the north end of the park; because the pool is only 3 feet 8 inches deep there is a no-walking rule for the swim. That race fills early too. I also enjoy the American Memorial Triathlon, held in September at Greenwood Lake, New York. A grassy lake swim is followed by a hilly bike segment, which is followed by a run that is hilly for the first half, nice and flat for the finish.

Among my other favorite local races was my first, the Mighty Hamptons, held in Sag Harbor, New York, in September. I have done that race twelve times. Because of scheduling conflicts, after the 1998 race I could not get to it again until 2005. But doing it then felt like old home week. When I could tolerate really cold water, I always enjoyed the Montauk Triathlon, held in early June. There are now several races held throughout the summer in that fun and picturesque area of eastern Long Island. A different early-season race that I thoroughly enjoyed was the Katterskill Spring Prelude, a long Sprint quadrathlon held at Ski Windham in New York State. It began with a ¼-mile "run" in the snow with ski boots on, followed by a 1-mile downhill ski, a 17-mile road bike, and a 10k run. One time when I was coming in last, 20 minutes behind the next competitor in front of me, the volunteers came out and put up a tape for me to break as I crossed the finish line—to their cheers. (What did I tell you about finishing last?) Unfortunately, that race is no longer run. The New York City Triathlon, held in early July with the swim in the now-clean-enough-to-swim-in Hudson River, is a spectacular race, with a great bike ride on the Henry Hudson Parkway's northbound lane, that is closed to cars for the race. I grew up overlooking that parkway. I felt as though I was riding in my front yard. I have done that race three times. The only problem with it is the logistics of getting to the race headquarters in a midtown hotel, then over to the transition area at 79th Street and the Hudson River. But if you can deal with such problems, the experience is well worth it.

As for my less frequent out-of-region races, all of my Long and

Ultra Course races have been done in other parts of the country, from the East Coast (Massachusetts's Cape Cod and Martha's Vineyard), to the West (California's Sonoma Valley). Although I have done it only once, St. Anthony's in Saint Petersburg, Florida, an Olympic-distance tri held in late April (and filling within 3 days of the opening of the Web site for entries on December 1), is a race that I hope to get back to in the future. It is major league all the way, held in a beautiful location full of historic Americana. My wife has family there, and my dear friends Don and Carol Ardell live there, so we have more than one reason for going. I did an International Masters Games Triathlon at Hagg Lake, outside of Portland, Oregon, in 1998. Hagg Lake regularly hosts triathlons, I understand. The course is challenging, but a good, doable challenge even for Ordinary Mortals like me. I have done one other race in the Northwest, the Age-Group National Championships at Coeur d'Alene (CDA), Idaho, in 2002. CDA is also home to a number of triathlons, held in gorgeous mountainous surroundings. I highly recommend it. Vermont Sun, whose Aqua-Bike I did in 2005, provides a delightful setting in Branford State Park, where they run races of various lengths.

I have been to one race abroad, the Age-Group Triathlon World Championships, held on Madeira Island, Portugal, in May 2004. The eligible-competitor numbers worked right for me at Nationals the previous year, and I made Team USA, as slow as I am. Unfortunately, I became somewhat hypothermic in the swim, and I could not finish the hilliest bike course I have ever been on. Nevertheless, Chezna was with me, and we had a most enjoyable week on that beautiful island with its friendly people, had a fun time with my teammates, and ate some really good food. Being on Team USA was a thrill that I hope to repeat one of these years, perhaps when I age up the next time at 70. I also look forward to other Age-Group National Championships in other parts of the country.

Some Last Thoughts to Help You Get Started and Keep Doing It

Triathlon/duathlon is one of the few sports (marathoning is another) where you get credit just for going around the course. For most of us, being there and crossing the finish line, no matter how far behind the winner we are, is the name of the game. In addition, even if you do not cross the finish line in a particular race, if you did your best on that particular day, if you truly tried, you get credit too—especially if you do not give up but try again. For as Dave Scott is quoted as saying at the beginning of this book, "The trying is everything."

Further, triathlon is the only event other than marathoning where the absolute amateur, the entirely recreational athlete, even the slowest person in the race, can get onto the same field of play and compete with some of the best in the world, not directly by time but on the same course in the same conditions. The Ordinary Mortal baseball, football, or basketball player, golfer, or tennis player cannot get out there with Pedro Martinez or Brett Favre or Shaquille O'Neal or Tiger Woods or Lindsay Davenport. However, the Ordinary Mortal triathlete can get out there with the very best. Oh, what a feeling!

I cannot overemphasize the importance of setting goals that are reasonable and rational for you. If you are going to be successful at this endeavor (and indeed most other endeavors in your life), it is vital at the outset to set clear goals for yourself: what you want to do, why you want to do it, what you think you will get out of it, for whom, primarily, you are doing it. (Goal setting will work for you only if your goals are primarily for yourself, not anyone else.) What will you have to give up to get where you want to go? Is it worth it for you?

Furthermore, those goals must make sense for you. They must be achievable in the context of your current abilities, your available time to train, and the accessibility of races suitable for you. At the beginning, especially, you should think small. Set a goal in terms of time, distance, and type of event (triathlon versus duathlon) that you think you have a good chance of achieving without doing something that for you would be absolutely extraordinary. Once you achieve that first-level goal, you can always set another that is more demanding, *should you choose to do so*. Then another, and so on. But take it one step at a time. If you set a goal at the outset that is clearly too much for you, when—as is likely—you fail to achieve it, you will probably be disappointed and discouraged and may very well quit. As you start out on this great adventure, you want to succeed, not fail. By setting reasonable, rational goals, you can be virtually certain that you are setting yourself up for success, not failure.

As for me, my future goals focus on remaining active in the sport indefinitely. When I did my 100th multi-sport event in the spring of 1999, I set my sights on doing my 200th by the age of 75. By the end of the 2005 season, I had done 103 triathlons and 164 multi-sport races overall. The new goal of 220 races by age 75 is well within sight, as long as I do not sustain any serious injuries. Also back in 1999 I set a goal of crossing the finish line as a member of the 80-plus age-group in triathlon or duathlon. Stay tuned! Barring injuries, I have a shot at making that one too.

Why have I been able to stick with it for so long, especially since I did not become an athlete until I was 44 years old? Why do I think I have a good shot at achieving the goals I established for myself at age 62? There are five main reasons for my longevity in multi-sport racing. First is what it has done for my body, my mind, and my spirit. Second is that I have consistently set goals that I can achieve with a reasonable amount of focus and dedication. Third is that although I am consistent in my training, I do not train a lot of hours, nor do I pound and stress myself. I work, but I keep it comfortable. So far, I have been injured only infrequently and not seriously, and I do not hurt much. Fourth, by going as slowly as I do in the races, I do not get overstressed. Finally, as you know well by now, I am racing simply to have fun. For the recreational triathlete, that is the secret: Have fun! As long as you do, I guarantee that you too will keep coming back for more.

Appendix I

REFERENCES

Chapter 1

George Sheehan spoke about "energy, clarity, and self-esteem" in a talk given at the Presidential Sports Fitness Festival, in Dallas, Texas, on December 3, 1983.

Jim Curl was quoted in "Triathlon: Sport of the 80s?" by Margaret O. Kirk in *The Boston Phoenix* of February 28, 1984, p. 1. Jim was the cofounder of the Bud Light United States Triathlon Series, one of the first sets of races, for elite and amateur triathletes, held all across the country.

Sofia Shafquat's article "Is Running Fun?" appeared in the *New York Running News,* June/July 1984, p. 13.

Rod Dixon's article "Reaching Your Peak: Consistency Is the Key to Better Performance" appeared in *The Runner,* March 1984, p. 22.

Jim Fixx's classic is *The Complete Book of Running.* New York: Random House, 1977. His story is from p. 3. The Mao quote is from Jim's book as well, on p. 24.

Chapter 2

My book on medical education, *Medical Mystery: The Training of Doctors in the United States,* was published by W. W. Norton in 1978.

Chapter 3

E. C. Frederick and Stephen Kiesling's article "The Semi-Tough Triathlon" appeared in *American Health*, June 1984, p. 56.

Chapter 5

Bill Bowerman's "10 Principles" are found in Chris Walsh's *The Bowerman System*. Los Altos, CA: Tafnews Press, 1983, Chapter 3.

Ardy Friedberg's *How to Run Your First Marathon* was originally published by Simon & Schuster, New York, 1982. It was more recently available from Fitness Enterprises, 175 Fifth Avenue, New York, NY, 10010.

One of Dr. Ken Cooper's several books on aerobics was *The Aerobics Program for Total Well-Being*. New York: M. Evans and Co., 1982.

The quote from Dr. Tom Bassler was from his article "The Child Marathoner," which appeared in the *American Medical Joggers Association Newsletter*, October 1983, p. 38. In a 2005 communication, he assured me that he still stands by it—if anything, more so.

David Oja's "Six Rules of Rest" appeared in his article "Everything You Wanted to Know About Rest," published in *Footnotes*, Spring 1984, p. 14.

Rod Dixon published his "Ten Rules of Running" in his article "Reaching Your Peak: Consistency Is the Key to Better Performance," *The Runner*, March 1984, p. 22.

Chapter 6

The (original) *Runner's Handbook*, by Bob Glover and Jack Shepherd, introduced me to running in the early 1980s. The 2nd revised edition (written with Shelly-lynn Florence Glover) was published by Penguin, New York, in 1996.

Appendix II

RESOURCES

National Organization

USA Triathlon, 1365 Garden of the Gods Road, Suite 250, Colorado Springs, CO 80907-3425, phone (719) 597-9090, fax (719) 597-2121, e-mail Info@USATriathlon.org, Web site www.usatriathlon.org.

Regional and Local Organizations and Clubs

Both national triathlon magazines (see below) periodically list the regional and local organizations and clubs, usually toward the back of their issues. Many of the organizations/clubs have Web sites. An example is the New York Triathlon Club, found at www.nytc.org. Clubs may also be found listed in *USA Triathlon Life* and on the USAT Web site.

National Magazines

As of 2006, there were two:

Inside Triathlon, 1830 North 55th Street, Boulder, CO 80301-2703, phone (303) 440-0601, fax (303) 444-6788. Subscriptions: it-subscrip tions@insideinc.com; customer service U.S. and Canada (800) 494-1413;

international customer service (303) 442-4966; fax (303) 444-6788; Web site www.insidetri.com.

Triathlete, 328 Encinitas Boulevard, Suite 100, Encinitas, CA 92024, phone (760) 634-4100, fax (760) 634-4110, e-mail feedback@triathletemag.com, Web site www.triathletemag.com.

USA Triathlon Life is a benifit of USAT membership.

There are also numerous regional and local triathlon publications. You could start your search by putting "Triathlon publications, regional and local" into your search engine of choice.

Race Calendar and Registration Web Sites

Both national magazines have Web-based race lists, as do many of the regional and local triathlon organizations and clubs. A comprehensive national race list is found at The American Triathlon Calendar (www.trifind.com), which has links to many of the listed races' own Web sites. Among the organizations that provide online race registration are, in the Northeast, Lin-Mark Computer Sports (www.lin-mark.com), and, nationally, Active.com (www.active.com/triathlon).

Books

On Fitness in General

American College of Sports Medicine (principal author, Walter Thompson, PhD; contributing authors, Steven Jonas, MD, and Dan Bernadot, PhD). *ACSM Fitness Book.* Champaign, IL: Human Kinetics, 2003.

Edwards, Sally. *Heart Rate Monitor Guidebook*, Sacramento, CA: Heart Zones Publishing, 2005.

Running

Fixx, Jim. *The Complete Book of Running.* New York: Random House, 1977.

Glover, Bob, Jack Shepherd, and Shelly-lynn Florence. *The Runner's Handbook.* 2d rev. ed. New York: Penguin, 1996.

Hanc, John. *The Essential Marathoner.* New York: Lyons and Burford, 1996. Now available from Globe-Pequot Press. Equally as good for the beginning marathoner as Ardy Friedberg's book (see page 244).

———. *The Essential Runner*. New York: Lyons and Burford, 1994. Now available from Globe-Pequot Press.

Sheehan, George. *Running and Being: The Total Experience*. New Jersey: Second Wind II, 1998. This is the 20th-Anniversary Edition of this classic work.

Bicycling

Baker, Arnold. *The Essential Cyclist*. New York: Lyons and Burford (now Globe-Pequot Press, out of print).

———. *Smart Cycling: Successful Training and Racing for Riders of All Levels*. New York: Fireside Books, 1997.

Phinney, Davis, and Connie Carpenter. *Training for Cycling: The Ultimate Guide to Improved Performance*. New York: Perigee/Putnam, 1992.

Swimming

Katz, Jane. *Swimming for Total Fitness Updated*. Garden City, NY: Doubleday/Main St. Books, 1993.

Tarpinian, Steve. *Triathlete's Guide to Swim Training*. Boulder, CO: Velo Press, 2005.

Triathloning

Friel, Joe. *The Triathlete's Training Bible*. 2d ed. Boulder, CO: Velo Press, 2004.

Jonas, Steven. *The Essential Triathlete*. New York: Lyons and Burford, 1996.

Williams, Jayne. *Slow Fat Triathlete*. New York: Marlowe & Co., 2004. Endorsed by yours truly.

INDEX

Page numbers in *italics* refer to illustrations.